In the Pilot's Seat

ALSO BY BOB WORTHINGTON
AND FROM MCFARLAND

*The Making of an Army Psychologist: From Fighting
in Vietnam to Treating Fellow Veterans* (2023)

*Fighting Viet Cong in the Rung Sat: Memoir of a Combat
Advisor in Vietnam, 1968-1969* (2021)

*Under Fire with ARVN Infantry: Memoir of a Combat
Advisor in Vietnam, 1966–1967* (2018)

# In the Pilot's Seat
*A General Aviation Memoir and Guide*

BOB WORTHINGTON

McFarland & Company, Inc., Publishers
*Jefferson, North Carolina*

The author passed away on May 9, 2023, shortly after
delivering the final draft of the manuscript to McFarland.
His daughters worked tirelessly to bring it to publication.

Unless otherwise noted,
all photographs are from the author's collection.

ISBN (print) 978-1-4766-9083-4
ISBN (ebook) 978-1-4766-5183-5

LIBRARY OF CONGRESS CATALOGING DATA ARE AVAILABLE

Library of Congress Control Number 2025017207

© 2025 ER & Anita E Worthington Trust. All rights reserved

*No part of this book may be reproduced or transmitted in any form
or by any means, electronic or mechanical, including photocopying
or recording, or by any information storage and retrieval system,
without permission in writing from the publisher.*

Front cover image: © Tyler Olson/Shutterstock

Printed in the United States of America

*McFarland & Company, Inc., Publishers
Box 611, Jefferson, North Carolina 28640
www.mcfarlandpub.com*

To all the pilots and their spouses I have met and flown with since 1975, especially those members of the United States Pilots Association and the New Mexico Pilots Association.

Keep the shiny side up!

And to my three daughters, who continuously support and encourage me.

# Acknowledgments

As a writer I depend on several other people to help me produce the best work I can. Friends of mine (experts in what I am writing about) read every chapter and give me feedback. They point out my mistakes, suggest different (and better) ways to rewrite what I have done, and tell me what works and what does not.

My three readers for this book are all professional pilots, are all former military aviators, and all have their airline transport pilot certificate. Kathi Durst is a senior captain for a major airline, Lucy Young is a recently retired senior captain for a major airline, and Mike Wright is an aviation accident investigator. My readers have contributed much of their time helping me make this book a better read. I cannot thank them enough for their support and excellent comments.

For the medical portions of this book, I asked my former FAA aviation medical examiner, Doctor William Baker, DO, to read what I wrote about the medical aspects of being a pilot. He provided the feedback necessary to ensure that what I said is correct.

I am a writer; I love writing. But my manuscripts must be in a prepared format per my publisher. Plus, 75-year-old photographs must be restored and enhanced to meet the standards for print publication. These tasks are beyond my capabilities, so I have relied on Nithzia Pena to do these chores that are so necessary but not my strong suit. Lastly, books like this one owe their existence to work by publishers, who turn thumb drives of digital images and text files into award-winning products. My heartfelt thanks to everyone at McFarland who worked so hard to bring my words to life and produce this book you are about to read.

# Table of Contents

| | |
|---|---:|
| *Acknowledgments* | vi |
| *Preface* | 1 |
| *Introduction* | 3 |
| **One.** The World of General Aviation | 5 |
| **Two.** Becoming a Pilot | 19 |
| **Three.** Aviation Organizations and Associations | 39 |
| **Four.** Buying an Airplane | 47 |
| **Five.** Owning and Maintaining an Airplane | 61 |
| **Six.** Financing | 92 |
| **Seven.** Aviation Journalism | 113 |
| **Eight.** Aviation Psychology | 119 |
| **Nine.** FAA Investigations | 126 |
| **Ten.** Advanced Proficiency Training | 145 |
| **Eleven.** Nontraditional Landings and Survival | 156 |
| **Twelve.** Flying Warbirds | 174 |
| **Thirteen.** Flying Outside of the United States | 183 |
| **Fourteen.** Aging | 193 |
| **Fifteen.** Remaining a Safe and Proficient Pilot | 216 |
| *Epilogue: My Aviation Life After Open-Heart Surgery* | 237 |
| *List of Aviation Organizations* | 241 |
| *Index* | 243 |

# Preface

I have been involved in aviation for over 60 years. My introduction to aviation was in the Marine Corps, trained in what was called "vertical envelopment." It began for the Marines after World War II, was tested in the Korean War, and by the late 1950s was part of Marine tactical doctrine, where helicopters transported combat troops to the fight and kept them supplied with food and ammo.

In the early 1960s I was an Army officer assigned to the 11th Air Assault Division at Fort Benning, where assault helicopters were tested for combat. While a combat advisor to the South Vietnamese Army, I flew on aircraft every chance I got. I was not a military pilot but flew combat missions as a passenger or a crew member. The aircraft was a tool of war used for combat assaults, reconnaissance, or special operations missions.

In the 1970s my job as an Army clinical psychologist required considerable travel, so friends who were military pilots suggested that I learn to

Bob, age nine, standing in front of a Piper J3 Cub at the Peter O. Knight Airport in Tampa, Florida, in 1947.

fly, which I did. I also became an aviation psychologist. After retiring from the Army in the early 1980s, I became an aviation journalist.

To become a pilot, I joined an Army flying club. Since then, I have joined several other aviation organizations, assuming leadership roles.

Many pilots do not share their passion with their families. Two aspects of my flying career will remain with me forever. The first is the memorable flights I will never forget. The second, but most important, was my constant companion sitting beside me in the right seat, my late wife, Anita. Her passion equaled mine, and she enjoyed several thousand hours next to me. Anita worked the radios, helped navigate, and watched for traffic, and during instrument approaches she would look for the runway as I focused on the instruments. We were a team. Once when we lost our engine, I had to make an unscheduled, off-airport landing that destroyed the plane. I very quickly replaced that plane. There was no hesitation or fear as Anita climbed into the right seat for our first flight in our "new" plane. She was as eager as I was for our next aerial adventure. Without a doubt, her sitting beside me has been what I miss most about flying. Our flights together will never be forgotten.

I became a pilot at age 38, not because of a love of aviation, but as a means of easier travel, to gain more control over my ability to get from here to there. But very quickly I fell in love with aviation. It took me places others can only dream of. For 40 years I occupied the left seat where the airplane pilot sits, owned nine planes, and savored a passion like no other. I have seen and been a part of extraordinary changes in aviation, flying, and planes. Through this book, I want to share what I have learned, my passion for flying, and hopefully an appreciation for some of the most fun a human being can ever experience. It is my pleasure to share with you what I have learned, loved, and lived.

# Introduction

## *Why Read This Book?*

I presume you either have a desire to learn to fly or are already a pilot. My plan is to share information with you that I have gathered in my 40 years as a pilot—my excitement, my passion, my successes, and my sorrows, which were very few. With over seven thousand hours in the sky, as a pilot, an aviation journalist, an FAA safety counselor presenting safety seminars, and an aviation psychologist, I have accumulated considerable knowledge regarding aviation. I have flown my own planes in all states except Hawaii, flown into three foreign countries, and owned nine airplanes. During this time, I have experienced quite a bit, learned a lot, and written hundreds of articles on all facets of aviation. I became a pilot at age 38 and stopped abruptly at age 78. I experienced how the aging process affects flying, remaining insured in my later years, and have endured three FAA investigations—successfully.

Pilots in the United States enjoy a greater freedom to fly than pilots anywhere else in the world. We have fewer restrictions on flying and fewer governmental impediments than any other country. Yet our rules, regulations, and professional practices allow us to navigate in the safest aeronautical system on the planet. I have personally seen flight activities accomplished in the United States that were prohibited outside our country.

This book will guide you through the process of how to become a pilot, how to remain a safe pilot, how to advance in pilot certificates and ratings, and how to continue to fly safely while getting older. I will even discuss ways to have someone else cover part of your flying expenses as a private pilot.

Throughout this book, the emphasis will be on general aviation (GA). I was a GA pilot, so most of my experience relates to that portion of our aviation community. Yet I do cover aspects of being a professional pilot and how to become one as either a military or civilian commercial pilot. While the focus is on general aviation, this book covers many aspects of aviation, especially describing the different pilot certifications, training, and the aviation industry.

## ONE

# The World of General Aviation

## *The Aviation Industry*

The vast, majestic, magical machine of general aviation in the United States is comprised of thousands of moving parts. It is one of the safest and most regulated industries in the world. Yet at the same time, as a private pilot, I had unfettered access with my airplane wherever I wanted to go in our nation. There are some prohibited areas for national security and restricted areas requiring special permission to traverse. Yet, avoiding them or receiving permission to cross is not difficult. This chapter introduces you to what makes general aviation so great, how it operates, and how all the pieces mesh, allowing civilian pilots to fly in the greatest domain in the world. Many foreigners who want to become career pilots come to the States to learn to fly. It is easier and cheaper, and often our weather is better for flying than that in their home countries.

## *What Is Aviation in the United States?*

Our aviation is divided into three parts or tiers. The smallest aviation fleet in the United States is our commercial aircraft with approximately 8,200 (2024) planes. These are the airliners and cargo planes that move people and products. Next is the world's strongest military fleet (our Air Force, Navy, Army, Marines, and Coast Guard) with 13,043 (2024) aircraft. The largest segment of aviation in the United States is our general aviation fleet with 204,405 (2021) planes.

The general aviation aircraft include jets owned by the superrich, which can cost over $100 million, down to used ultralights and light sport aircraft worth a couple thousand dollars or less. General aviation aircraft are owned by businesses and corporations, government agencies and institutions from the federal level to states and municipalities, to privately owned aircraft. General aviation is categorized from business and government usage to personal (private) and recreational travel.

The aviation industry in the United States contains many factions, each functioning singularly but each a valuable component that must interact readily, easily, and effortlessly with every other part. No element can operate independently; each must rely on the others to function. Obviously, the aviation industry needs pilots to work. But pilots need aircraft, and aircraft need airports. Airplanes also need airspace to fly. This airspace needs people to manage it along with rules and regulations to operate safely. Airplanes need manufacturers, and the industry needs people at every level to function.

This chapter will define and describe each segment and explain how each complements the others and how, together, they comprise the largest and safest industry in the world. As I cover each segment, please note that both the internet and other topic-specific books will provide more in-depth information. I will explain each aspect sufficiently to illustrate how it fits into and functions as an integral part of aviation.

## *Aviation Rules and Regulations*

Throughout this book I will be referring to the regulatory citation that governs what I am describing. If I state, "a pilot must do this," I will cite the regulation so that you, the reader, may look up this regulation on the internet if you desire more details. This section begins by describing those rules and regulations that everyone in aviation should be aware of and must comply with. One studies these rules and regulations in ground school (the academic portion of pilot training) as well as flight training with a certified flight instructor (CFI).

The United States is governed by two different sets of laws: legislative and statutory. The United States Code is a compiled list of legislative laws created by our federal legislative process, referring to laws that are general and permanent, meaning they apply to everyone and have no associated time limits. These laws are divided into 54 different titles.

The other set of laws are statutory, called the Code of Federal Regulations (CFR), and created by federal agencies and departments. These also are divided into 50 different titles. In this book I will cite those statutory rules and regulations found in CFR, Title 14, "Aeronautics and Space," which regulates the aviation industry. These are legally binding laws, published annually each January.

Originally, in 1958, these were called the federal aviation regulations or FARs. Confusion arose because another list of rules was called the federal acquisition regulations, so the acronym FARs was dropped from all government usage. The term "FARs" remains in popular use today, however.

## One. The World of General Aviation

A volume of many often-cited parts of CFR Title 14 is published by Aviation Supply and Academics, Inc. as the FAR/AIM (*Federal Aviation Regulations/Aeronautical Information Manual*). So throughout this book you will see the regulations referred to by either the CFR Title 14 Part *xxx* or FAR Part *xxx*.

As a student pilot, my understanding of the FARs and my appreciation for their value to me as a pilot did not extend beyond my passing my private pilot FAA written exam. I wanted to learn how to fly not become an aviation attorney. But when I became an aviation journalist, my editor demanded that I cite the pertinent FAR regulation. This forced me to pay more attention to the FARs and understand them better. When I became an FAA safety seminar instructor as an FAA safety counselor, I had to become better educated in the FARs. My knowledge of the FARs eventually assisted me in having the FAA dismiss investigative charges, which is rare, resulting in no fines or issues (see Chapter 9).

I have not committed any FARs to memory, nor can I cite every part in the regs. But I do know where to locate a reg and understand its meaning. Do not be like me and delay your understanding of the FARs until you're forced to study them. From the beginning of your pilot training, embrace them and read those that pertain most to you and the flying you do until you become comfortable in locating and understanding what they mean.

The second volume of valuable information is called the *Aeronautical Information Manual* (AIM). This is an FAA-compiled official guide to basic flight information and air traffic control procedures. It contains 11 chapters and is published twice a year in April and October.

The AIM is not regulatory but provides information that pilots need to know to fly airplanes and to become a participant in the world of aviation. The AIM contains information on airports, aviation communication procedures, weather, aviation charts, maps and other FAA publications, licenses and registrations, and other areas necessary for functioning as a pilot. While technically not regulatory information, pilots may find themselves in trouble if they ignore it. Parts of the AIM restate or amplify federal regulations.

Everything is quickly available on the internet. I no longer use a print edition of the FAR/AIM but just Google what I need, and the official FAA document appears on my screen. A print copy is still available, but whatever form you prefer, get it, read it, and know how to use it. It can become the most valuable source of information in your aviation career—it was for me.

Now let me present to you the different components that make up aviation.

## *The Pilots*

The various kinds of pilots (or levels of professional training) run the gamut like the range from grade school to a doctoral degree. If one wants to be an attorney or physician, one must graduate from law school or medical school. But probably no other profession has as many different career trajectories as does aviation. Chapter 2 will cover how to become a pilot.

In many professions, one's experience is measured in years of practice. The benchmarks for pilot experience are certificates and ratings earned and hours of flight time. Military pilots with 20 years or more typically accumulate two thousand to three thousand flight hours. If they flew combat aircraft during wartime, their hours may be more. The hours flown also depend on the aircraft flown. A cargo pilot can amass more hours than a fighter pilot. An airline pilot during a 40-year career may log 25 thousand to well over 30 thousand hours, depending on what and where they flew. For the private, general aviation pilot, the number of hours accumulated during 20 to 40 years of flying covers an expansive range. Most private pilots fly 55 to 80 hours a year. Thus 25 years of flying may yield 1,375 to two thousand hours. Some dedicated GA pilots end up with five thousand to 10 thousand total hours. But these are the exceptions. In my 40 years in the sky, I flew 7,050 hours.

To become a pilot in the United States, a person must undergo a minimum specific type of training (both academic and actual flight training in an aircraft) and pass two FAA exams. One is a written/computer exam on the academic side of aviation, and the other is demonstrating flight proficiency and competency to an FAA-designated examiner in an aircraft. Upon successful completion of the training and passing the exams, the person is issued a certificate that never expires.

The FAA has various levels of pilots, depending on their stages of training and proficiency. The FAA also has terms (rating or endorsement) that define additional levels of flying authorized by the certificated pilot.

The FAA has seven levels of pilot certificates—for details see FAR 61.3:

1. Small Unmanned Aircraft Systems: FAR Part 107—certification to fly small drones. Written exam only. As drones become more valuable and prolific due to increased business usage, these regulations may be revised.

2. Sport Pilot: FAR Part 61.313—limited flight privileges and aircraft allowed to fly. Requires academic and flight training plus exams in both areas. Medical certificate not required, can train and fly using driver's license. Used mostly for recreational flying. Incorporated in 2004, it was an introduction to flying with limited privileges.

3. Private Pilot: FAR Part 61.109 (a)—requires a medical certificate and a minimum of 40 hours of flight training. This also requires considerable academic work, called ground school. The private pilot certificate and an instrument rating, plus an endorsement or aircraft type rating, allow a pilot to fly most anywhere in the world.

There are two more pilot certificates to become a professional pilot (i.e., flying airplanes for pay): commercial and airline transport pilot. There are restrictions on what a private pilot can do with a plane and be reimbursed. Primarily a private pilot cannot be paid to fly. To do that a pilot must hold at least a commercial certificate. But a private pilot can use a plane for one's business (see Chapter 6).

A pilot is issued a certificate by the FAA that gives the pilot the privilege to fly a specific aircraft, known as category and class, such as "Airplane Single Engine Land." This pilot certificate is commonly referred to as a pilot's license (like a driver's license). But the government never uses the word "license." Perhaps the word "certificate" is used because a certificate is defined as a document certifying that a person has completed the training required to practice or function in a specific profession or field.

While I mentioned that an FAA certificate never expires, there is a catch to that. To exercise those flight privileges authorized by the certificate, the pilot must be current, i.e., complete specific flight requirements within specific time periods and possess a current medical certificate or valid state driver's license, as required by the type of flying being done.

Once a pilot has earned a pilot certificate, they can obtain endorsements or ratings. An endorsement is achieved by completing a specific amount of training and then showing a flight examiner, usually a certified flight instructor, that you are competent to do that type of flying. An example of an endorsement could be for flying a tailwheel airplane or a complex airplane. The FAA defines a complex aircraft (FAR Part 61.1) as having retractable wheels, flaps, and a controllable pitch propeller. An endorsement is verified by a pilot logbook entry.

A rating is an additional FAA-issued authorization added to a pilot's certificate. A rating specifies how or what a pilot can fly. A rating requires specific additional training, both academic and flight, and FAA testing.

I have an FAA private pilot certificate with an instrument rating for airplane, single-engine land. I have endorsements for complex aircraft (FAR 61.31[e]) to fly an airplane with flaps, retractable gear, and a controllable pitch propellor; high-performance aircraft (FAR 61.31[f]) to fly a plane with an engine over 200 horsepower; and the U.S. Air Force high-altitude program (FAR 61.31[g]) to fly pressurized aircraft over 25 thousand feet above sea level. I have never flown a pressurized aircraft. I took the course to learn more about flying at altitudes where oxygen is needed and to be a safer, more educated pilot. This combination of certificate, instrument rating, and endorsements allowed me to fly my plane almost anywhere in the world. It was all I needed, since all my flying would be for me, my family, my friends, and my business.

A pilot's logbook is a multipage document listing every flight completed by a pilot. The pilot signs the bottom of each completed page, certifying the flight information (what plane was flown, where the flight was, hours flown, weather conditions, and other pertinent information) that becomes the official (legal) documentation of a pilot's flying career. Most of my logbooks are only for a single year for income tax purposes, but collectively they contain the total history of my 40 years in the sky from my first flight to my last. Pilots can use an electronic (online or computer) form for recording flight time.

Earning a pilot certificate allows a person to enter a world few people ever join. Some people simply fly for fun. Others earn their living by flying. Most of the U.S. pilot population falls somewhere in between. Their motivation to fly may be travel for their business, vacation with friends or family, or using a plane like a family station wagon or SUV to visit fun places. Becoming a pilot allows one to join a group of very friendly people, all sharing the same passion for flight.

## *The Airplanes*

Planes allow us to fly. Airplanes come in a variety of packages. The cheapest are used ultralight aircraft selling for a few thousand dollars. Note that no FAA pilot certificate is needed to fly an ultralight, but all FAA flight regulations must be complied with. Moving up the scale of aircraft, light sport aircraft (LSA) are next. Now we are talking in the range of tens of thousands of dollars. Some small and older airplanes (built in the 1940s or 1950s) qualify as a LSA and can be found for under $20,000. New ones can be purchased for well over $100,000. The typical general aviation airplane is a single-engine vehicle seating two to four people. Some have fixed gear where the wheels remain down, while others have retractable wheels that tuck up into the wings or fuselage after takeoff. These planes, both old and used, can sell for between $20,000 and $50,000 at the low end and up to several hundred thousand dollars. The price depends on the plane; its age; the number of hours on the engine and the airframe; its radio, navigation and other flight equipment on board; and its condition.

A new general aviation four-seat aircraft can run from $400,000 to $500,000 or more. Most GA pilots who want or need a plane can find something they can afford. Ownership is not mandatory, as many pilots rent or belong to a flying club. As I describe in Chapter 4, locating and purchasing an airplane that will meet your flight requirements is mostly about compromises, striking a balance between what you want and what you can afford. In my 40 years of flying, I was always able to find the plane I wanted to complete the flight missions needed, and within my budget. I did this nine times.

Speed and distance in airplanes today are noted in knots (speed) and nautical miles (distance). A knot is approximately 15 percent greater than one mile per hour. A nautical mile is 15 percent greater than a statute mile. The speed gauges in older planes are marked in both knots and miles per hour.

Since planes in our general aviation fleet are generally between 40 and 50 years old, pilots will find most of the panel instruments to be analog gauges (referred to as steam gauges). The planes coming off the assembly lines today have digital instruments and are called glass cockpits. The old round gauges have been replaced with modern computer screens that can display much more information than the old gauges. The introduction of computer screens on the instrument panel began in the 1990s with navigation equipment and became prominent when the GPS (global positioning system) equipment became accepted. While navigation for the U.S. military using satellites began in 1958, it was not authorized for civil aircraft usage by the FAA until 1994.

An analog cockpit instrument panel. Note all the round gauges, called "steam gauges."

**A modern "glass cockpit" showing several multifunctional display screens (pxhere.com).**

The "glass cockpit" is a multifunctional, electronic flight display screen mounted on the instrument panels of aircraft. Using electronic and digital technology, more information on the aircraft, its engine(s), and navigation is displayed in easy-to-read formats on computer screens. Glass cockpits began in the late 1960s in military aircraft. By the mid–1970s, commercial planes began to use this technology. By the late 1990s, new general aviation airplanes came off the assembly line with electronic flight displays. Manufacturers found this equipment to be reliable and efficient, providing more feedback to pilots than analog technology.

When digital technology first began, aircraft also had analog basic flight gauges placed at the bottom of the instrument panel in case the digital equipment failed. These were steam gauges that provided information on airspeed, aircraft attitude, and altitude. Today these are supplemental digital equipment.

The display screen works like your desktop computer using touch-screen programs. What the National Transportation Safety Board has found is that proficiency in using this equipment calls for more training than analog created information. One reason is it provides so much more data. When many general aviation aircraft are retrofitted, digital packages replace some analog gauges. This is especially true for corporate and business aircraft. Much of the smaller general aviation fleet flown by private pilots will be equipped with a hybrid combination of steam gauges and some form of electronic flight displays. Most will be for navigation, but some provide more digital data for the pilot. If you are attending a larger flight school or college, your planes will most likely be digital. Flying clubs, small flight schools, and individual certified flight instructors will probably have a combination of both analog and digital equipment.

In addition to electronic flight displays there are electronic flight bags (see FAR Part 91-78, Advisory Circular 91-78, and AC 120-76D). In the twentieth century, pilots carried all their pilot/flying gear in a cloth flight bag, sort of like a cross between a small backpack and a briefcase. Prior to electronic flight bags, carrying paper charts could be quite cumbersome.

For example, often my wife and I would fly a lengthy cross-country flight, taking several weeks over more than half the United States. We would begin at Las Cruces, New Mexico, and fly to Atlanta, where our youngest daughter and her family lived. Then to Washington, D.C., where Anita's parents lived, then to Connecticut where my parents lived, and finally to Chicago where our middle daughter and her family lived. Then back to New Mexico. Our flights would cross 20 states, necessitating IFR charts (navigational tool used for flying under Instrument Flight Rules) and approach plates for each of those states plus those for adjacent states we might need to transit due to weather. These paper products weighed some 40 pounds, requiring a good-sized duffel bag to hold them.

I read an article where the U.S. Air Force eliminated tons of printed materials by using electronic tablets with applications and programs. I did the same. Now I could have every IFR chart for the entire lower 48 states, every approach plate for every IFR airport, and VFR charts (visual navigational tools using terrain and other visual references), also for every state. Now the flight information is in a tablet weighing a pound or so, less than 12 inches square. Another bonus is that the tablets are updated automatically. The paper charts were published several times a year to remain current; unfortunately, if that date arrived while I was en route, I would have to fly with outdated information. The downside is that you have to keep the tablet charged; I flew with extra battery packs and had a solar battery charger for the plane. Planes today have onboard chargers.

When I began flying in 1975, cross-country navigation was accomplished by following specifically designated airways (straight lines called Victor airways) between radio-identified ground-based navigation points known as VORs (very high frequency omnidirectional range). They look like an upside-down ice cream cone. An instrument on the panel allows the pilot to dial in a VOR's frequency, and the instrument is used to determine the heading to the VOR station. Today more than half the VOR locations have been decommissioned and replaced with GPS-identified navigation locations displayed on FAA navigation charts.

Since I began flying, aerial navigation has changed considerably. With GPS a pilot can enter any designation in the plane's navigation system and then fly directly to that location. In aircraft-congested airspace such as the upper East Coast or Southern California, air traffic control probably will not permit "direct" flights but require aircraft to follow Victor airways, like an interstate highway in the sky, as a means of controlling the skies.

## *The Airspace We Fly In and Those Who Control It*

For safety, everywhere an airplane goes in the sky or on the ground is regulated by the FAA. Airports have rules and regulations with which pilots must comply. This information is in the *Aeronautical Information Manual* (AIM). Airports have signs and markings on the runways and taxiways providing information on what pilots should do. Once in the air, there are six classes of airspace control (Class A through Class E and Class G) as well as other forms of airspace control.

The airspace in the United States is a part of the National Airspace System (see Chapter 3 of the AIM and FAR Part 71). This is a joint effort between the U.S. military and the FAA as well as airports, navigation facilities, and all the equipment and people (air traffic control or ATC) who make this work. Our airspace is divided into two categories: regulatory (Class A through E and restricted and prohibited areas, subject to rulemaking to establish strict standards) and non-regulatory (another way to establish regulations without the rulemaking process). This includes military operating areas (MOAs), warning and alert areas, controlled firing areas (CFA), and national security areas.

Airspace is also defined by type: controlled, uncontrolled, Special Use Airspace, and other. FAA charts identify these different airspaces, and it is up to the pilot to understand what requirements must be followed. Two airspace areas that seem to give pilots the most navigation problems are those for which special fly-through permission is required—such as the Washington, D.C., air defense identification zone (ADIZ)—or temporary flight restrictions (TFRs). While this may seem like "Big Brother" is watching you to catch you making a mistake, this is not happening. These regulations are for safety. These areas are defined and noted by permanent or temporary regulations. This avoids aerial conflicts where military aircraft are training, aircraft are fighting forest fires, or for security purposes. One can easily cross our country north to south or east to west with appropriate planning without hassle.

## One. The World of General Aviation

The ADIZ are areas defined for national security, and if you fly through them, the federal government must know who you are, where you are, and why. They are clearly marked on aviation charts and electronic GPS instruments. Avoiding them is readily accomplished. Entering an ADIZ without proper permission can lead to serious trouble (see Chapter 9). The TFR is the definition of a specific piece of land over which air traffic is not allowed, except for authorized aircraft. This includes places like where the president is visiting, forest fire areas, or stadiums full of people such as over the Super Bowl. The purpose is to keep out all aviation traffic except those authorized to be there for safety reasons.

Another important aspect of airspace is the airplane's altitude. Elevation on topographic maps is determined by height above sea level. But another concept of heights involves how high a location is above the ground. For example, the elevation of my local airport is 4,457 feet above sea level. A plane flying two thousand feet above the airport could have its altitude described two ways in aviation terms. Being two thousand feet above the 4,457 feet of the airport, it is 6,457 feet MSL (mean sea level or above sea level). The plane is also at two thousand feet AGL (above ground level). MSL is a reference, so all planes understand how high they are. AGL is typically used in reference to height obstacles near a plane in the air or low altitudes above ground.

Most aircraft are being followed by a controller somewhere, observing the flight on radar and ensuring that planes do not converge. If the pilot elects to work with the air traffic controllers, the ATC provides aircraft separation and tells pilots where to fly to avoid other aircraft or provide guidance to land at an airport.

While all of this seems confusing and difficult to learn, it really is not. For non-pilots, this is a different world that initially makes no sense at all. But as one goes through the educational process of becoming a pilot (see the next chapter), it begins to unravel and becomes understandable.

Flying a plane across our nation involves transiting a variety of different airspaces. Understanding and knowing airspace requirements is not difficult. In most cases I had the controllers in ATC guiding me safely through airspace where I welcomed help. I did not have to memorize Chapter 3 of the AIM or FAR Part 71 to fly safely and legally. I did have to know what I could or could not do in the airspace I was flying through.

As a non-pilot reading this book, you might find the prospect of understanding airspace regulations daunting, but it is not. Ground school, safety seminars, aviation magazines, computers and the internet, and other aeronautical resources keep you abreast of what you need to know. Additionally, simply flying through different airspace cements this knowledge in your brain. Believe me, while it may seem complicated, it is not.

Consider this: there are almost 10 thousand planes in the skies over the United States at any given time. The purpose of airspace control is to help pilots not hinder them. Safety is the prime directive.

## *Airports*

It is obvious that without airports there would be no aviation. Aviation in the United States blossomed after World War I in 1918. Transient pilots from the war, flying old military aircraft, were called barnstormers. Barnstorming refers to pilots selling rides or performing stunts (aerobatics) in their planes. Aviation was unregulated, and pilots would fly to where they could attract crowds for scenic flights or performing flying circuses. They would land in pastures or open land when possible. In 1926 the Air Commerce Act was passed, regulating aviation. Pilot certifications, aircraft regulations, and flight standards were now mandated, ending the era of barnstorming (due to many unnecessary and regrettable accidents). This act made aviation safer for both pilots and those on the ground. With regulations came the creation of permanent airports. Airplanes now had a stable location to function from. Businesses founded to service aircraft were termed "fixed base operators" (FBO) because they gave pilots established locations from which to operate their businesses. Today, the word FBO is still common in aviation. As aviation became regulated and airports were established, pilots and their aircraft became regular tenants at a single airport. Today FBOs provide fuel, parking, hangars, and maintenance for airplanes. Services are available to both local aircraft based on the field and transient aircraft passing through. FBOs are granted authorization by the airport to do business there and must comply with both the regulations of the airport owner and the FAA.

Within the United States and its territories are 20,081 airports, heliports, and seaplane bases. Airports come and go, so no figures are completely accurate. For example, in 2023 there were 5,217 public airports, but in 1990 there were 5,559 airports. Airports are classified as public (anyone can land there), private (these 14,556 airports are privately owned with some not open to the public), and military (308 airports). Airports are also classified as commercial, reliever, and general aviation (88 percent of all airports are GA).

The federal government has a National Plan of Integrated Airport Systems (NPIAS) that identifies those airports vital to national transportation, national security, and protection of air travel in the United States. Government funding is available to support those designated airports.

Public use airports are owned by cities, counties, or states and all must comply with both the laws of the city or county and the state as well as the federal government. The airport must operate following FAA regulations, again for safety reasons. If commercial air travel is available, then Homeland Security will also have additional rules to follow.

Many airports do not have control towers to direct local air traffic. The amount of local air traffic usually determines if an airport will have its own tower. Sometimes a smaller airport in the vicinity of a larger commercial or military airport will receive a degree of control support from the larger airport's control tower.

The larger the airport, the greater the services to aviation available, such as ATC control or direction. For example, a small, non-towered county airport may offer self-service aviation fuel at a low cost but no other services. If a pilot needs overnight lodging, a rental car, and a hangar to place the plane, the small county airport may not suffice. Readily accessible are apps, websites, books, and other tools that provide current information on services and resources available, including current fuel prices.

## *Aviation Service Industry*

To keep us in the air, we need the support of the aviation industry. This includes every business that sustains flying. It begins with those businesses that manufacture our airplanes and those who sell them. We cannot function without those who make the parts for our planes and those who maintain them. We need aviation charts, electronic flight bags, headsets to hear, survival equipment, and the list goes on and on. We need flight schools, simulators to train on, computer programs to teach us, and textbooks to read. Fuel for our planes is different from our cars and trucks; although, I should point out that some aircraft engines have been converted to use regular gas. Diesel and electric engines are growing in number.

General aviation as a consumer of aviation services is small. In 2021, 2,646 general aviation aircraft were sold in the United States. During that same period 15 million vehicles were sold. Aircraft parts and equipment must be certified by the FAA. For many businesses, the aviation market is too small or too expensive to enter. A narrow consumer base and often FAA-mandated requirements result in higher costs. The COVID-19 (2020–21) epidemic created supply and personnel disruptions that took time to resolve. Additionally, insurance requirements also affect flying. Fewer insurance companies, higher premiums, and stricter eligibility requirements may impact who flies.

While the U.S. aviation industry is not large, it does provide a valuable service to our country, supporting 11 million jobs, grossing $1.8 trillion, and generating over 5 percent of our nation's gross domestic product. Also, these businesses provide support, service, and safety—and they keep us flying.

## *The People Who Staff the Aviation Industry*

We cannot become pilots without airplanes, flight instructors, maintenance facilities, air traffic controllers, and everyone else who works in the aviation industry. These are the people who have found a career working to serve and support us, the pilots and the students desiring to become pilots.

Just one example. For thousands of hours, I have flown in bad weather, needing to avoid thunderstorms, lightning, or heavy rain. One day on a common flight, my wife and I were alone, transiting West Texas, six thousand feet above the ground. We were in and out of rain clouds, with limited forward visibility. On an instrument flight plan in harsh weather, we had two choices: turn around and land or continue forward. In the plane I had limited knowledge of what was in front of us.

But I did have a radio and was speaking with an air traffic controller who was watching my progress on her radar. She also had weather radar. She advised me that if I made a 90-degree turn to my right, in 10 miles I would be out of the weather and could continue directly in the clear.

This is but one instance of all the professionals dedicated to a career in the aviation industry, all working to make our flying safer.

## *General Aviation Summary*

In the United States we have the world's largest general aviation fleet, about 210 thousand aircraft. Since there is no statistical accounting for general aviation pilots, it is estimated that approximately 80 percent of all our 720,605 pilots fly as GA pilots, meaning that we have about 577 thousand GA pilots.

This book will focus on a common sort of nonprofessional pilot, an individual who flies for personal pleasure, sometimes for personal business reasons, who may own a small plane or rents one, and flies enough each year to stay safe.

Now that you have a basic understanding of what general aviation is, let us find out how to become a pilot.

# Two

# Becoming a Pilot

## Ways to Become a Pilot

For most vocations, careers, or professions, one must learn what to do. The instruction may take the form of on-the-job training or some type of educational program, such as a trade school, college, or professional school. Pilot training is regulated by the federal government (the FAA) or the military. There are diverse ways to become a pilot. The type of education a pilot-to-be selects is usually dependent on what kind of pilot the student wants to be or the type of flying they desire to do.

Flight training comes in two separate flavors: civilian or military. Civilian pilot education is controlled by the FAA, while the military is controlled by the branch doing the training. While military flight training is done in military flight schools, civilian flight training may be obtained from an individual flight instructor, FAA-certified flight schools, colleges, universities, or in accelerated flight programs.

## Military Flight Training

Military flight training is conducted by the Army (mostly helicopters), the Air Force, and the Navy, which also conducts the Marine and Coast Guard initial pilot training. Each military branch has its own pilot candidate selection criteria (age and education) as well as rigorous physical standards. Flight standards and physical qualifications may change from time to time. Some branches may offer waivers for disqualifying issues. Do not disqualify yourself before checking with the military service.

The Air Force, Navy, Marines, and Coast Guard require their pilots to be commissioned officers, which normally requires a college or university degree. The Army has commissioned officer pilots, but most Army aviators who are warrant officers, where a high school diploma is the minimum education requirement.

Current selection procedures can be obtained from the military branch recruitment offices or college ROTC programs. Another option is to apply for and be selected to attend one of our military academies and, upon graduation (if qualified), take flight training. Often selection criteria depend on the military's need for pilots. Right now, the U.S. military needs pilots, with shortages expected into the 2030s.

Military flight training, regardless of service, follows similar patterns from start to finish on the path to earning their wings. The initial training is to generate basic pilots. The new military aviators next move to specific training for the aircraft they will fly—be it bombers, advanced helicopters, fighters, cargo, or whatever—and how to fulfill their military missions. Military flight training is very rigorous, rigid, strict, and formal. But our military pilots are the best in the world.

## *Civilian Flight Training*

Civilian flight training can vary from a 60-year-old farmer who is a certified flight instructor (CFI) with a grass strip on his property flying a 65-year-old Cessna 150 to the most modern flight schools with the newest glass cockpits and equipment. Any CFI with access to a small airplane can teach someone to become a recreation, private, or commercial pilot. Most smaller airports in the United States have a CFI or two who charge by the hour for flight training. Learning to fly an ultralight or a light sport aircraft may be more difficult as approved instructors and training aircraft are not that common. But teachers and suitable aircraft for the recreational, private, or commercial pilot are easily located at most airports.

Many airports house small flight schools or flying clubs individuals can join to learn to fly. Learning to fly comes under two FARs: Part 61 (Certification: Pilots, Flight Instructors, and Ground Instructors) or Part 141 (Pilot Schools). Part 61 defines what training and experience is required to become a pilot. Part 141 defines what flight training schools must do to train pilots. An individual CFI trains a student pilot under FAR Part 61. A student pilot who attends an FAA-certified flight school is trained under FAR Part 141. But a student pilot may also attend a flight school under FAR Part 61 rules. Both regulations for becoming a pilot comply with the same standards. Part 61 training is up to the CFI, while Part 141 training is prescribed by the FAA. What is the difference?

Part 61 training is administered by an individual CFI, while Part 141 training is provided via an FAA-approved syllabus by the school's CFIs.

Part 61 training can be tailored by the CFI to meet a student pilot's needs and availability. Part 141 is strict and regimented, closely following FAA guidelines. In Part 141 the student must comply with what and how the school instructs. It is a much more disciplined course of instruction. If one wants to become a professional pilot, the Part 141 school may be the best route to take as it is a very rigorous and regimented process. And because Part 141 schools are more rigorously monitored by the FAA, fewer hours of flight time are required to become certified.

There are about 120 four-year and two-year colleges and universities in the United States that offer degrees in various aspects of aviation that include becoming a professional pilot. Since these include both private and public schools, costs vary considerably. Most airlines prefer their pilots to have a four-year degree. But there are other ways to become a professional pilot besides colleges and universities.

Airline pilot students may attend accelerated aviation programs at professional flight schools to acquire the necessary certificates, ratings, and flight hours to become an airline transport pilot (ATP). Some of these programs allow one to receive their ATP with fewer flight hours. These programs are full-time, and the students become immersed in aviation and flying. With no time off between lessons, learning is accelerated, and it takes less time to become certificated.

Flight training is not cheap. Becoming a private pilot requires both flying lessons and ground school, typically taking several months. This may cost from $8,000 to $15,000, depending on how you train and how long it takes. Training spread out over time costs more because learning recedes over time. Lost time between training flights requires relearning and more flying to get back up to speed. Therefore, the more time off between lessons, the more training required and the higher the cost.

Where does one get the money for flight training? Personal savings, grants, loans, scholarships, or working at a flight school. For advanced flight training after the private pilot certificate, a veteran can use the GI Bill or Veterans Administration (VA) funding, but a student must possess a private pilot certificate as the funds from the GI Bill or VA are for a profession, meaning commercial certificate and higher. Many flight schools or degree programs use their advanced students (now CFIs) to instruct new students, so the former get paid. Some professional pilot schools or programs have arrangements with airlines that provide financial support for advanced students.

Information on where to get flight training is found on the internet or by contacting the University Aviation Association (UAA). UAA is an organization comprised of more than 1,200 colleges and universities worldwide that offer degrees in the aviation industry.

## What Training Is Required to Become a Pilot?

### Ground School

There are several ways to complete the academic portion of flight training. Attend an FAA-approved course in a Part 141 school or a weekend program offered by a flight school, college, or university. Complete a course provided by an FAA-authorized instructor. Or take a home-study program using books and a computer or an online study program. King Schools and Sporty's Pilot Shop offer several of these programs for home study.

The ground school program covers aerodynamics, which is the theory of how airplanes fly. Cockpit instruments are explained. Since all flights should begin and end at an airport, operations, signage, and runway markings are covered. Weather, airspace procedures, aviation rules and regulations, aircraft operations, and navigation are among the subjects taught. At the completion of the ground school, one must take the FAA airman knowledge test and pass with a score of 70 percent or more.

This test has 60 multiple-choice questions with three answer choices per question. One has two hours and 30 minutes to complete the test. The ground school prepares each student to pass the test. Is it hard? The FAA says that 90 percent of the test takers pass on their first try. There are books available or computer programs with guidelines about taking the test and sample tests. To be eligible to take the test one must have proof of completion of an approved ground school program (for Part 141 schools), or Part 61 students can receive approval from their CFI. The tests are taken at a computer testing center. The FAA provides information about where and when one may take the test.

### Flight Training

This is the fun part of learning to become a pilot. This is where you fly a plane. You are taught how to take off and land, how to climb to and hold an altitude. You understand how to turn, climb, descend, and taxi on the ground. You discover how to maneuver the plane, navigate by instruments (and visually observe terrain), watch the instruments in the panel while looking all around for other traffic, switch radio frequencies, and talk on the radio! All at the same time. Everything learned in ground school is applied in the air.

At first, this appears to be daunting, impossible even. Eventually, over time, the vastly different pieces begin to fall into place. Eventually you find that you can scan the instrument panel and watch for traffic outside, all at the same time. You can also switch radio channels, talk, and keep track of where you are, simultaneously. As time passes, and you gain flight hours and experience, it all begins to make sense and what was once impossible is accomplished easily and correctly.

My initial flight training was at Fort Polk, Louisiana, in a non-towered environment. I joined the Army Flying Club to learn to fly. The Army airfield only had a single radio frequency, so switching frequencies was not done. Before I had completed my training, I was transferred to San Antonio, Texas. Now the Army Flying Club was at an old Army airfield with no tower. So, no one on the ground to talk to.

But to the east was an Air Force training airfield. To the south were two Air Force airfields and a busy civilian airport. To the west was another civilian airport. Almost immediately to the north was San Antonio International Airport. Everyone had their own airspace. Flying around the city might require the pilot to speak to controllers at five different airports.

My first flight with a CFI almost caused me to quit flying. It seemed as if all he did was switch frequencies to talk to somebody. I swore I could never learn to do that. Guess what? After a few flights around the city, covering several hours, I became adept at doing this, and soon it became second nature. It just took time and practice.

You are trained to fly solo and navigate cross-country (FAR Part 61.1[b] [3] [ii] a flight of 50 miles or more), which is a requirement to become certified. Additionally, you must learn how to take off, fly, navigate, and land at night. One time as a business professor, I accompanied a group of students to a collegiate business research paper session. They drove to another university, some 150 miles away. I flew. The session terminated in the early evening, so I was going to fly back that night. One student wanted to fly back with me, so I said okay. She then asked how pilots and planes could see at night. She thought that airplanes had headlights like cars to light up the sky. I explained that planes flew in the dark, that planes had no headlights, only landing lights. The landing lights were turned on when landing, only to light up the runway and for taxiing to parking. She thought about that for a few minutes. Her only experience was driving at night in a car where headlights are necessary. Somehow, she could not conceive of any vehicle moving at night without headlights showing the way. Upon confirmation that I would not fly at night with headlights, she decided to return by car. It had headlights.

The more often you fly, the quicker you learn. During my flight training, I would fly early in the morning before work or after work and on the weekends. During my initial eight weeks of flight training at Fort Polk I was flying about an hour a day, five or six days a week. Then I went for a month without flying while being transferred. Over the next six weeks after moving to another Army post, I flew 19.3 hours or about three roughly hour-long flights each week. Keep in mind that also during this time, I had taken on a new job, had to rent an apartment for our family (wife, three daughters, ages 15, 11, and 7), and bought a house.

My actual flight training took three months where I accumulated 68.6 hours flying six different Cessna 150s. In all, while training for my private pilot certificate I was averaging flying about five hours a week. The more often one flies, the quicker the learning, the more retained, and thus the faster the training process. For my ground school I attended a weekend private pilot seminar. We students received by mail text study materials to read before the weekend (this was in 1975, before personal computers). We met Friday evening and began our ground school. The class ran all day Saturday and Sunday, and we took the FAA written exam on Sunday evening. I received a score in the mid-nineties. Weekend ground schools are available in cities around the United States.

## The Training Airplane

What is on the instrument panel of the plane you train in is usually related to who owns the plane. Larger, modern flight schools (and colleges and universities) usually have the current technology (glass, computerized, digital panels). Smaller flight schools, flying clubs, and CFIs often have older planes still with original equipment. The typical general aviation plane for training is 40 to 50 years old. Yet, most planes will have a combination of both older engine gauges and new navigation equipment.

Does it matter? Probably not. What is taught at the private pilot level consists of learning the language and laws of aviation and how to fly a plane. Either an analog or digital panel will be new and different, so one can learn equally on both. If a pilot begins on an analog cockpit and then moves into a glass panel digital plane, transitioning will be easy and intuitive since most pilot candidates today grew up in a digital world.

## Flight Simulators

Flight simulators come in a variety of sizes, costs, and capabilities, and they are a way to become more proficient and competent. A flight simulator is a device which replicates the cockpit instrument panel of a plane and attempts to simulate flying an airplane. Today some simulators are as simple as a desktop computer connected to a yoke, or control column, and rudder pedals; others are massive machines on hydraulic rods that control motion, with the flight crew sitting in an actual cockpit of the plane the simulator emulates.

## Two. Becoming a Pilot

The first flight simulator, also called flight training device (FTD), was created in 1910, but the first practical one was invented by Edwin Link in 1929. The U.S. Army eventually purchased 10 thousand Link trainers between 1939 and 1945. This FTD became the primary flight simulator for World War II. In fact, it was still being used by some foreign countries into the 1970s.

Analog simulators were created in the 1950s, but by the 1960s, the U.S. Air Force was using full-motion flight simulators. The airlines also began using these simulators, and in the 1970s, screens outside the cockpit simulators were used to replicate the outside world, allowing pilots to fly visually or completely on instruments.

In the early 1970s a company called Analog Training Computers, Inc. (ATC) created an analog desktop simulator (21 inches tall, 29 inches wide, 17 inches deep, weighing 37 pounds) representing a typical small general aviation single-engine airplane. Electrically operated, it came with a yoke, throttle lever, and rudder pedals. It looked exactly like the instrument panel of a small plane (and operated exactly like one). It could produce any type of instrument approaches (GPS was not available then). The FAA authorized this device to be used to log instrument training under both Parts 61 and 141.

I purchased an ATC-510 simulator from a defunct flight school in the late 1970s and used it for training for over 20 years. When I bought it, I

Bob practicing on his ATC-510 analog flight simulator. The headset is attached to a recorder playing a tape of ATC instructions that are linked to the instrument program in the simulator.

was a new instrument rated pilot and flew all over the country. I did not buy it to log time for credit but to maintain instrument proficiency and to remain a competent pilot. It helped me do just that.

A few days before a trip, I would program the simulator for the various instrument approaches at my destination airport. When I arrived, I had already made several different practice approaches, so the real landing usually was uneventful. In 20 years of ownership, I estimate I put over two thousand hours on my simulator.

As the dawn of personal computers blossomed, a crude flight simulator program was developed in 1979 for Apple computers. Microsoft purchased the program in 1982, and it has continued to upgrade the program since then. Now it has several competing similar flight simulator programs.

While the military and airlines have the most complex and expensive simulators, there are smaller devices available for general aviation training. The FAA has approved the use of less complex flight training devices, also known as basic aviation training devices (BATD), and the full flight simulators, or advanced aviation training devices (AATD), for FAA training credit. Requirements for FAA-approved flight simulators are covered in FAR Part 141.41 ("Full flight simulators, flight training devices, aviation training devices, and training aids"). BATDs and the AATDs are found at many flight schools.

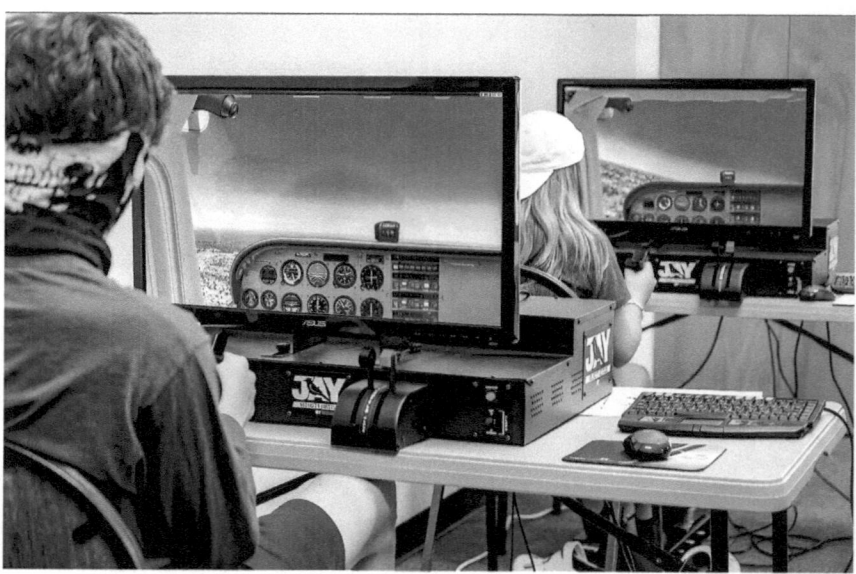

**Students using a modern digital flight simulator with large computer screens (rawpixel.com).**

Basic aviation training devices typically consist of aircraft flight controls (yoke, rudder pedals, throttle quadrant, and panel) and a computer screen. Prices usually begin at several thousand dollars. Frasca International, Inc. and Redbird Flight Simulations, Inc. are two companies that produce and sell FAA-approved flight simulators. Prices for full flight simulators begin around $50,000 and can reach the hundreds of thousands of dollars. These simulators are enclosed and involve motion. Simulators for the airlines can run into millions of dollars due to their size, complexity, and variety of training scenarios.

One can also purchase computer-controlled simulator packages (yoke, throttle quadrant, pedals, computer, and screen) to train and practice on. While not FAA approved for flight credit, they do allow flight training at no cost other than purchasing the equipment (around a few hundred dollars). Whatever device one buys or uses at a flight school, it allows a pilot to remain sharp and proficient. It paid off for me.

## Being a Private Pilot

Being a private pilot allows you to fly by visual flight rules (VFR), day or night. CFIs will always say that "getting a private pilot certificate is just getting a license to learn." This means that receiving your private certificate allows you to fly alone or with passengers, day, or night, but always in clear weather. New pilots have little experience. This comes by building hours in the sky—safely—and staying within the limitations of your certificate and the aircraft you are flying.

Flying in marginal weather. Landing in considerable crosswinds. Discovering less power in extremely hot weather. Flying into strong headwinds, taking longer to reach your destination. Encountering these events should create a "lessons learned" scenario where the pilot learns—firsthand—what to do or not do.

Flying, over time, provides the experience necessary to remain safe. Yet another form of gaining experience is to train for advanced certificates and ratings. One gains a high degree of additional sophistication and competency, becoming a more proficient pilot.

# *Advanced Ratings and Certificates*

## Is Advanced Training Worth It?

The answer is: "It depends."

If one desires to be a professional pilot, then advanced certificates and ratings are required. I have two other thoughts on the subject. If a pilot wants to become better, obtaining higher levels of pilot training is certainly one way to accomplish that. In addition to making one a better pilot, the training makes one a safer pilot. The academic portion of advanced training increases one's understanding of aviation. While certainly increasing the skill level of your aviating, your knowledge also grows. Besides, the more certificates and ratings earned, the lower your insurance premiums. My other thought is: if a private pilot has an instrument rating, and has no desire to fly for hire, additional certificates are not necessary. There are other less costly ways to remain safe, competent, and proficient. To be honest, I must confess that twice I enrolled in a flight school commercial pilot program and never finished. It also took me three sessions with an FAA flight examiner to get my instrument rating.

I have friends who are ATPs yet will never sit in the cockpit of an airliner. I know CFIs who have never occupied the right seat teaching a student pilot, and I have friends with commercial certificates who have never earned a dime as a pilot. I am not against advanced credentials to improve a pilot's expertise, but there are separate ways to become better pilots. Chapter 10, Advanced Proficiency Training, covers diverse ways to accomplish this.

The chapter you are reading addresses the typical advanced ratings and certificates most commonly sought including the instrument rating (allowing a pilot to navigate and fly through clouds using the plane's instruments), commercial pilot certificate (the authorization to fly for hire), certified flight instructor (CFI: authorized to teach students to fly), multi-engine rating (being able to fly a plane with more than one engine), and the most senior aviation certificate: airline transport pilot (ATP: needed to fly airlines). Professional flight schools teach all the above in their professional pilot training program. From 1,000 to 1,500 flight hours, depending on the type of flight school, are required to receive an ATP certificate. Flight schools use their newly minted CFIs to teach the school's private pilot students to build flight hours.

These ratings and certificates are a requirement for anyone desiring to become a professional pilot, and this training will make any pilot safer, more proficient, and more competent.

## My Own Experience with Advanced Training

A couple of years after I received my private pilot certificate in the mid–1970s, I had a 300-mile Army trip planned. Usually, I would depart late the day before so I would be there early the next day to work. Unfortunately, my home city was overcast with low clouds, prohibiting flying visually. Therefore, I had to drive. Between 20 to 30 miles out of the city, the weather cleared, totally. The clouds were only around one to two thousand feet thick. With an instrument rating I could have departed and in a few minutes been out of the clouds and enjoyed a visual flight the rest of the way. And this was not the first time I was grounded because of a few feet of overcast. Without delay I decided to get my instrument rating.

## Why It Took Three Tries to Become Instrument Rated

I had the GI Bill I could use for instrument and commercial training. At the time, I was a low-time private pilot. I had used my GI Bill benefits to get two masters' degrees and a PhD, so I did not have enough left to complete the commercial/instrument course requirements. Still, I enrolled in a local Part 141 aviation school for their Instrument Commercial course, where I studied and flew as a student throughout the summer of 1977. All I needed was the instrument rating, but the two subjects were taught as a single course. Four months later my GI Bill money was spent, and I had to drop out of the program. I did not receive either the instrument rating or commercial certificate.

I continued to postpone some trips due to IFR weather that grounded me. In December 1977, I bought a 10-year-old Cessna 172, a VFR-only plane. It was purchased since the reliability of scheduling rental aircraft was risky for someone who had to adhere to a rigid travel regime. Until my plane was set up for instrument flying, I had to continue to use rental planes for my instrument training. I found an avionics shop that could convert the plane for instrument flight (see Chapter 4 for details).

With my instrument training completed I had an afternoon appointment to fly with an FAA examiner to get my rating. We met, and the verbal interview went perfectly. We climbed into a rental C-172 for the flight test (after a thorough preflight). As soon as I started the engine, someone was banging on the examiner's door. Opening it, he was told that his wife had just been in an auto accident. Telling me to shut down, he ran away.

Toward the end of the week, I rescheduled the flight test after work hours. The day of the exam was remarkably busy and demanding for me. When I arrived, I was as worn out as he was, due to his wife's accident (she was bruised but okay). Again, we began the flight test in a rented 172. But clearly I was not ready. The examiner's mind was also elsewhere. I made minor mistakes (which were immediately corrected) even before we made it to the test area. It was evident to the instructor that I was not ready this early evening, so he said to return to the airport. He said he would not record any of our two sessions, so they never officially happened. I never failed an instrument flight examination because I never took one.

A friend was a certified flight instructor-instrument (CFII) who took me under his wing. He was excellent, and he signed me off as competent to take the instrument rating exam. On May 29, 1979—a Tuesday—I flew my now instrument-equipped 172 to the airport where the examiner had his office. I had a late afternoon appointment for the instrument flight test, but he was not there.

Apparently, before I arrived, another pilot showed up for the instrument rating test without an appointment, and the examiner, thinking he was me, went flying with him. When they returned, he discovered his error. Being nice, he agreed to take me up for the exam. Not so good as he tried to complete the test in about 30 minutes. I could not do it. He recognized that he was rushing too fast. We returned to his airport, the test incomplete. He apologized and said we could do it again on Saturday, June 2. I explained that my instrument written exam would expire on May 31, and that I could not take my flight exam with an expired written. Thinking for a few minutes, knowing the regulations as thoroughly as he did, he asked for my pilot logbook. In it he wrote, "Instrument flight Test incomplete due to mechanical problems." He said we would resume the test on Saturday morning and that if I completed it my rating would be effective on May 29, the day the test began. Smiling, he said he would save the entire afternoon just for me.

On Saturday morning, June 2, 1979, I flew 1.7 hours with my CFII, going over everything I would be evaluated on. Returning home for lunch, I was worried. Twice before I had not completed my instrument flight exam. I had not done well with either one. I was a clinical psychologist in the Army and had successfully used clinical hypnosis on anxious patients. As a sport psychologist for a U.S. Olympic team I had used it to increase confidence and enhance personal performance. After lunch I induced self-hypnosis to relax me and calm me down. I had about an hour to accomplish this. It worked.

I showed up and we took to the air. Both of us were relaxed, calm, and into flying. The examiner was not rushed, and we took our time. I was perfect. On the ground he entered in my logbook, "Instrument Flight Test passed satisfactorily." Now I was an instrument rated pilot, no more being grounded for a little cloud cover. Over the next 36 years, I logged 1,054.4 flight hours of flying in actual instrument weather. I did not log time when doing instrument training or time flying on an instrument flight plan in VFR conditions, only time flown under IFR conditions. The instrument rating made all the difference in the world for me. It allowed me to conduct flights in conditions that would previously have kept me grounded.

## My Commercial Pilot Training

My first experience with the Part 141 Commercial/Instrument program in San Antonio, Texas, took four months but was never completed.

In 1990 I had not flown for six months due to a motorcycle accident that had destroyed my left leg. Because of the accident, I only flew 47 hours that year. I did not own a plane as I had sold it before the accident (see Chapter 5).

In August 1991 I enrolled in another Part 141 school to get my commercial pilot certificate. As an aviation writer I thought an advanced certificate would give me more credibility. It was a full-time program, which I began on Sunday, July 8, 1991. I received all my study books and materials. Our training plane was the 1985 Cessna Cutlass RG, a retractable 172. For a few weeks I went to school every day, doing both classroom work and flying. Despite not being able to walk, I could fly.

I missed not having my own airplane. The Part 141 school was expensive, but I had the savings to cover the cost. I had sold my last plane two and a half years prior. During this time, the motorcycle accident and beginning a new tenure-track teaching position resulted in two separate six-month periods where I had to quit flying. I missed that, and flying in the Part 141 school reminded me how much.

A physician on the field owned a Grumman Tiger, a low-wing, four-seat, single-engine plane with a sliding canopy, which he let me fly with his instructor. I could preflight the plane, and with the sliding canopy, entering and exiting the plane was easy even with my leg disabilities. I found one for sale (see Chapter 5). I had enough money for a considerable down payment with my savings for the flight school. So, what was more important? My commercial pilot certificate or owning my own plane? I bought the Grumman Tiger and quit flight school. For the five and a half months left in the year I put 134.2 hours on my Tiger. I could not walk, but I could fly. I really missed flying. My attempts to earn my commercial pilot certificate ended forever when I bought my Tiger.

## *Are Advanced Ratings and Certificates in Your Future?*

Does a private pilot need advanced ratings and certificates to be a better pilot? Probably not. I certainly agree that pilots with advanced credentials should be safer pilots. Undeniably, commercial pilots are trained to higher standards than private pilots. But is a commercial certificate needed to be a safer pilot? Absolutely not. See Chapter 10 for ways to become more proficient as a pilot.

Research shows that flight experience makes a pilot safer. Motivation, responsibility, understanding personal limitations, good judgment, and decision-making skills are attributes that make pilots safer. While advanced credentials improve these attributes, this is not the only way to go.

## *The Instrument Rating*

In my opinion, this rating is the most important for a private pilot. It allows a pilot to fly safely in times of reduced visibility. Often, my wife and I had to remain on the ground when others departed into white puffy clouds or punched through a thousand feet of overcast into clear, blue skies above. Insurance companies adore the instrument rating. Instrument-rated pilots can navigate in times of limited visibility when unexpected severe weather surfaces, or when a non-instrument pilot pushes the limits in failing weather to get home.

What is flying on instruments? What does it entail? Flying visually is like driving a car in that the driver must be aware of the road conditions; other traffic; potential hazards such as pedestrians, bikes, and motorcycles; road signs indicating curves or incoming traffic; and stop signs and traffic lights. If on a new road or street, signs provide information and guidance on which way to go. Today's cars have GPS systems telling the driver what to do to get somewhere. Flying visually is like this without the traffic (except when landing at a busy airport). The pilot is not following a road but visually observing terrain below and following either GPS or compass headings. Flying on instruments usually means that these external visual cues are gone due to limited outside visibility.

An instrument pilot is trained to interpret the flight information provided by instruments in the plane indicating speed, spatial orientation, attitude of the plane, heading, altitude, and configuration of the plane in the air as well as movement. The pilot understands what the instruments are indicating about what the plane is doing in space relative to what the pilot wants the plane to do. At the same time, the pilot may be talking to an air traffic controller who can provide feedback on the plane's performance. Additionally, the controller can provide information on weather conditions, traffic, and expected future flight requirements. Flying by instruments usually means the pilot is talking to someone else to provide guidance and respond to questions regarding flight conditions, weather, or instrument procedures. The pilot is not alone; someone else is watching the flight on radar and available to help in any way needed.

For most pilots, learning to fly on instruments is not difficult. Yes, it is complicated at first, but soon it becomes an intuitive process, and with practice it becomes easy and almost second nature. To remain safe, the pilot must fly on instruments often, practice, and/or fly simulators. One typically does not obtain the instrument rating and immediately start a night flight in total clouds and heavy rain. Usually new instrument pilots begin by flying through benign clouds or in conditions where visibility is semi-obscured. Flying by instruments is being done, yet sufficient visual outside cues are available, if needed. As time passes and experience is gained, instrument flying becomes easier, and confidence is established. Soon, night IFR flight becomes easy.

Sometimes I would depart and fly in visual weather. But nearing our destination, IFR weather would prevail, like rain, clouds, or overcast. Knowing the weather an hour or so away, I would just ask for an IFR clearance to continue and, when approved, adjust to the proper IFR altitude, study my instrument approach plate for the runway in use, and arrive at my destination with no problems. I did not fly in thunderstorms, ice, hail, or dangerous winds. A wise pilot avoids such conditions unless the aircraft is equipped to manage that sort of weather. But I would advise to never fly into thunderstorms (or even close). I seldom encountered such ferocious weather. If I did, I could stay on the ground or fly a different route. After receiving my instrument rating, few flights were canceled. Delays occurred, routes changed, sometimes I did not fly, but overall, the instrument rating made flying easier, less traumatic, safer, and much more enjoyable.

## Some Further Thoughts

Advanced training becomes expensive. Aircraft rental and fuel top the list of costs. Some pilots train in their own planes, which reduces expenses somewhat. An instrument rating may cost $8,000 to $15,000 (again using your own plane may reduce the cost somewhat). The commercial pilot certificate may run from $25,000 to $35,000, while a multi-engine rating may cost $10,000 to $15,000.

These costs can depend on how often you train, whether your education is under Part 61 or Part 141, if you use your own plane or rent, and how fast you absorb what you are learning. There are many variables and cost variances. Training full-time under a Part 61 CFI may cut costs considerably, but flying only a few hours a month can raise the cost greatly. There are loans, grants, and scholarships available for flight training. Other chapters in this book show how to remain proficient without advanced ratings or certificates.

If one wants to be a professional pilot, then many ratings and certificates are required. If one wants to be trained as a professional pilot but not work as one, the higher advanced training may be the way to go. But as this book will explain, there are many ways to become and remain highly skilled as a pilot and to be as safe as possible. The key is not how many ratings and certificates one possesses, but how often one flies and how often one practices what they fly. The safest pilots in the world are those who fly our airlines and military aircraft. They train and fly constantly. There are ways to emulate this training and experience while keeping the costs low. Fly simulators, attend safety seminars, fly with different CFIs, get the flight review every year instead of bi-annually, or fly with safety pilots. Taking online courses or safety programs and reading aviation books and magazines are inexpensive ways to increase your aviation knowledge and make you a better pilot.

## *Flying with Family*

Most new pilots are eager to share their new skills with family or friends. For those like me, we want our significant other to share our joy of flying and the ability to use a plane to visit fun destinations.

Usually, our special passenger will have some anxiety unless, of course, they come from an aviation background. This anxiety is the result

Bob's wife, Anita, in the right seat, eagerly awaiting another flight.

of apprehension of flying in a small airplane and the knowledge that the pilot has minimal experience and has just learned to fly. The mission of this flight is to show and convince your "other" that small planes are safe and your skills as a pilot are exemplary. This is not the time to play daredevil!

I had heard several horror stories where a new and young pilot wanted to take a friend, spouse, or special other for a flight. Unfortunately, the new pilot wanted to show off their aerial skills, so they took the passenger through stalls, steep turns, and other stomach-turning maneuvers, so scaring the person in the right seat that they vowed never to ride in a small plane again. I learned to fly so I could fly myself on trips for the Army, but I also wanted my wife to accompany me.

## My Wife's First Flight with Me

I wanted to introduce Anita to flying as a comfortable, enjoyable mode of transportation to travel to fun places quickly and safely. I selected a very calm, clear Saturday for her first flight. Discussing the preflight inspection of the Cessna 150, I explained details so she would understand that this procedure would ensure that the plane was safe. Preflight completed, I helped her in the plane, showing her how to buckle up. Moving around the plane, I entered, closed my door, and strapped myself in. Describing the starting process and demonstrating the checking of the control surfaces and the run-up to check all the instruments and the health of the engine relaxed her. Slowly moving down the runway, I rose very gently, the transition from wheels on the ground to flight so smooth it went unnoticed. We cruised around San Antonio, making my performance appear like a professional pilot. We both had headsets, so she could hear everyone I spoke to. We did not go very high, the turns were gentle and fully coordinated, and our flight brought us back to the airport in under 30 minutes. My pattern was high and wide, so the turns were slow and easy. The landing was almost perfect; I parked the plane and tied it down. Anita thought the short flight was fun and safe.

## What You Should Do

A CFI friend said that the significant other's first flight should be with a CFI, an experienced pilot with the capability to demonstrate how safe and gentle a small plane can be.

I do not agree with this. Yes, a first flight with a CFI should do exactly that. My disagreement centers on the fact that the significant other's flying trips will not be with the CFI (hopefully) but will be with the new pilot. I believe, psychologically, that the first flight with the new pilot would best demonstrate that both the plane and the skills of the pilot are safe.

There are exceptions to this. If your "other" has a profound fear of flying or small planes, probably a first ride with an experienced professional would be best. If your "other" accepts flying as fun, then you can step in and demonstrate your skills as a safe pilot. While my wife had never flown in a small plane before, she knew I would never do anything to harm or scare her. She was right.

## Flying with Family Is Fun

Flying with family members can be great. In some families, the love of aviation passes from one generation to the next. In other families, the pilot has no one who shares their passion.

When I became a pilot in 1975, I was a 38-year-old Army major. Our three daughters were Suzi (15), Julie (11), and Karen (7). They knew I was competent, and their mother excitedly described her flights in an airplane. So, when I invited my girls to fly with me, I have no recollection of any first flight with them. I assume it was safe and interesting for them. Flights became so common that our youngest thought for some time that every family had an

**Bob and Anita's daughter Suzi sleeping in the back seat.**

aerial station wagon parked somewhere. Like riding in the back of our car on long trips, it became boring. The customary behavior exhibited by our daughters was to fall asleep, waking up upon approach to landing.

One younger daughter had a friend who wanted to fly with her. After convincing the friend's mother that I was a safe pilot, a Saturday morning was scheduled for a trip to another airport for the proverbial $100 hamburger. The little girl's mom was a nurse, telling me her daughter never suffered from motion sickness (yet she gave the girl some Dramamine before our trip).

Bob and Anita's daughter Julie asleep in the back seat.

Upon leveling off, the little girl became so sick, she vomited all over the back of the plane. Forced to return to my home base, we spent much of the day cleaning the rear of the plane. Lesson learned: don't take your kid's friends flying.

One problem. Anita and I had three daughters, and all my planes would only seat four people. Most trips I flew only had my wife as a passenger. Until our oldest went to college, one had to remain home. This never became an issue because the girls usually were involved in so many activities that staying behind was no concern. Sometimes Anita would stay home so dad and daughters could bond in the sky.

## Going Away to College

For those pilots with kids, nothing beats general aviation for checking out colleges or visiting your child at their school. Suzi knew she wanted to go to a women's college in New Orleans. It was about 550 miles away from San Antonio, Texas, so we would stop in Lake Charles, Louisiana, for fuel and food and then continue. The trip by car would take 12 to 14 hours, but by plane it was six to seven hours. Now the four of us left behind could fly together to visit Suzi.

When it was Julie's turn to select a college, I suggested Northern Arizona University in Flagstaff, where I had received a master's degree. The two of us planned a visit, a dad-daughter fun trip. We would fly from San Antonio to Lake Powell, Arizona; camp there a couple of days; fly to Flagstaff; and then fly back home.

Karen was the last to leave for college. Her quest for schools initially focused on California. Living in Canyon, Texas, near Amarillo, Karen had five schools she wanted to visit located in the Los Angeles and San Francisco areas of California. General aviation was the only way we could travel three thousand miles in a week.

Flying with family can be an uncomplicated way to travel. My wife occupied the right seat for thousands of hours, while my daughters slept hundreds of hours in the back. But to enjoy flying with family, they must be introduced slowly and with minimal drama. Allow them to enjoy flight without fear, anxiety, or remorse. Carefully show them how much fun a small plane can be and how it is a hassle-free means to get to fun destinations for fascinating vacations. As an aside, none of my daughters or my wife ever got sick in our planes.

## Three

# Aviation Organizations and Associations

Without our aviation organizations, we in the United States would not enjoy the freedom of flight we have. Aviation organizations are the backbone, the ultimate promoters of our industry. They support our ability to fly in the safest aviation system in the world and protect our right to fly. In addition, they advance the technology of our industry while interfacing with our government to ensure aviation is dealt with fairly. Every pilot should join some of these organizations and become an active participant. These organizations are the mainstay of our industry.

## What Is an Aviation Organization?

Across our country there are hundreds of organizations, associations, and clubs devoted to aviation. They range from the international to national, to state and local levels. Memberships run from several hundred thousand people to a dozen or fewer. All originated to serve the needs of pilots, crew members, aviation service people, and those who enjoy aviation. While most were created to fill a specific need in aviation, all seem to also serve a social purpose. All members share an interest in a specific area of aviation.

These organizations range from local airport flying clubs to international professional groups. They may represent a vocation, aviation businesses, labor organizations, various specific groups of pilots, aviation professions, specific variants of aviation, owners of specific manufactured aircraft, and many other unique factions of the aviation world.

For almost five decades I have belonged to several aviation organizations: one international association of aviation writers (as a director), three national general aviation organizations (one as an officer and director), two state pilot associations (cofounder, officer, and director of both), the local chapter of a national organization, and four flying clubs. As a professor at a state university, I created a student flying club that belonged to a national collegiate aviation organization (I was the faculty sponsor and advisor).

A review of the various aviation associations and organizations over the past 50 years reveals the changes that have occurred in general aviation.

## *What Are They? Where Are They?*

Some organizations are associated only with a specific brand or even model of aircraft. Others represent various aspects of aviation and are typically national in scope. State organizations represent general aviation pilots within a state. Some organizations focus on a specific segment of aviation such as experimental (homebuilt) aircraft, while others deal with education and safety aspects of aviation. Many cater to the professional tier of aviation, while the largest associations specialize in general aviation.

All these organizations have a specific purpose created to meet the needs and expectations of pilots, mostly within a narrow framework. The bigger the organization, though, the broader its benefits to its members. Most active pilots and aircraft owners belong to several aviation organizations simultaneously to reap greater benefits.

The two main national general aviation organizations are the Aircraft Owners and Pilots Association (AOPA) and the Experimental Aircraft Association (EAA). AOPA has almost 400 thousand members, and EAA has more than 220 thousand members and more than 900 local chapters scattered across the nation. Both cast a broad net for general aviation pilots. Then there are aircraft brand specific associations that provide all sorts of information for owners of a specific make of plane such as Piper, Cessna, Beechcraft, Mooney, Daher TBM, and Cirrus. State pilot groups usually do two or three things. They plan fly-ins for their members, they host aviation safety seminars, and they liaise with the state aviation divisions to keep each other apprised of aviation needs and pilot desires within the state.

Local flying clubs are a group of local pilots who share what they do with their hangar mates. Some clubs own aircraft that the members maintain and fly. Some pilot organizations are large enough where they are for-profit businesses and are staffed and managed by paid owners and employees. Others are nonprofit and run by nonpaid volunteers.

Larger aviation organizations also are designed to make money, but their purpose is to serve and represent a segment of aviation. Nonprofit organizations cannot lobby Congress to promote legislation, but a for-profit aviation-related business can become involved in the legislative process. But even for-profit aviation organizations usually seek out volunteers to do specific jobs related to aviation such as being an airport representative or teaching safety seminars or assisting at various meetings or fly-ins the organization sponsors. Some create separate political action components to pursue aviation interests. Others may create foundations to bring in money to support special interests. The larger organizations tend to be IRS 501(c)(3) tax exempt organizations.

Most state and local (and some national) pilot organizations are managed by unpaid volunteers and funded by dues and donations, but most national aviation associations have paid staff. The membership dues typically do not cover expenses, so they have industry sponsors. They are also involved with industry tie-ins that provide benefits for members such as insurance, rental cars, industry discounts, etc., which earn commissions for the association. Some have foundations that can raise funds to support various association events such as pilot safety seminars.

There are also many charity aviation organizations that provide, voluntarily, aircraft trips to shuttle animals such as rescue dogs, or people who need medical treatment, or goods and supplies for emergency relief projects. Some use volunteer pilots and planes to provide medical personnel for care around the world.

## *The History of Aviation Organizations*

AOPA was founded in 1932 to promote general aviation. Today it is the premier voice of general aviation in the United States. The Experimental Aircraft Association was founded in 1953 to promote and support people who built, repaired, or flew home-built recreational aircraft. Today it has expanded to encompass a full spectrum of general aviation aircraft owners and pilots besides just those built by people, not manufacturers.

Aviation in the United States came about in the 1920s after World War I when military pilots returned home eager to continue in this new mode of transportation. As the U.S. aviation industry grew and developed, airplanes went from open cockpit, wood- and cloth-covered vehicles to being totally enclosed in metal. World War II came along in the 1940s, and hundreds of thousands of men and women were trained as military pilots. When the war ended, aviation flourished. The U.S. peak in aviation was in the early 1980s. We had 827 thousand pilots, and the general aviation fleet consisted of 208 thousand planes. Forty years later in 2020, the number of U.S. pilots had decreased to under 700 thousand.

A membership ad for Aircraft Owners and Pilots Association.

In the 1970s and '80s, general aviation was increasing, and small aircraft were used to get pilots, families, and friends from where they lived to a fun place for a day, sometimes for a weekend or a week's vacation. Corporations transported businesspeople across the nation to ply their professions. Flying was not as expensive as it is today; flying was affordable for many people.

Aviation organizations 50 years ago focused on the fun aspect of flying. As the late '80s and '90s rolled around, general aviation grew smaller. Fewer new planes were being built, government rules and regulations demanded more of aviation, and safety education was needed. In the '80s and early '90s, aviation organizations lacked volunteers to assist in the management of these organizations. In the late 1990s and the beginning of the twenty-first century, the number of general aviation planes and pilots began to shrink. The Covid epidemic in 2020 and 2021 was devastating to aircraft travel, both commercial and private.

Membership in most aviation groups also decreased. While safety education remained a strong focus of aviation organizations, most became involved in tackling the tasks related to the rising cost of owning aircraft and flying and the increase of government regulations negatively impacting pilots.

Many pilots and aircraft owners of today are flying less because of the cost. The average age of the general aviation pilot is increasing (mid-forties). This expansion of aging aviators produces another problem, passing the FAA physical exam. The typical age of the smaller general aviation aircraft is more ancient, 40 to 50 years old.

New general aviation aircraft are too expensive for many pilots, so we own and fly legacy aircraft. Because of many demands on our time (careers, family, life), finding aviation organization volunteers is difficult. What aviation organizations did to attract and hold members 30 to 40 years ago no longer suffices. So national organizations must change tactics, e.g., doing away with big (i.e., expensive) annual meetings and instead spreading the meetings all over the United States to cater more to local pilots.

There are still pilots and airplane owners who can afford to use their planes to have fun over a weekend, visiting places. General aviation is making a comeback. More people are becoming interested in flying. One good aspect of Covid was the increased need and appreciation for safer and more convenient transportation by private aircraft. People and businesses found that travel by private air was quicker, safer, and more expeditious than by commercial means. General aviation is on the rise again.

## Why Belong?

The two biggest problems with the lower end of general aviation are government regulations that cost pilots considerable money and the high expense of owning and flying. It becomes more difficult to justify the expense of aircraft ownership.

Aviation organizations are vital to the industry. They represent our passion for flying, work with the government, and support aviation. Pilots should join and serve in leadership positions in these organizations. Much of what I know about aviation has been because I belonged to pilot groups. As president of the United States Pilots Association, I spent years working in aviation at the national level. A major learning experience. As cofounder of two state pilot associations (Texas and New Mexico), I have worked with state aviation officials and served pilots and aviation within the state. As a member of several local flying clubs, I have enjoyed sharing adventures, stories, trips, aircraft, and knowledge with pilots much more experienced than I am.

A noticeably big benefit to joining an aviation organization pertains to networking and financial aid. Many organizations provide mentoring programs for new pilots or those who are interested in aviation careers. Grants and scholarships may be available to assist in paying for flight school and aviation training. Aviation association members may help people who want a career in aviation to overcome hurdles, cut through red tape, provide professional advice, or otherwise assist students to finance training or find sponsors.

Over 40 years ago, I founded a student flying club at West Texas State University (now West Texas A&M). I was also a contributing editor for the weekly aviation newspaper *General Aviation News*. I have authored articles

Bob receiving the United States Pilots Association (USPA) Outstanding Member of the Year award from the USPA president, Robert L. Gamble.

## Three. Aviation Organizations and Associations

> Page 4—Canyon Sunday News
>
> **U.S. Pilots Association**
>
> # Worthington named outstanding
>
> ALBUQUERQUE, N.M. — Bob Worthington, noted aviation writer and West Texas State University management professor, was awarded the 1985 National Award for the Most Oustanding Member of the United States Pilots Association.
>
> This annual award is presented to the member who has contributed most to general aviation. The USPA consists of over 3,600 members representing several state pilot associations. Each state nominates a candidate for the award and the USPA selects one from this group. The award was presented at the USPA Annual Meeting on May 31 and June 1 at the AMFAC Hotel in Albuquerque, N.M.
>
> Worthington is a charter member, newsletter editor, and director of the Texas Pilots Association and also serves as a director of the USPA. He was selected as the TPA candidate for his contributions to promoting aviation which includes serving as an officer and board member; and organizing and hosting the following events: a fly-in weekend in Amarillo in August 1984, a conference with the Aircraft Owners and Pilots Association Annual Convention in Nashville, TN, in October 1984, a quarterly USPA Directors Meeting in San Antonio in February 1985, and a conference to be held at the 1985 AOPA Convention in Washington, DC in October of this year.
>
> In addition to work directly related to the USPA, Worthington promotes general aviation as a writer for numerous aviation publications. He is contributing editor of *General Aviation News*, author of the "Airport Business Quarterly Review" published by *Airport Services Management* magazine, a columnist for *Cessna Owners' Magazine* and staff writer for *Freebird Flyer* and *Flying Review* magazine. His research and reporting on aviation activities require him and his wife Anita to travel throughout the U.S., flying about 40,000 miles each year in their own aircraft.
>
> The USPA, headquartered in St. Louis, MO, is a non-profit association of state pilot organizations and their members. The purpose is to represent, on the national level, state pilot associations that promote aviation safety and education, and provide an influential body of knowledge for local, state and national levels of government regarding general aviation.

**A newspaper article about Bob receiving the United States Pilots Association 1985 Outstanding Member of the Year award.**

about the creation of the university flying club. At that time, in 1982, several pilots—who had read my articles—were in the process of forming a Texas state pilot organization, and they invited me to join. They were being mentored by the U.S. Pilots Association (USPA), a new organization.

USPA was created in 1981 as a replacement for a failed national aviation organization. The purpose for USPA was to assist states in forming state pilot organizations, promote general aviation, and support flying safety education. I joined USPA and helped cofound the Texas Pilots Association. A few years later, I was a cofounder of the New Mexico Pilots Association.

Over time, my memberships in a variety of aviation organizations have resulted in lifelong friendships with an amazing group of pilots. My passion for aviation has been nurtured and blossomed because I belonged to a group of like-minded people. Many of my most memorable flights were taken with other pilots and their spouses. I have visited several federal aviation institutions and agencies, flown simulators of the largest airlines, and toured most major general aviation aircraft manufacturing plants, all because I belonged to the U.S. Pilots Association.

I cannot emphasize enough the benefits (both personal and professional) of becoming a part of an aviation organization. I suggest that AOPA be on the top of your list. It will be the best source for aviation information and be able to perfectly answer any question you may have. Once the FAA investigated me for violating probably the most secure airspace there is—around the U.S. capital. The AOPA legal staff assisted my response, and the FAA dismissed the charges. I describe what happened in Chapter 9.

Check the list of aviation organizations at the end of this book. I am sure you can find some perfect for you.

## Four

# Buying an Airplane

## *How and Why I Bought My First Airplane*

Purchasing a plane is a large investment, ranking between a house and a car—well, for most of us anyway! Often it is hard to justify owning a plane. A house is needed to live in, and a car gets us to work. But for the average general aviation pilot finding a solid reason to spend a fortune on

Bob's first plane, a Cessna 172 (before it was painted).

a plane becomes an almost impossible task. Yet pilots can rationalize why aircraft ownership surpasses renting or leasing or belonging to a flying club. To make a point, aircraft ownership is not mandatory.

In 40 years of flying, I have owned nine planes. My first plane, a 1965 Cessna 172F Skyhawk, was purchased in 1977. I must have had a good reason I needed to own it because my wife agreed it was necessary.

Stationed at Fort Sam Houston in San Antonio, Texas, I was assigned to the staff of the Army Health Services Command, which was responsible for all Army medical services and medical facilities throughout the United States. As the clinical psychology consultant, I was responsible for everything involving Army psychology within the entire United States. A major part of my job involved visiting Army medical facilities that had psychologists, about one every other week.

Commercial air travel usually was a day-long adventure because few Army posts are near big-city airports. This meant flying from San Antonio to Dallas–Fort Worth, then to another big city, followed by a shorter commuter flight. As a pilot belonging to a local flying club, I could fly myself in rental aircraft in less time, and the Army would reimburse me. But that became a hassle as I would have a plane reserved only to find it unavailable due to some sort of aircraft problems or scheduled maintenance.

## My First Plane

One day, George McKee, owner of the flying club, said he had the answer to my scheduling difficulties. He had just bought a 12-year-old, VFR-only Cessna 172 in excellent condition. He would sell it to me for $8,500.

On December 26, 1977, I took my first flight in N8233U; the tachometer had 1,393 hours on it. My checkout flight took 30 minutes with one landing. It flew perfectly. But first I needed to determine its condition, and Mr. McKee provided me with his pre-buy inspection, only a few days old. I made an appointment with the San Antonio FAA Flight Standards District Office and met with a maintenance inspector. I was able to borrow all the plane's logbooks, and he went over every maintenance logbook and explained what it meant. An entry indicated that a wing had been severely damaged when another plane ran into it. It was repaired, and the inspector said he knew the shop that did the work and that they had an excellent reputation. Based on the maintenance records, the inspector deemed the plane to be well maintained. Looking at the pre-buy report, he said that he did not see any maintenance issues or concerns. I bought the plane on December 30, 1977. The total cost to me was $8,960, including a $25 title search, $425 in taxes, and $10 for registration.

## Four. Buying an Airplane

The 172F had a Continental six-cylinder O 300 D, 145-horsepower engine with a time between overhauls (TBO) of 1,800 hours or 12 years. The calendar TBO just expired, but the engine was in excellent condition with 1,400 hours. It was not instrument equipped but came with two Narco Mark 12 Nav/Comms, a King KR 86 ADF, and a Narco AT 50A transponder.

Over the next four years, I put slightly over 800 hours on it, had it IFR equipped and painted, and had the engine rebuilt. I flew it from Texas into Canada, from California to Maine, and to almost every state in between.

Occasionally the city of San Antonio would be covered with clouds, too low for safe VFR flying but only a couple thousand feet thick. Thirty miles from the center of the city, it would be clear. This happened often enough for me to realize that I needed my instrument rating.

In mid–October 1978, I took my plane to an avionics shop to have it IFR equipped. The shop had used avionics for instrument landing system (ILS), VOR, and localizer approaches but explained that the plane's electrical system was not designed to support the additional avionics. The simple solution was to replace the 1965 generator system with a Cessna 152 alternator system. The total cost to make the plane IFR compliant was $1,000. Now my instrument training could begin.

When it was time for the 1978 annual maintenance and after getting the plane IFR equipped, I decided to also have it painted. The annual was $379 and the paint cost $2,020.

Throughout my first year of ownership, I flew 163.5 hours. Because I flew for Army business, the Army reimbursed me to fly my plane, but not all flying costs. The Army would reimburse me what an airline ticket would cost, not what I would spend for the flight. The total cost to own and operate N8233U for 1978 was $4,347, or $26.59 per hour. Aviation gas, or avgas, ran between 85 and 93 cents per gallon, and tie-down at Nayak Aviation on San Antonio International Airport where it was based was $20.20 per month.

By 1979, expenses increased quite a bit. Tie-down was now $25.25 per month, while fuel ranged between $1.05 and $1.30, depending on where I bought the gas. The total cost for the plane in 1979, flying 243.5 hours, was $17,034.39. But this is grossly misleading, because I spent $4,169.28 on avionics and $6,955.80 on rebuilding the engine. Additionally, I was reimbursed $1,148 for Army flights. Therefore, if the Army reimbursement was subtracted from my total cost of owning and operating N8233U, my actual out-of-pocket costs were $65.24 per hour, an increase of 41 percent over two years.

I retired from the Army in the fall of 1981, joining the business faculty at West Texas State University, in Canyon, Texas, just south of Amarillo.

In late November, my wife and I were flying to Las Vegas, where our football team was playing the University of Nevada. The headwinds were so strong that cars on Interstate 40 below were passing us. My wife casually inquired if it would be possible to get a faster plane. In less than two months I had found a like-new, two-year-old 182. On December 11, 1981, I took my last flight in N8233U, flying it to San Antonio to trade for a 1979 Cessna 182Q, IFR equipped.

In 1981 I flew N8233U 190 hours. While the cost of fuel for 1979 averaged $1.95 per gallon and the Nayak tie-down had increased to $35.35 per month, for the past two years I had no major aircraft expenses. The plane was painted, its engine was rebuilt, and it had perfect avionics. The hourly cost for 1981 was $33.23. In four years of ownership, I had put 810 hours on the plane. Its replacement cost $39,500 with N8233U's trade-in value $14,000.

## But Why Buy the Plane?

I mentioned two reasons why I bought my first plane. Commercial air travel took a long time; essentially a day was lost while spending considerable time waiting for connecting flights. Rental aircraft cut my downtime quite a bit, especially for flights under one thousand miles. But occasionally reserved aircraft were unavailable, and replacements were not on hand. Sometimes I could catch a commercial flight, but usually the trip was rescheduled. This was a rare occurrence, but when it happened, it created a real mess for me.

My wife could see how frustrating this was. Also, because sometimes she accompanied me on these trips, she was disappointed when a flight had to be canceled or I would fly alone on an airliner. Additionally, she recognized the advantage of being able on a moment's notice to drive out to the airport for an unscheduled or unplanned flight to lunch at a resort on a lake in Austin or an overnight weekend campout on the beach at Padre Island. She enjoyed flying with me, and the plane expanded our ability to go places in an hour or so that could require half a day by car. This was my wife's rationale for owning a plane. Instant transportation, always available.

So, together we started considering owning a plane. Could we afford it? With our daughters being 17, 14, and 9, my wife looked forward to working again. In addition to the Army, I was also teaching at local universities. Besides, the Army would reimburse me partially for flying my own plane. So, yes, we could afford to own and operate a plane. An older, smaller, used plane, though.

The biggest advantage to ownership was complete control. I would know when the plane had engine or equipment issues and when planned maintenance would occur and could schedule any trips accordingly. And if I bought a good plane, it should function without problems. When the sale of N8233U was presented to me, my wife and I agreed that buying would be in our best interests.

## How to Buy an Airplane

### Basic Considerations

As a pilot I have owned nine airplanes, spread over 39 years. Purchasing a plane is easy; all you need is money or good credit. Purchasing a "good" plane takes time, planning, and money. Every plane I bought was in excellent condition. This section will cover what I did to make sure, to the extent possible, that I did not buy a lemon.

Let me make this perfectly clear. Owning a plane is not required to fly. A pilot can rent or lease a plane, belong to a flying club, or share ownership with flying partners. Depending on how often one flies, owning may be the costliest option. If you decide to own a plane, this section will explain the buying process.

Most of us do not have unlimited funds. Our ability to buy centers on our income, financial obligations, our financial credit, and what we can afford each month. Buying a plane is almost always a compromise.

Of the nine planes I owned, seven were bought either from friends or through friends, some of whom were also aircraft dealers. Two were purchased from dealers who were reputable but unknown to me. One dealer was 1,100 miles away and another 1,200 miles away, and the distance meant that considerable extra money was required to complete the purchase. Two were local buys, and five were 400 to 600 miles away. The closer the buy, the cheaper and more convenient the purchase process.

The prospective owner must consider what is wanted, what is needed, what is affordable, and what is available. Financial situations determine the upper limits within your means. What is available in your price range presents the choices to select from. Emotions should be swept aside, and a fact-based spreadsheet type of approach favored.

Part of the process is becoming educated. The astute buyer does considerable research regarding potential makes, models, and years. There are numerous pamphlets, articles, chapters in books, videos, internet information, and promotional literature that offer advice on how to go about buying a plane. Specific make and model aircraft clubs or associations may publish buying guides regarding a particular airplane. *The Aviation*

*Consumer* magazine often publishes up-to-date articles as a buying guide for a make and model. This publisher also sells *The Aviation Consumer Used Aircraft Guide*, a series of books containing everything you might need to know about the airplane being considered.

The easiest and most comprehensive source of information on used planes is the internet. YouTube videos can be an excellent source of valuable information but may have limitations. The ones I have watched are like a pilot friend sharing the information related to their plane. Watching their videos with a pen and paper for notes yields considerable details about ownership issues, performance details, and costs.

Books and articles on how to buy an airplane are much more detailed than the YouTube videos. Buying information is plentiful from the internet. All the knowledge and materials needed to be an informed buyer are available in multiple formats. The choice is yours.

There are specific steps necessary to complete the "ideal" purchase. Most are done in conjunction with each other. Part of deciding what to buy must also include consideration of how much money is available for both the purchase and the cost of owning and maintaining the plane. Then what is available should be reviewed. What you want may be too expensive … back to the drawing board. Not available … back to the drawing board.

One must accept that in almost all instances, an aircraft purchase is about concessions. What you want versus what you need. What you want versus what you can afford. What you want versus what you are trained to fly. Can you afford additional training if needed? What you want versus what is available. Considering an affordable plane but in need of modern avionics. New versus used. Low-time engine with high price versus cheap cost but with run-out engine. The list continues, but most of the time compromises must be reached to purchase a plane.

One more point. Some people purchase a plane to learn to fly. So, for the most part they have zero experience flying a plane. Yes, this is possible, and it can be a way to save money when learning to fly. An additional bonus is that when you become a certified pilot, you will also be an expert in flying your own plane.

Often this first airplane purchase is not for a simple two-seat trainer. It is usually a step or two up because it will be your transportation vehicle, not just for training.

To buy a plane to train in, you need expert advice. Usually this would be a flight instructor and, perhaps, someone else who is experienced in the process of evaluating and buying a plane. Despite your lack of knowledge about planes and flying, doing the research listed in this section and discussing what you have learned with other experienced pilots should make your quest a more informed one. Good luck.

There are two other major considerations that should be contemplated. Do you have a secure place to park your new plane? Don't buy a plane and find that long-term parking doesn't exist at your airport. Before acquiring a plane, have a place to park it (Chapter 5 has more details on parking). Also, verify that you can get affordable insurance for the plane before purchase. Talk with your insurance company to learn what they will allow and what it will cost (Chapter 14 has details on insurance).

## Analog Versus Digital Technology

When I first began buying planes in the 1970s and 1980s, my choices were pretty much limited to equipment I needed and what I could afford. Today, though, the used plane buyer has more serious choices, namely analog versus digital. The average age of our smaller general aviation aircraft is between 40 to 50 years old. New planes employ digital technology. Therefore, many older planes have been upgraded so they have both analog and digital equipment on board. Sometimes, attempting to combine the two technologies can create a disaster.

Because of what digital technology is capable of, the overall cost for the benefits is less expensive than analog technology. Bottom line, analog technology for cockpits is going away and digital is in. But as we are aware, embracing modern technology comes at a price: understanding the enhanced learning curve necessary to be proficient in modern technology.

Most of us older nonprofessional general aviation pilots are used to and comfortable with analog technology. The new digital technology can make flying so much easier and safer for us that if we can afford it, we want it.

# *Steps to Buying a Plane*

## The Mission

When buying a plane my first step is to determine what is needed. A plane that will suit the most common missions. IFR or just VFR? How many seats are needed? Who will fly with you? What type of flying? Mostly local or long cross-country trips? For work or just pleasure or both? Where? Paved, big-city airports or back-country grass strips? What is most important? Speed? Performance? Carrying capacity? Economy? Do you want to buy a worn-out engine, rough interior, and old VFR-only analog gauges that you can rebuild with a new engine and digital panels? Or do you prefer an older plane that someone else has rehabbed? In my experience, buying someone else's work is much less expensive than doing it yourself, assuming the work was performed properly and you can see that it all operates correctly.

If this is your first buy, you will probably take your time and step cautiously. But if this is not your first buy, you should have valuable experience behind you, making this buy easier.

Therefore, the buying process begins with a clear and verified understanding of what you want the plane to do. Once you have determined what kind of plane will best satisfy your flight missions, then everything else comes into play.

## The Money

Financing should be arranged before looking, insurance requirements and costs investigated, estimating actual flying and maintenance costs, contemplating the flying missions you habitually do, and deciding if ownership will be solo or shared as in a club or with partners.

Where you physically buy the plane may make a sizable difference with sales taxes. I bought a new Tiger from an American General dealer in San Diego, California. I lived in Las Cruces, New Mexico. I flew commercial into San Diego and inspected the plane. I had already flown the plane for an article a few months previous. The sales manager and I flew the plane to Tucson, Arizona, where all the paperwork was completed and I wrote a check for the plane; I paid cash, no loan. Thus, the plane was purchased in Arizona, not California, and its new home would be New Mexico. This avoided any sales tax, although the state of California hounded my wife and me for a variety of taxes for two years, which we were never liable for.

Other costs associated with a plane purchase are title and escrow fees, prepurchase maintenance inspection of the plane and logbooks, and the cost of either you flying to buy the plane or the cost of having the plane delivered to you. If you are obtaining a loan to purchase the plane, the lending agency may work out the details to cover all these extra purchase costs. Before looking at planes, make sure either you have the money in your bank account or you have confirmed approval of a loan and your purchase is insurable.

## Deciding on a Plane

With today's internet, details about and photos of planes for sale are right at your fingertips. Before you start looking for a plane you should clearly understand what you need the plane to do. Recreational local

## Four. Buying an Airplane

flying can be done with a light sport aircraft, but is the same plane good for a couple to use for long, cross-country missions? Do you need speed? Weight-carrying capacity? Two, four, or six seats? VFR or IFR?

Based on what kind of flights will be most common, make a list of aerial attributes you believe are necessary. Then research those planes that have the attributes you have listed. Now create a list of those planes being considered for purchase.

Used plane buyers' guides, aircraft owners' groups, and the internet should all have valuable information on the pros and cons of planes on the list. At this point I also talk to friends or friends of friends who currently own or once owned what I am considering. I also talk to mechanics to get their opinions.

How much you have to spend dictates what you look at. The dollar value of planes relates to the year it was manufactured, time on the engine, how it is equipped, and its condition. So, if you have a $150,000 budget and the make and model you want sells for $500,000 brand new, you will probably be wasting your time looking for models five to 10 years old. You may have to start your search for planes 20 to 30 years old.

To match my flight needs with aircraft capabilities, I go to *The Aviation Consumer Used Aircraft Guide* website (aviationconsumer.com) to obtain data on airplanes and reviews; however, you need to be a subscriber to obtain this information or buy the books. This provides me with a list of aircraft that match my flying requirements. I try to limit my search to within 500 to 600 miles. The further afield you search, the more expensive the logistics of purchasing the plane become.

Of course, you will have your own concept of what to buy. It might be a new plane that is typically more expensive but less costly to operate and maintain than a used plane in good condition, which may be cheaper to buy but have higher operating and maintenance costs, or a worn-out plane to rebuild from scratch. The last option can be expensive but allows you to have a like-new, used plane at only part of the cost of a new plane. In most cases, buying a used plane with the equipment you want is cheaper than having to add equipment that you need but that is not in the plane you purchase. I have done all three and not one was a better deal than the others.

My favorite internet sources for used planes for sale include: *The Controller*, *Trade-a-Plane*, *Aero Trader*, and *Barnstormers*. I use other websites to comb local airports, FBOs, flying clubs, aviation newsletters, airplane organizations, et cetera. When beginning the search, how much money you have to spend becomes the most important ingredient in your decision process. If you are seeking the best deal available, then your budget's upper limit becomes the ceiling for your search.

Some search considerations include time on the airframe versus cost, engine size, speed, weight carrying capacity, equipment, and overall condition. A plane with hefty hours may have been consistently flown, while a low-time plane may have sat for extended periods of time. The time on a plane relates to how it was used. Some planes with thousands of hours on the airframe may be worn out, others flown and maintained on a regular basis. A plane with few hours may have been flown and maintained on a regular basis but taken no long trips or perhaps it sat in the sun, parked for a year or more. The logbooks will reveal a plane's usage history. All of these factors relate to the asking price of a plane.

Here the AOPA website offers plenty of help. It has tips for buying a plane and a computer-based program (VREF) that, fed all the details of a used plane, will produce a dollar value for it. This is an excellent means to obtain a negotiating start for any plane you are considering buying. Aircraft values are also found in *Aircraft Bluebook*.

## Tips on the Search for an Airplane to Buy

In 2005 I bought a worn-out complex airplane, a 1981 Cessna 182 with retractable gear. It had 24-year-old avionics, a run-out engine, tons of hours on the airframe, a ratty interior, and a 20-year-old paint job. I bought the plane to be completely rebuilt—engine, interior, panel, avionics, and paint. I turned a $75,000 relic into a state-of-the-art IFR, like-new cross-country dream. The rehab cost another $126,000.

I had planned to keep the plane for several years; however, in 2013, returning from a business trip in Washington, D.C., to New Mexico, I stopped in Birmingham, Alabama. Taxiing to parking, my nose gear collapsed. The front went down, propeller spinning. Moving forward, the prop bent, the lower cowling was torn apart, and the front bottom severely damaged. Why the nose gear failed was never ascertained (see Chapter 9 for details).

Cessna manufactured the 182 from 1956 to present with two interruptions, building more than 23,000. But in the eight years from 1978 to 1986, when the 182RG was built, only 2,032 were produced. In fact, during its last model year, only 20 were constructed.

The plane could not be completely repaired because (1) it was out of production and (2) not enough were made to create a sizable stockpile of salvage aircraft to provide spare parts. I also learned that from one year to the next, aircraft parts changed. Sometimes a parts supplier to Cessna ceased business or quit making the Cessna part. Then another vendor would be procured, but the new parts would not mate with the old. Being long out of production also meant new parts were no longer manufactured.

The FAA tends to frown on handmade parts placed on aircraft.

Replacement parts must comply with FAA requirements and inspection conditions. Thus, major repairs must meet all FAA regulations. See FAA Advisory Circular No. 20–62E: Eligibility, Quality, and Identification of Aeronautical Replacement Parts.

The moral of this story is to recognize that aircraft long out of production, and/or those with minimal production, may be exceedingly difficult to return to flying status if damaged in an accident or incident. I recommend not considering purchasing a plane unless enough were made so aircraft salvage yards have plenty of wrecks on hand.

All my planes were fully insured, and I never had any problems recovering all costs on my two planes that crashed. Neither accident was my fault. Working with the insurance companies was easy and pleasant, with no conflicts. One plane was totaled, while the other was repaired.

More tips. Before purchase, locate a maintenance facility that can take care of your plane, preferably at the airport where your plane is based. Have evidence that you and your plane can be insured. Sometimes an insurance company will not allow you solo flights in your plane unless you have received $x$ hours of dual training by a CFI experienced in your new plane.

When I bought my 182RG my insurance required a one-hour checkout, despite the fact I had over five thousand hours total time, several hundred hours in a 182, and thousands in retractable aircraft. It helps to have a local CFI who has experience in your plane.

Okay. Now you have decided what planes to look for. You have access to the money, have an insurance broker that will insure your plane, have confirmed that your local maintenance shop can service the plane, and have made parking arrangements. You are ready to buy.

## Checking Out the Plane

When a plane has been located you need to see it. Once I bought a plane without seeing it, but that is another story as others did the looking for me. I am not so interested in me flying the plane as I am watching the owner fly the plane and operate all the equipment onboard. I want to focus on how the plane flies, how it performs and operates, and how well the equipment on the plane functions. I may fly a pattern or make a landing, but mostly I want to observe and take notes on how everything in the plane behaves. If you have not done this before, make a list of everything you want checked out in flight and then have the pilot demonstrate how the equipment functions.

Many of today's used planes for sale combine both analog technology (all the round gauges right in front of the pilot) with digital, such as the navigation equipment in the center stack. For the digital equipment to work, often it must mate with analog technology in the plane. For the most part, avionics shops have this uncertainty under control. But sometimes it does not work well. Since most older used planes are a hybrid of technology, take the time for the seller to show you that it all works as planned.

If satisfied with the plane's performance, next examine all the logbooks. For your first plane it may be best for a mechanic to go over each logbook with you. This exam can reveal how well the plane was maintained and point out potential problems. If everything is thus far okay, next is the pre-buy inspection.

This should be accomplished by a mechanic who knows the make and model being considered. The pre-buy inspection should not be done by the plane's mechanic, nor done as a pre-purchase annual arranged by the owner. Because most planes have their own quirks and various models have known problems that should have been fixed, these items should be on a pre-buy maintenance checklist. I have had pre-buy inspections done by friends, my mechanics, dealers selling me the plane, and mechanics I did not know and had never met. Five planes I bought from dealers who did the pre-buys for me. All dealers were friends; I trusted them, and not once did they fail me. Two inspections were made by my mechanic, another one by a mechanic recommended by the association for the plane owners done about 1,200 miles away, and the last done by a good friend who knew the plane and was an A&P mechanic. But do get a pre-buy inspection from a trusted mechanic who has experience on the plane being considered.

If the in-flight performance is fine, the pre-buy reveals nothing wrong, and the aircraft has the equipment you want, the final negotiation begins.

## Buying the Plane

The legal aspects of buying a plane are sort of between buying a car and a house. Planes are bought and sold at the federal level, not state. Planes are registered with the federal government, the FAA. But some states may require that they also be registered in that state or taxed like real estate. If the plane checks out okay and you and the seller agree on a price, you should ascertain that the seller owns the plane outright and has the legal right to sell. If the plane is owned by a business, corporation, or partners, you may want to seek the advice of an attorney with experience in this area. You can collaborate with a company that executes the selling and buying of planes, or you can do it yourself. All nine of my aircraft buys were either done by me or a dealer. One key is to do a title search to ensure that the seller has the legal right to sell the plane and there are no liens against the plane.

In my experience an institution lending money to someone to buy a plane will file the FAA form AC 8050-98 (Security Agreement) in a New York minute. Yet, once the lien has been paid, they fail to refile the form stating that the debt has been satisfied. Once I bought a plane with no debts, yet the FAA had a form AC 8050-98 still indicating that the mortgage was not paid. Contacting the lien holder, a bank, I was able to get a letter stating that the debt had been paid, but the bank failed to notify the FAA. The seller had the paperwork verifying that the loan was settled. I bought the plane, and eventually the bank filed the loan payoff with the FAA. A title search is especially important.

Two other FAA forms must be executed: AC 8050-1, the Aircraft Regristration Application, and AC 8050-2, the Bill of Sale. The seller and buyer should create a sales contract clearly outlining what each party will receive. AOPA has a sample sales agreement on its website.

The title search can be done yourself, but there are companies that specialize in doing this for a fee. Another service available is both title search and escrow services for a fee. A third-party company checks all pertinent documents involved in the sale, collects all funds for the sale, does the title search, prepares the documents, and issues the funds when buyer and seller are satisfied. For additional fees, they can obtain accident/incident documents or major repairs or alterations on FAA form 337.

The proper process of buying a plane should be well planned. It may take considerable time and can get expensive if done the right way. Sometimes I would fly to the seller to check out the plane. Other times the seller would fly to me, and I would agree to share gas expenses. If I bought a plane delivered to me, I would pay the commercial airfare for the pilot's return trip. A quick, dirty, cheap pre-buy is a waste of money. Allow the mechanic the time to do a thorough inspection and to study the logbooks. Never be rushed when researching a potential buy. Take your time to do it right. Plan with the seller to have the time. The honest seller of a good plane should not begrudge the time you take to examine their plane. If the seller insists on a speedy inspection, hindering a comprehensive assessment, it may be best to just say no to any deal.

If a maintenance issue arises during the inspection, your mechanic may be able to estimate what it could cost to remedy the situation. Sometimes only a rough approximation of the extent of the problem can be determined and it may be better to just back out of the purchase.

Sometimes when a severe problem is found and verified, and your mechanic can provide a firm cost to fix it, you may negotiate a lower price. I have never encountered this happening. My research on the model and my thorough review of the logbooks usually reflects the care of the plane and whether it was maintained as it should have been. My pre-buys were usually able to confirm what I already believed through my research of the logbook. The pre-buy is a necessary step to confirm what already appears evident. If problems or issues are found, these should be resolved before buying the plane.

With the mechanic's inspection, sometimes I have taken three or four days to completely check out a potential buy. But I never bought a lemon.

While I have never used this service regarding aircraft purchases, the AOPA legal service can examine purchase documents to offer legal advice. Purchase contracts must comply with both state laws and FAA regulations.

One last caveat. Some people have a revokable family trust. This is a document containing one's assets with binding instructions on the disposition of those assets. While there are several reasons for a trust, one is to avoid the probate process. A trust contains one's assets and has a trustee responsible for seeing that the conditions of the trust are met. Assets such as investments, cars, houses, boats, and aircraft are placed in a trust. Usually this is not an issue or problem. With the FAA it can be.

Typically, a trust stipulates how assets will be divided. Say a person has a trust, with all the assets going to that person's three daughters, equally. If there is an airplane in the trust, ownership goes to the three daughters. This is where the FAA becomes involved. U.S. law (49 USC 44102) does not allow a non–U.S. citizen to own a U.S. registered aircraft. Therefore, if a U.S. aircraft is to be registered in a trust, the FAA must vet the trust to ensure that future owners are all U.S. citizens. If you want your plane to be part of your trust, ensure that all beneficiaries of the aircraft are U.S. citizens.

If all has been properly accomplished, you are now a plane owner.

# Five

# Owning and Maintaining an Airplane

## *The Joys of Ownership*

Let's face it. Owning a plane is not cheap, not if you want to be safe. When I lived in the Texas Panhandle where I was a university business professor, several of my students came from exceptionally large ranches. Some of these ranches used airplanes to survey their land and keep track of their cattle. One student had over 600 hours of flight time but never even possessed a student pilot certificate. I learned that this was common. Small planes were just another form of a ranch pickup and treated as such. A quick peek at the engine would see more parts from AutoZone or NAPA than Continental or Lycoming. The plane was another tool flown only across the ranch property. The ranchers perceived this as just doing business, not of any concern to the FAA.

But I could not accept that understanding. I wanted my planes to be as safe and legal as possible. This means spending money. But a pilot does not have to be a millionaire to afford a plane. One friend was a captain in the Air Force and loved to fly cross-country trips with his wife. They owned a two-seat Grumman TR-2. Captains were not rich. He had a sergeant who was also an FAA certified A&P mechanic with inspection authorization, as well as being a pilot. The captain and the sergeant made a deal; the sergeant would maintain the plane, and the captain allowed him to fly it. Chapter 6 covers ways to achieve income from your plane to help pay for it.

This section will describe what expenses arise from owning and maintaining a plane. Throughout 40 years owning nine planes I never skimped on costs that would impact safety, and, after all, I am still around to write about it. Many of my flights were with my wife in the right seat, and I would not risk her health or life traveling somewhere. Never would I take shortcuts to her safety.

I loved flying so much that I wanted total control over when and where I would fly. This meant having my own plane. It also meant being financially responsible for its well-being. I never owned a plane I could not afford. I loved flying so much that in addition to my regular full-time position, I held other part-time jobs to help pay for owning a plane.

Having our own plane provided my wife and me a degree of freedom and a sense of personal satisfaction nothing else could provide. We decided early in my flying career that owning our plane was the way to go. And we vowed that we would financially make that happen. And we did.

## Why Planes Can Be Expensive

Owning and flying your own plane costs more than a car.

Why are planes expensive, yet cars are not? Two primary reasons. First, aviation is one of the most regulated industries in the United States. For manufacturers, the cost to remain compliant can be high. This cost is shared with the users (pilots and aircraft owners). To place this in sharper perspective, consider this. In 2021 America sold slightly more than 15 million new vehicles. Yet, in that same year the General Aviation Manufacturers Association stated that only 1,393 new piston airplanes were sold. The higher the sales volume, the lower the price. According to the FAA, the total size of America's piston engine general aviation fleet is well under 200 thousand aircraft. New airplanes are expensive. Since the number of all general aviation aircraft is low compared to our 285 million registered vehicles, spare parts and overall support is restricted. Limited suppliers, vendors, and manufacturers mean higher costs.

Replacement parts for airplanes must be FAA approved or maintain the same level of safety. This means that replacement parts should not be purchased from your local auto parts store. In the 1980s, the popular electronics store, RadioShack, sold light bulbs identical to those used in my Cessnas 172 and 182. An electrical engineer, who was also an A&P mechanic, created a list of Cessna light bulbs and their RadioShack equivalents. The difference? The Cessna bulbs were FAA approved and the RadioShack bulbs were not. Also, the Cessna bulbs could cost $20 to $40, while the RadioShack bulbs cost a couple bucks.

The FAA requires replacement parts to be approved. Sometimes non-approved replacement parts can do the job but are not authorized for aircraft usage due to size or weight, or incompatibility with the other aircraft components. Stick with FAA-approved replacement parts, even if they do cost more. They are safer, and legal.

This level of aircraft maintenance and inspections increases the cost

## Five. Owning and Maintaining an Airplane

of operations. A faulty part in a car mostly means cruising to the side of the road and calling AAA for help. A faulty part in a plane at five thousand feet does not allow pulling over to a cloud to call for help. Therefore, maintenance requirements and replacement parts are highly regulated for safety reasons.

The older the plane, the more it has been used and the more costly it can be to fly. The older the plane or the fewer manufactured, the harder it is to locate approved parts. The more hours on the engine or airframe, the more likely something will wear out and need to be replaced.

The theory is, the newer the plane, the fewer the maintenance issues. In most instances this should be true, but not always. Once I bought a new plane, a 1992, IFR-equipped American General Tiger (AG-5B). This was the first and only new plane I ever purchased. Almost a year after my purchase the FAA issued an airworthiness directive (AD), a decree requiring action be taken to remedy an unsafe aircraft condition. The AD called for an inspection of where the wings joined the fuselage; if there was wear or excessive clearance, repair was required. The inspection could be done by most A&P mechanics, but repairs could only be done by approved maintenance shops. The inspection and any needed repairs had to be completed within a specified time or flight period.

My local mechanic inspected the plane and found excessive clearance. The wings had to be removed and shims emplaced. The nearest facility to do this was a Grumman and American General repair station, Fletcher Aviation, in Houston, Texas, almost 800 miles away. Unfortunately, the Tiger manufacturer went out of business, so there was no warranty. I flew the plane to Houston and left it there to be fixed. Three weeks later I returned to get my plane, and the cost came out of my pocket.

There are two sets of "costs" related to owning and flying your plane. One set of costs is called fixed costs. These are annual costs that are based on ownership and are not related to how often you fly. These include your airplane insurance, parking or hangar costs, taxes, electronic data subscriptions, aviation organization dues, magazine subscriptions, the annual inspection, and other costs that you pay because you own a plane. The second set are variable costs because they are dependent on the hours flown. These include fuel, cross-country overnight parking charges, airport landing fees, regular maintenance such as oil changes, any work required from the annual inspection, and other airplane operating expenses.

There are other possible costs that are not required, rather they fall into the want category of upgrading and modifications. As a pilot and airplane owner I was constantly looking at ways to make my plane better: quieter, faster, safer, more comfortable, easier to fly, prettier. This costs money, and there are dozens of vendors who sell products that can do all of this and more. Over a lifetime of airplane ownership, I have spent a few hundred thousand dollars making my planes better and safer. A reminder, though: it is doubtful you will ever recover the money spent on making your plane "better." But, during your years of ownership, you can enjoy your improvements.

## *Fixed Costs*

Probably the most expensive fixed costs are parking and insurance.

There are four usual places to park an airplane: outdoor ramp tie-downs, overhead shaded parking, shared hangar, and single hangar. I have used all. Outdoors ramp parking is the most brutal. In the Southwest, paint deteriorates, rubber disintegrates, anything inside the plane becomes baked. Next to the ocean, salt water corrodes everything metal; in colder climates, ice and snow can make flying almost impossible. Yes, the cost is cheapest, but nice planes can deteriorate quickly. Sunshade parking means overhead protection from rain, snow, and sun but open sides. Clearly much better than open ramp parking.

Next are community hangars where several planes are in one building. These can be owned privately or by an FBO. Both require constant moving around of planes in the hangar, commonly resulting in hangar rash, scuffs, small dents, or scratches, the result of planes shifted to allow a plane to exit or enter the hangar. In privately owned hangars the plane owner usually must do the moving. In an FBO shared hangar the line people usually move your plane in or out per your request.

The ideal is a single hangar, just for your plane. This provides the best security protection as access is limited to only those you allow. High-wing airplanes, like a Cessna 182 with full fuel, may require a gas or electric tug to move your plane in or out. Hangars can be rented or owned. Figuring the cost to buy or build a hangar has too many variables to quote prices. If hangars at your airport are scarce, costs can be high. If there are hangars vacant, costs can be low. The size of the airport and its location affect costs, as well as who manages the airport, public or private.

One point if desiring to own your hangar. When buying a home, the purchaser usually obtains a deed and title showing legal ownership of the parcel of land and everything physically attached to it. Essentially one owns both the land and the structures built on it. Not so with most airports.

Public use airports that have received any federal funds or grants must comply with various rules and regulations. This money obligates compliance with federal grant assurances (see 49 U.S. Code Part 47107).

## Five. Owning and Maintaining an Airplane

These assurances govern how the owner of the airport must manage the airport in a manner to provide fairness to all users, tenants, pilots, and vendors.

Typically, airports grow and get bigger. To accommodate any future expansion, airport management must control the land. Therefore, management cannot sell airport land for hangars, which would transfer ownership away from the airport management. So, a long-term land lease is arranged for someone to build a hangar. If the length of the lease is too short, the hangar owner may lose their investment—not a fair deal. If the length is too long, it may extend beyond the useful life of the hangar—not good for the airport.

Buyers of existing hangars should understand the leasing agreement with the airport. Also carefully examine the future master plan of the airport. It could be that a new runway is planned to be constructed where the hangar you are seeking to buy is sitting. Not a good idea to buy a hangar and have it torn down after purchase. Even pilots engaging in long-term hangar subleases should examine what kind of lease agreements the hangar owner has with the airport.

Insurance costs depend on several variables to include the plane, the pilot, the airport, parking, location, and aircraft usage. These variables are discussed in detail in Chapter 14.

The other fixed expenses are relatively minor compared to parking and insurance.

## Variable Costs

Airplane engines are nothing like the engine of your car. I drive a five-year-old Jeep Cherokee that I bought used at one year old. It uses synthetic oil and goes in for maintenance once a year. In all my planes, oil was changed every 25 to 50 hours. My aircraft records reveal that each year about 66 percent of all costs for owning and operating a plane were fuel and maintenance expenses. Flying is not cheap. And the more you fly, the more it costs. The more one flies, the more fuel consumed and the quicker the parts wear out. I calculate that in my 40 years of flying I probably consumed about 90 to 95 thousand gallons of aviation fuel. During this time, I had five airplane engines rebuilt. In the years where I replaced engines, maintenance costs were around 50 to 55 percent of the total annual aircraft costs. Between engine rebuilds, fuel costs accounted for about 50 percent of my total annual aircraft expenses.

Upgrades or modifications were another large expense for my planes. Most involved equipment related to aircraft operations, such as newer radios, navigation equipment, or instruments to make flying easier like weather detection instruments or an engine analyzer. Modifications are great, but they can also result in trouble as described later in this section. Using unapproved parts is risky because they may not provide the same degree of usage or safety as the approved parts, and they are not legal. Therefore, stick with approved parts.

If one flies often like I did, fuel and maintenance will be your highest expenses along with engine rebuilds. Most years I averaged around 200 hours a year. Some years I flew little, mostly due to being severely injured in a motorcycle accident. But in 1994, after a lean year or two, I added more than 400 hours to my logbook. So, for me, fuel and maintenance were my biggest costs of owning and flying my planes.

The FAA often regulates the maintenance of aircraft ownership. Installed accessories, replacement parts, and maintenance must be recorded in aircraft logs specifying that the maintenance complied with FAA regulations. These procedures are not common to non-aviation personal vehicles such as cars, bicycles, motorcycles, or trucks. Yes, our other motor vehicles must comply with a variety of safety regulations but nothing compared to what aircraft require. Compliance with FAA regulations certainly increases the maintenance costs.

The single most costly maintenance expenses can be the FAA-mandated annual inspection of a plane or replacing a worn-out engine. More on these later.

Thus far, my comments on ownership costs have seemed harsh. But owners can do considerable maintenance themselves to reduce costs.

## *Owner Performed Maintenance*

The FAA allows owners of personal aircraft to perform considerable preventive maintenance themselves. This includes removing and cleaning spark plugs, replacing light bulbs, changing engine oil and filter, changing tires, and much more. The authority for doing this is in FAR Part 43, Appendix A, Subpart C. Additional help explaining what a pilot-owner can and cannot do is in FAA publication Maintenance Aspects of Owning Your Own Aircraft (FAA-P-8740-15) and Advisory Circulars AC 43-12A Preventive Maintenance and AC 20-106 Inspection for the General Aviation Aircraft Owner.

Pilots who can do these maintenance items can save hundreds to thousands of dollars annually depending on how many hours are flown in a year. A pilot can also reduce the costs considerably by preparing their plane for the annual or 100-hour inspection. Legally, only those people certified to do the annual or 100-hour inspection can assist in an inspection.

Pilots must remember to properly list in the aircraft logbooks what maintenance they performed.

## The Dreaded Annual

Every pilot who owns an aircraft has read or heard of the pilot who left their plane at a mechanic for an annual and the horrors that followed. Usually, the pilot does not know the mechanic and only a verbal contract was issued. The pilot expects a $2,000 to $4,000 invoice for the work and is astounded to receive a bill for $20,000 or more. Luckily, this never happened to me, and I will explain why.

The FAA requires aircraft to undergo an annual inspection. Planes used for hire or flight training face other inspection requirements such as each 100 hours of flight. The purpose is to perform an inspection to confirm that the aircraft meets all airworthiness standards. This inspection must be conducted by an A&P mechanic with inspection authorization (IA). Other people, such as an A&P or the pilot, may prepare the plane for the inspection, such as by removing inspection plates, opening cowlings, and removing aircraft parts to get at items requiring inspections. But the inspection must be done by an A&P with the IA. See FAR Part 43.7 for authorization on who can do the inspection.

There are several regulations governing the conduct of the annual inspection. FAR Part 91.409 and Part 43, Appendix D describe what the inspection consists of. If an annual inspection is not completed 12 months after the last inspection, the plane cannot be flown. Actually, an inspection can be completed beyond 12 months. Normally the inspection can take a week or so, not counting any more downtime to accomplish required repairs. The regulations allow the inspection to be conducted until the end of the twelfth month. If the plane's last annual inspection was finished on October 5, another inspection must be completed by October 31 of the next year.

Other components of a plane also require periodic inspections. The emergency locater transmitter (ELT) requires inspection every 12 months, the transponder every 24 months. If flying IFR and in controlled airspace, the aircraft's static system, altimeter, and automatic altitude-reporting (Mode C) system must be inspected every 24 months.

FAR Part 43.15 states that the annual inspections must follow a checklist. The checklist may be from the aircraft manufacturer or created by the inspector. But the checklist must include the details listed in Part 43, Appendix D.

An annual inspection also includes the aircraft logbooks to ensure proper documentation of all required services and compliance with all required airworthiness.

Mike Busch, A&P with IA, and noted aviation maintenance writer, advocates that any annual inspection begin with a written contract between the owner and the inspector to clearly specify what should be done. For most, the annual inspection is conducted in two parts. First is the inspection to determine the condition of the aircraft. The second part is to fix what is not airworthy so the aircraft can pass the inspection. And this is where most problems occur. Usually, these problems happen when the shop or inspector is not known to the pilot. Also, typically the instructions by the pilot are just a verbal: "Do the annual."

I have never had an annual done by a shop or inspector I did not know. I would begin with my own list of items to be checked. I would have a typed list of what I wanted done. First, I wanted the inspection conducted and a list created of problem areas. Nothing else, just do the inspection and make a list. I would request that this list be comprised of three areas. First those items that needed work to be airworthy, then those that should be corrected to be safe or where continued neglect could result in more expense or an unairworthy condition. Lastly those items that needed repair or replacement but would not create problems if left uncorrected.

I would then go over the list with my mechanic and decide what needed to be done and what could wait. A deciding factor for what would be done, obviously, could be cost. My process avoided unexpected "end of annual" expenses because I was a part of the annual inspection procedure. Occasionally an expensive issue would be discovered such as a bad cylinder. Then the inspection would be halted, I would be contacted, and we would discuss options available.

During my ownership of nine airplanes, I would guess that I paid for about 38 annuals. I can never recall any time when I felt blindsided by any annual findings or costs. Yes, there were rare times when my expectations of costs were exceeded. But again, I never experienced an annual that cost more than I could afford to pay. All were reasonable and there were no damning surprises. But I knew the shop, and the annual began with the inspection and then proceeded to repairs. No surprises at the end.

## *Engine Rebuilds*

If one flies often, eventually the engine will wear out. Five times I had an engine either overhauled, rebuilt, or replaced. Each provides a higher quality product and of course each escalates in price.

## Five. Owning and Maintaining an Airplane

The most expensive way to replace a worn-out engine is to install a factory-built new engine. Replacement engines fall into three categories: new, rebuilt, or overhauled. FAR Part 43.2 defines the difference between a rebuilt engine and an overhauled engine. The rebuilt engine meets new engine limits and tolerances and can only be rebuilt by the manufacturer or a designated agency. This results in a new logbook called a "zero-time engine," just like a new one. The third option is an overhauled engine.

An A&P mechanic can overhaul an engine. But the overhaul is to lesser limits than the factory rebuild. Additionally, an overhauled engine does not start life over again—no new logbooks. The overhauled engine continues with the time on the engine it had prior to being overhauled. This is the least expensive way to resuscitate a worn-out engine. While I have had both overhauled engines and factory rebuilt engines, there are pros and cons about both procedures. A good shop can overhaul an engine that will cost less but function as well as a rebuilt or new engine. Often, when an engine is overhauled locally, the overhaul can be completed quickly.

A factory can rebuild or overhaul your engine. You can send them your engine and have it rebuilt (zero-time) or overhauled, or you can purchase a factory rebuilt engine, sometimes called a remanufactured engine (not an FAA term), that originated from someone else's airplane. From my point of view the time and perhaps cost makes the difference in having your engine rebuilt or replaced. If you send in your engine, it will take time to complete. If time is of the essence, buy an already rebuilt engine from the factory. You order; they ship. You have a replacement engine quickly. Additionally, by purchasing a rebuilt engine from a factory or factory-approved shop, a significant discount may be received by providing them your old engine assuming that it is not damaged.

Following FAA regulations, engine replacement is rather simple: factory new, rebuilt, or overhauled. Unfortunately shops that offer overhaul services have created unfamiliar terms and advertising words, with discount prices that seem unreal. They can be deceiving. On the other hand, there are shops that specialize in rebuilding airplane engines to factory-new tolerances that do excellent work.

Deciding what to replace your worn-out engine with can be a daunting endeavor. Decisions are based on cost, time involved, and your knowledge of the reputation of the company doing the replacement or rebuild. Experts suggest that price should not be the deal-breaker. Quality, safety, and reliability should be top priorities. I can honestly say that I never had a problem with any of my replacement engines.

## Aircraft Modifications

This is one area where an owner can spend more than the plane is worth and most likely never recover that cost. We all want our planes to look nicer, fly faster, be safer, and have all the bells and whistles we can afford. The aviation industry is engulfed with companies and businesses that offer only one specific product: a modification for an airplane. Sometimes the modification is so great the airframe manufacturer adopts it for future models.

One example is the 1982 Mooney 231 I bought in 1986. It was fully IFR equipped and had a stock turbocharged engine. It had a problem of overheating at altitude. I purchased it for its speed (realistically 190 plus knots) and service ceiling (24 thousand feet), but to keep the engine cool up high, I had to consume excessive amounts of fuel.

This problem was resolved by Turboplus, a company that designed and sold an intercooler, a product that kept the engine cool, regardless of the altitude. I sold the Mooney two years later. I did not buy an intercooler.

In 1996, I purchased a 1979 Mooney 231, in excellent condition with an almost new factory rebuilt engine, but this plane was modified with an Airflow intercooler. The plane ran cooler, faster, and consumed less fuel than my first 231. An intercooler is not cheap. One costs around $6,000 and requires one to two days of labor to install. But the mod is worthwhile as the fuel burn is less and the cool engine will last longer.

The FAA must approve mods. The mod design is typically evaluated on a stock model airplane to receive the FAA blessing. Herein lies a potential problem. Even though your plane is the same make and model as the plane the mod was tested and approved on, your plane most likely is different from the plane the mod manufacturer used. What? Why?

We seldom buy a brand-new plane and immediately begin modifying it. Usually, it is an older plane we want to make better. And often our older plane has previous mods that may not be compatible with what we want to do. Or perhaps an upgrade or modification, though legal, simply will not work without more modifications.

Sometimes a shop can tell you why a mod will not work without additional work. Sometimes, after a mod has been made, you are the first to learn that it will not work as advertised. In the planes I have owned and mods I have had installed, I have experienced all the above.

A VFR plane I owned was to be converted to IFR usage. I selected the radios and navigation equipment to be installed. The shop told me that the electrical system on my plane could not manage the additional electric requirement of the added equipment. Therefore, first my electrical system had to be modified to safely operate the additional load. This was done, and the new radios and navigation components worked perfectly.

Another time I added some more navigation equipment, but, at altitude, after flying for several minutes, my radio receivers began buzzing. Hearing clearly became difficult. The radio shop located the problem and, by installing a filter, got rid of the noise. But this anomaly was unknown until I flew for a few minutes. The problem was a slight incompatibility with other equipment added earlier.

Mods are great, and I find that many can really turn a plane around to make your flying easier, faster, or more comfortable. But a word of caution: before investing hundreds or thousands of dollars in a modification, do your research. Make sure the installing shop has expertise in this area. Discuss the mod with other owners. Read articles or search the internet to learn what others think of the mod. Taking the time to learn as much as you can about a mod may save you heartaches and lost money. Not all mods work as advertised. Or they can cost you more than they are worth.

## *Is the Cost of Ownership Worth It?*

I can say, without qualification, yes! The convenience of having your airborne steed always in the stall (hangar) waiting for your desire to fly at any time, to me, is well worth the extra cost. I never regretted owning and paying for any plane. One way or another my wife and I were able to afford what we wanted. Sometimes owning can be less expensive than renting. This option was never a consideration for us. We owned because we wanted our own plane, just for us and always available. Twice we sold a plane and did not replace it immediately. We had our reasons, which I will explain in the next section. Bottom line, nothing beats owning a good airplane. It is all yours and always ready to take you on a magical trip, quickly, safely, and without the hassle of the airlines.

## *The Planes I Owned*

Buying a plane can be a scary experience. They are expensive, and most of us cannot afford a new plane, so we buy used ones. Determining if a plane we want to purchase is a good buy is an arduous task. And the process of guaranteeing the buy is worthwhile is almost impossible. Added to this mix is that most pilots do not possess the skills or knowledge to inspect the mechanical condition of any airplane. I know I certainly was not able to ascertain the health of any plane. And then the logbooks. Technical and legal understanding of aircraft logbooks is beyond the skill set of many pilots.

For this reason, most pilots must rely on the expertise of many other aviation and legal experts to determine if a plane is a good buy. Like most other pilots, I required the assistance of several other aviation folks to help me assess every plane I bought.

I was asked often, "What is your favorite airplane?" My response was always the same, "What I am now flying." Why? Every plane I owned was selected for the type of flying I planned to do at time of purchase. I should note that every plane purchased had to also be approved by my partner, my wife Anita. What I mean is that we both had to agree that what we would buy would be equally acceptable to both of us. We both agreed that I would be the aircraft expert, but that financing and maintaining the new plane was a decision we both had to agree on, which we did for every purchase. Our decision-making process avoided future disagreements; therefore, we never had any arguments on any single plane we owned. We both loved to fly.

A chronological examination of every plane I bought, in conjunction with my status in life at the time of purchase, should reveal that each buy had a clear purpose, related to my aviation needs, my financial situation, and my age.

## N8233U, a 1965 Cessna 172 Purchased in 1977

N8233U cockpit.

## Five. Owning and Maintaining an Airplane

**N8233U (after being painted).**

When I bought my first plane in 1977, I was a PhD clinical psychologist in the Army's medical department with the rank of lieutenant colonel. Additionally, I was also an adjunct professor at a local university. Clearly, I was not broke. I had three young daughters, and my wife was employed full-time.

I bought the plane because renting was not reliable. I was a fairly new pilot with my private pilot certificate about 25 months old. At this time, I had 289.8 hours in my logbook with 197.1 hours of pilot in command time. I was not instrument rated, so I only needed a VFR plane. We paid cash for the plane. Two years after purchase it was converted into an instrument-capable aircraft. In 1978 I received my instrument rating. This plane transported my wife and me throughout much of the United States and eastern Canada.

Over 80 percent of my flying in the Army was work-related: visiting Army medical facilities, presenting research papers, attending military and civilian psychology conferences. Most trips were to fascinating locations or large cities or inviting resorts (aside from the hospitals at smaller Army posts). My wife flew with me on most of these trips.

Our daughters were old enough to manage themselves during the day, and we would arrange for an adult to stay with them during the nights and weekends.

As I gained experience and flew more IFR, my wife and I decided we needed to explore something that flew faster. N8233U was traded in for a faster Cessna.

## N96551, a 1979 Cessna 182 Purchased in 1981

I had retired from the Army in the fall of 1981 and was now a business professor at West Texas State University (WTSU) in Canyon, Texas, a few miles south of Amarillo. I had my Army retirement pension, a salary as a professor, part-time writing income, and my wife and I both worked for our management consulting business. Our oldest daughter, Susan, was a senior in college on a full U.S. Air Force scholarship. Our middle daughter, Julie, was at WTSU with a partial scholarship and faculty tuition discount. Our youngest daughter, Karen, was in the local high school. Financially stable, we considered our next plane.

At age 44, I had 912.1 flight hours with 66.5 actual IFR. I wasn't sure what would be best for me, so I consulted with a good friend who owned Stinson Aviation in San Antonio, Texas. He said that he was able to acquire a two-year-old, IFR-equipped 182 with around one thousand hours on it.

He explained that moving up in a Cessna would be easy since I had some hours in a 182. The plane was in excellent shape and had the latest instrument panel with an autopilot. The 182 would fly 25 knots faster than the 172 and fly higher. I trusted my friend, so we agreed to trade in my 172 for the 182. His shop would do the pre-buy. The price for the 182 was $39,500, and the trade-in value for the 172 was $14,000. The plane was financed by Cessna Finance Corporation. It was purchased with 1,080.4 hours on December 11, 1981, four years after I bought the 172.

In April 1983, with 1,402.1 hours, the engine had to be rebuilt. The contract with a local repair facility was to overhaul the engine to factory limits in accordance with FAR Part 42.3 and TCMs and current service bulletins and manuals. The total cost, which included an annual, was $7,575.33.

As we moved into the mid-1980s, my flying was increasing, I was doing more magazine writing, and we were traveling all over the United States chasing stories. About 75 percent of my flying was business-related. We realized that a faster plane would be more economical since we would spend fewer nights en route.

## N1159G, a 1982 Mooney 231 Purchased in 1986

At the end of 1986 I was only teaching half-time and writing full-time. Two daughters were married and working, and the third daughter was a

## Five. Owning and Maintaining an Airplane

**N96551 and Anita.**

freshman in college on a full scholarship. Our travels in the 182 totaled well over 200 hours a year, but we were expecting our travel needs for writing to increase in the immediate future. Three quarters of our flights were work-related. The other quarter were just plain fun trips to vacation destinations, resorts, or the homes of friends and relatives. By December I had accumulated 1,921.3 total hours with 210 instrument hours. We needed a faster IFR airplane, so my friend at Stinson Aviation was contacted again. I explained what I needed.

He said he could get a fully IFR equipped 1982 Mooney 231 in excellent condition with just under 500 hours on it. As before, his shop would do the pre-buy inspection. I explained that I didn't know how to fly it, and he said he would teach me. He was a good friend and lived a couple of blocks from me in San Antonio before I retired from the Army where we both were lieutenant colonels in the Army's Medical Department at Fort Sam Houston. He was also a CFII and herded me through my instrument rating. He said that if I bought the plane he would spend as much time as needed to teach me to fly it.

On December 11, 1986, we purchased the 231 with 495 hours on it, a Century 31 autopilot, complete King IFR radio/navigation package, Hoskins FT101 fuel flow meter, and WX 10 Stormscope (weather detection). This was the most complete and complex IFR equipped airplane I ever saw. It cost $61,000, and I received a trade-in of $13,000 for the 182. I had owned and flown the Cessna for five years putting 1,071.3 hours on it.

**N1159G.**

For two days my friend and I flew in the Mooney. After eight hours of flying, including two hours at night and a couple hours in the cockpit on the ground, I was deemed competent and safe for day or night IFR flights.

It was 45 knots faster than the 182. Its service ceiling of 24 thousand feet MSL required using oxygen masks; nasal cannulas are not authorized above 18 thousand feet MSL.

One of the most memorable flights in this plane was flying over San Antonio, Texas, at 24 thousand feet MSL. We had the ADF tuned to a local AM station. We were IFR and skimming the tops of very wet and gray clouds. The sun above us was bright and warm. Below us, though, was a raging rainstorm, and, according to the radio, the city was undergoing considerable flooding. It was surreal. Almost four and a half miles below us, cars were stuck, homes were being flooded, and the rain was causing severe damage. Yet, here we were, safe and enjoying a smooth flight, in bright sunshine. Quite a difference from flying the 172.

But sooner or later all good things must stop. By 1987 my writing career was booming. My wife and I had completed two best-selling business books for a publisher and had a contract for a third book. I was writing for several aviation magazines. We decided I would quit teaching and write full-time. But not in the Texas Panhandle as the winds were too strong throughout the year and we missed the mild weather found further south.

After examining communities and cities in southern Arizona and New Mexico, we choose Las Cruces. It had a major state university for my research and an instrument airport with hangars, and, for us, an ideal climate. A friend who was the head of the Management Department in the New Mexico State University (NMSU) School of Business knew I was moving to Las Cruces. He convinced me to accept a visiting professorship for two semesters covering for two teachers on sabbatical. My responsibilities were to teach three classes a week totaling nine hours and be available for two hours a week to see students. For this I was paid around $22,000. Add to this my Army retirement pension and writing income, and I was not poor. Also, only one daughter was still in college and on a full scholarship.

My writing expanded from aviation to motorcycles, firearms, and off-road magazines. With teaching and writing, especially the non-aviation writing, I found myself flying less.

In 1987, the first full year of my 231, I flew 213 hours. In 1988, though, my first full year in Las Cruces, I only flew 95.2 hours. My full-time position as a visiting professor ended in June 1988. I was spending a lot of time on the road on my motorcycle and on off-road four-wheel-drive camping trips. The plane was flown mostly on work trips, but they were few because so many articles featured ground transportation.

Because my writing areas had changed to more non-aviation magazines, my wife and I decided that it was not financially feasible to keep the 231. I had owned the 231 for exactly two years, putting 364.4 hours on it. Kansas City Aviation Center bought it for $62,260 in December 1988.

## Between Planes 1989 to 1991

During this time, I joined a local flying club, and in 1989 I only flew 23.6 hours in the club's Piper Tomahawk (PA-38).

I missed teaching, but my writing kept me busy. I did some part-time teaching at night for the NMSU adult education classes, teaching writing. In the fall of 1989, I was hired for a tenure-track position as a journalism professor at NMSU. Once again, I was a full-time university professor.

In January 1990, I was riding my motorcycle on campus when a 19-year-old female student who wasn't watching where she was driving ran me down. The crash broke my left arm at the wrist and destroyed my left leg from knee to hip. After two major operations to put my arm and leg back together again, I spent several months hospitalized and then trying to learn to walk again, which I could not do as my left leg was three inches shorter.

I could not walk without crutches. I had a three-inch lift on my left shoe, so if I stood, both feet reached the ground, but I still could not stand or walk unaided. In June 1990, I convinced a CFI to allow me to occupy the left seat to see if I could fly a plane. While I could not walk, the CFI said I could fly an airplane.

My left leg had little lift capability when sitting due to the massive crushing damage done to the upper leg in the accident. The brakes for most small planes are on the top of the rudder pedals. I could not lift my left leg to activate the left brake. Resting my left heel on the floor in front of the rudder pedal, I could manipulate the rudder easily. To activate the left brake, I would grab my left pants just above the knee, pull up and place my toe on the brake. I became so adept at this that it became an automatic and unconscious behavior on my part.

Because of my intense physical therapy, my writing, and my teaching, I was too busy to fly. During 1990 I only added 47.3 hours to my logbook.

Over the 1990 Christmas break, I endured another operation on my left leg. I was unable to return to the cockpit for six more months. By then I was so comfortable flying with crutches, I decided that it was time for another plane of my own. The question was, what plane could be both preflighted and entered/exited easily by a guy on crutches.

Prior to the accident we were doing fine financially. After the accident, not so well. Before the accident I had multiple magazine article contracts. I also had a deal with a major publisher to produce my book on the Vietnam War. Additionally, I had a contract with a movie production company that would purchase a film I made while in Vietnam. I had a couple hours of footage I needed to edit into a 42-minute documentary for PBS.

Added to these requirements was the need to attain tenure. Most schools allow about five years for a professor to gain tenure. The main requirement was to conduct research and get published. Thus, the old saying in academia, "publish or perish."

Because of the accident, the hospitalization, and the physical therapy, I lost the book deal, the film contract, and most magazine contracts. I had no time to write, nor even do scholarly research. My focus was on trying to walk again.

I had met a local pilot who was a surgeon. Before medical school he was an Air Force fighter pilot. He owned and flew a Grumman Tiger. He claimed that in flight it felt like his fighter jet. He arranged for me to fly his plane with a flight instructor. I had spent several hours in the Grumman two-seat TR-2 trainer and loved the plane. The flight in the Tiger confirmed my feeling that I wanted one. On the ground, I was able to preflight the plane on crutches. All I had to do now was find one.

## Five. Owning and Maintaining an Airplane

### N4515U, a 1979 Grumman Tiger Purchased in 1991

As a 53-year-old well-abused pilot, I had 2,728.6 total hours with 278.9 hours of IFR flights by mid-1991. I wanted a low-time, IFR equipped Tiger, and I found what I wanted at FletchAir in Houston, Texas. Since this was my first purchase totally on my own, I knew I had to be very careful.

I never saw the plane, but after several phone calls to the owner of FletchAir, David Fletcher, I was convinced that the aircraft was exactly what I wanted. The price was $39,500. I prepared a two-page purchase contract that included stipulations that a pilot would fly the plane to Las Cruces, fly it with me, and then allow my mechanic to perform a pre-buy inspection. If the plane did not pass the pre-buy inspection and I declined to buy it, I would pay all travel costs to Las Cruces and back. If I bought the plane, FletchAir would cover those expenses.

N4515U had 950 hours, total time engine and airframe. It was fully IFR equipped and had a Century I autopilot. It was in beautiful shape, had no airframe damage, and flew perfectly. I bought it in July 1991, paying $14,500 cash and financing $25,000 with an aircraft loan from Maryland National Bank. In just under six months, I put 134.8 hours on the Tiger. I ended 1991 with a total of 143.4 hours with 34 instrument hours.

Due to the missed flying because of my damaged leg, I flew as much

N4515U cockpit.

as I could. In 1992 I flew 296.2 hours with 39.1 being IFR. Landing at other airports created a stir. On cross-country trips I would land and taxi to parking, slide the canopy back, and hop out onto the wing. I flew with the back seats folded down, so the entire back was open. Reaching in, grabbing my crutches, I would slip off the wing. With both feet firmly on the ground, I would place a crutch under each armpit and hobble off to the FBO office. Later I graduated to walking with a cane.

In the fall of 1992, Anita and I covered the AOPA annual aviation convention held in Las Vegas, Nevada. While there I visited the American General Tiger display at the AOPA meeting. I explained a story idea I had, to fly the new 1992 Tiger and do an article comparing the new and the old Tigers. The article was published in the December 1992 issue of *Flying Review*.

My article was not the first, as N1196L was the cover story in the May 1992 issue of *Private Pilot* magazine by Mary Silitch. The plane had been delivered to Crownair Sales in San Diego. It was completely IFR King-equipped with an S-Tec autopilot and a price tag of $141,649.

At the beginning of 1993, the leg became worse. Avascular necrosis was setting in, also called osteonecrosis. This is a condition where the bone does not receive enough blood and therefore dies. If not fixed, the bone would collapse, and I would not even be able to walk with crutches. Something had to be done. Plans were made for the Mayo Clinic in Scottsdale, Arizona, to rebuild the leg.

N4515U.

At age 55, there were no guarantees regarding this operation. My entire left femur would be removed from just above the knee, then prosthetic parts would be placed inside my left leg. There would be a titanium femur, a titanium hip ball joint, a polyurethane cup adhered to my pelvis, and then strands of stainless-steel wire wound around the metal femur to attach ligaments and muscles. Also, during surgery, the leg would be stretched three inches to its full length again.

Because of the unknowns regarding the outcome of the operation or how long rehab might take, Anita and I decided to sell N4515U. The market for well-maintained used Tigers was excellent. I quickly sold my Tiger to Indiana Aircraft Sales for $34,500 in June 1993. I had put 519 hours on the Tiger in the two years I owned it.

## N1196L, a 1992 American General Tiger Purchased in 1993

The July 1993 operation was a success. I healed quickly, and both legs now reached the ground again. A month later I flew a friend's 172 to the Mayo Clinic, where I was cleared to drive or fly or do whatever I could. I walked with a cane but got stronger every day. Now I needed another plane, and I knew just what I wanted. I had stayed in touch with the sales manager at Crownair about the Tiger I flew for my magazine article. It had not been sold.

Another factor in the decision was life. For well over three years, flying was at the bottom of my list of favored activities due to my physical disabilities and my inability to fly. Anita and I decided to make up for missed flights. Two daughters were married, and our youngest was in law school, which she was paying for. Anita and I were empty nesters, financially secure, and I did not do any teaching during the summer. We had time to have fun and fly again.

On August 20, 1993, at age 56, with 3,208.5 total hours, I bought my first and only new airplane, N1196L, for $119,000. I paid cash. As soon as I got home, I had installed a WX 900 Stormscope and a Trimble 3000T GPS and Loran. In the next four months I put 157.7 hours on the plane.

Three flights in N1196L I will never forget.

On March 7, 1994, Anita and I departed Fort Pierce, Florida, destination Walker's Cay in the Bahamas, 119 miles. We departed IFR because the water was totally obscured by low cloud cover. We were flying at five thousand feet above the Caribbean Sea and above the cloud cover.

For 40 minutes we flew in a straight line, our GPS counting down the miles to Walkers Cay, a very small island. Contacting Bahamas air traffic control, I requested permission to descend to one thousand feet. We

**N1196L cockpit.**

entered the clouds around three thousand feet and broke out around 1,500 feet above the water, with the airport dead ahead a few miles. That proved to me the worth of the new GPS navigation system.

That summer we went to Alaska. During a stopover in Fairbanks, we planned a day trip to Fort Yukon, just north of the Arctic Circle. Our scheduled day, July 18, 1994, was IFR. Clouds covered the sky, and it rained everywhere. We departed IFR on the trip in the Tiger, 138 miles away.

While Fort Yukon had several instrument approaches, it was a single dirt strip. I did not want to attempt an instrument approach to a muddy and wet dirt strip. Anita and I decided we would fly over the strip on instruments, just to say we had flown in the Arctic airspace. Over the airport, the clouds opened such that I could make a visual landing, which I did. On the ground we walked around, retrieved some rocks, boarded our Tiger, climbed up through the hole and received our instrument clearance back to Fairbanks, IFR all the way. Not many general aviation pilots can say they have landed in the Arctic.

One day, in the summer of 1995, we were flying from Memphis, Tennessee, back to Las Cruces. Our flight plan had us flying south down the Mississippi River to the Louisiana state line and then turning west toward home. The weather was perfect CAVU (ceiling and visibility unlimited) with a mild temperature aloft. Our flight plan was to cruise at six thousand feet MSL. But we were in no hurry to climb to our cruise level, so we

## Five. Owning and Maintaining an Airplane

N1196L.

just ambled over the river. We discussed just cruising, slowly over the river with the canopy open. Anchoring everything loose in the cockpit, I modified our flight plan, explaining that we wanted to follow the river around 500 feet AGL. Now I should explain flying the Tiger with the canopy open.

When Grumman created the Tiger, they had advertising photos of the plane in flight. One photo showed the plane flying with the canopy open about three to four inches, and early advertising promoted that. But the FAA said they were not certified to fly with the canopy open. So, Grumman received FAA approval but only for the distance shown in the promotion photo.

If the canopy is slid back in flight a foot or more, air currents swirling in the back of the canopy will force it shut. So, I cut one-inch-by-one-inch wood blocks, four inches long, and, upon opening the canopy in flight, slipped them into the canopy runners between the windshield brace and the front edge of the canopy. This would lock the canopy open four inches.

Our flight was so much fun, we continued down to Baton Rouge, landed for fuel, and then headed west. We spent the day flying low and slow, staying above cables crossing the river in perfect weather. The scenery was outstanding, with many Civil War–era plantations visible on the riverbanks.

My leg grew stronger, and I could walk again normally. I received tenure, and the freelance writing was picking up. We were flying to more places and more often, but the Tiger was too slow, and the service ceiling was too low. We needed a faster plane that could fly higher.

On January 26, I sold N1196L to an airline pilot, who bought it for his wife. In two and a half years I put 832.4 hours on the Tiger and sold it for $82,500. He paid cash.

## N4538H, a 1979 Mooney 201 Purchased in 1996

My Tiger was the most fun to fly, but it had its limitations. It struggled to get above 13 thousand feet MSL, and its cruising top speed of around 140 knots was a little too slow for us. I preferred to buy a plane I knew I could fly. Cessnas and Tigers were out—too slow. A Mooney 231 was expensive to buy and expensive to operate, especially at high altitudes. I had some time in a Mooney 201. It was not expensive to operate. It could reach 19 thousand feet MSL easily, and with full fuel along with Anita, and myself, we could still load 250 to 300 pounds of baggage. Besides it could cruise at 155 knots, 15 to 20 knots faster than my Tiger.

I could fly the Mooney 201; it seemed the answer to what we needed. Besides, we both loved the cross-country comfort of our 231, so we decided to find a good 201. My search this time did not follow my usual advice for finding a plane. During our prior Mooney ownership, we had joined the Mooney Aircraft Pilots Association (MAPA), an organization of very serious Mooney owners. They sponsored a multiday annual "Homecoming" in Kerrville, Texas, where the Mooney aircraft are built. Senior

N4538H cockpit.

## Five. Owning and Maintaining an Airplane    85

members sharing their knowledge taught classes at Homecoming, and the monthly magazine allowed newer members to learn everything about their Mooney. Additionally, it was the place to begin a search for a good, used Mooney. We rejoined MAPA.

Through MAPA assistance I located a 1979 Mooney 201 in Illinois with a full King IFR package, a WX 10 Stormscope, and a Century 41 autopilot. It had a total time of 2,452.7 hours and 656.4 hours on an overhauled engine, done by a nationally recognized shop. It was priced at $79,900.

Again, with MAPA's help, I arranged with a respected Mooney shop to do the pre-buy. The pre-buy showed that "the plane was in good condition, all logs and records appeared correct, and the previous maintenance was done in a fashionable manner." This Mooney appeared to be as advertised. The pre-buy cost $509.02 in February 1996. I purchased the plane for $77,000 in cash. The plane was delivered by the dealer, but I paid for the trip.

The first thing was to have my avionics shop install a Trimble GPS-2000 and interface it with the autopilot, which cost another $6,000, but now I had exactly what I needed. Currently, I was 10 weeks short of 59 years with 4,048.9 total hours and 449 actual instrument hours.

Two months after I purchased the plane, a crack in the crankcase was discovered. This required overhauling the engine, which cost $22,340. Two months into ownership, my $77K plane really cost me $106,000.

With the new engine, we flew all over the United States that summer, putting 120.2 hours on the plane. The Mooney 201 had a design flaw that I was not aware of. It had two magnetos but only one drive shaft connecting them to the internal parts of the engine. I learned of this flaw the hard way, when the shaft disengaged from the engine in flight, resulting in a stopped engine. The investigation revealed that the nuts holding the magneto in place had come loose. They had been improperly installed during the engine overhaul.

On August 25, 1996, Anita and I had departed Lubbock Airport in Texas for our last leg home when the engine quit. This accident is described in detail in Chapter 9. While Anita and I walked away, N4538H was totaled. The insurance company bought the wreck for $108, 526.87, as I had the plane fully insured.

### N231HB, a 1979 Mooney 231 Purchased in 1996

Anita was bruised from the landing, although I was not, and she vowed never to fly in another 201 after she learned about the magneto shaft backing out. We both loved the Mooney, so we decided to return to a 231. My friend who owned Stinson Aviation had become a partner in

**N231HB cockpit.**

All American Aircraft located at the San Antonio International Airport, which specialized in used Mooney aircraft. They had some 231s for sale, so I went to San Antonio, Texas, to see what they had.

One plane stood out. It was a 1979 231 with 2,300 total hours and 406 hours on a factory remanufactured (rebuilt) engine. It had a complete King IFR package, Century 41 autopilot, Stormscope, speed brakes, and—most important—an Airflow intercooler. The exterior and interior were in excellent condition. The price? $89,900. I spent two days checking the logs and other aircraft documents. I arranged for a local Mooney specialist shop to do the pre-buy. My own estimate of the value of the plane came to $120,300.

The pre-buy showed several very small items needing attention. I prepared a purchase contract requiring all airworthiness items be corrected and an offer of $88,600. All American counteroffered $89,000, which Anita and I accepted. On October 12, 1996, we became owners of N231HB. We paid cash. Over the next nine years N231HB served us well.

One flight will never be forgotten. Anita and I had been covering the AOPA annual convention in Las Vegas, Nevada, one fall. We departed Las Vegas in the early evening. We were IFR and at 23 thousand feet MSL. Over Phoenix we began to turn eastward for Las Cruces. We picked up terrific tailwinds well over 80 knots, so we were crossing the ground at over 300 miles per hour. That put us an hour away from home. This was the fastest I had ever flown myself. Shortly after passing Phoenix, I began my letdown for Las Cruces, still 300 miles away. Amazing!

## Five. Owning and Maintaining an Airplane

N231HB.

## N4696T, a 1981 Cessna 182 RG Purchased in 2005

As we moved along in the beginning of the twenty-first century, our age was beginning to show. The Mooney is a tight plane, not a lot of wiggle room, like in a Cessna 182. Entering the Mooney requires a body to twist and turn. As Anita and I slid into our mid-sixties, contortions we did in our forties and fifties were not so easy, especially for me with much of my upper left leg false.

N4696T cockpit.

We were in a dilemma: we wanted speed and a decent service ceiling, but at the same time easier entrance and exit and a roomier cockpit. We really liked our previous 182, but it was not fast enough. A friend suggested a Cessna 182 with retractable gear. Not as fast as our Mooney, but it was not slow; it could cruise at 150 to 160 knots, and it was roomy and easy to get into. My maintenance shop had a used, worn-out, 1981 Cessna 182RG with 6,450.1 total time with a run-out engine that had to be replaced. The exterior paint was worn, but much of the interior was new with leather seats. It came with the original Cessna IFR package and autopilot. The plane certainly needed a lot of work.

Anita and I decided this would be a good move. Our business usage of our plane had declined to just over 50 percent of all flights. Almost half our flying was pure fun. As in the past, it was not hard to combine both business and pleasure on the same flight. An example would be a business flight to Orlando, Florida, for three days, followed by a fun flight to a resort in Key West for the rest of the week, then back home to Las Cruces.

For insurance purposes we were moving to a less-complex aircraft. For our ages, we would be gaining an aircraft easy to get in and out of plus roomier inside. Before any deal was made, I joined the Cessna Pilots Association (I knew the founder) and received ample publications on the Cessna 182 and 182 RG. I knew what to look for in buying a used 182 RG as well as its performance capabilities.

**N4696T.**

I worked with my maintenance shop to decide what should be done to turn the worn-out plane into a modern IFR dream. We examined possibilities, studied costs, considered upgrades, and finally reached a decision. First the maintenance shop, El Paso Aero, would complete an annual inspection to determine the plane's airworthiness status.

A multipage contract was prepared outlining everything that would be done to the plane. A brand-new panel would be created with Garmin and King IFR equipment, an S-Tec autopilot, Stormscope, Garmin 430 GPS, engine analyzer and fuel flow meter, overhauled propeller, new windshield, and factory rebuilt engine. Since I needed the plane for another trip to Alaska, the painting would be postponed. The total price was $181,582 and the trade-in for N231HB was $105,000. We paid cash for the difference.

On June 18, 2005, the trade was made, and we now owned N4696T. At that time, I was 68 years old and had 5,868.5 hours with 828.5 actual instrument hours. In 1990 I had retired from university teaching at age 53 so I could spend more time flying and writing. Anita had quit working before I retired from teaching, so our income was from both our social security, my Army retirement, my retirement from New Mexico State University, some VA disability from combat injuries, our investments, and writing. Financially we were in good shape.

When I acquired my first Mooney 231, it took me eight hours of flying over two days to become safe and competent. With the 182RG it took me close to 100 hours of inflight training to feel safe enough to fly IFR at night. Learning the Garmin 430 GPS system, all the different coupled instrument approaches, and everything else in the cockpit took a lot of time. But I knew from personal experience that when something goes wrong, that is not the time to see how well you function. Practice and training were always my priority in flying.

On April 20, 2013, Anita and I were returning home from a business trip to Washington, D.C., Landing at Birmingham, Alabama, for fuel, I slowed down to exit the runway when the nose gear collapsed. That was our last flight in N4696T. It had taken us to Canada, Alaska, the Bahamas, and all over the United States. I had put 1,108.7 hours on the plane during our seven years and 10 months of flying.

Because of difficulty acquiring certified parts to rebuild the plane, it was in maintenance for one year before being purchased by an aircraft sales company in South Carolina. They purchased it before the plane was completely repaired, wanting to finish it themselves. The value of the plane at the time I sold it was complicated. My insurance had paid for some of the repairs. The unpaid repairs yet to be completed plus what the aircraft sales company paid me, amounted to $81,111.68 for a plane that couldn't fly.

## N9277G, a 1971 Cessna 182 Purchased in 2013

While N4696T was in maintenance, I rented a 182. But renting did not compare with owning. The biggest problem was that the rented aircraft was based 50 miles away, which was very inconvenient. The maintenance shop in Birmingham predicted the repair of the 182RG would take a very long time, most likely over a year, so Anita and I discussed our options. I was 76 years old with 6,970.1 hours flight time and 1,040.5 actual instrument hours.

I rented for seven months. My flying habits had changed considerably over the past decade. I did not fly any "hard" IFR anymore. I almost never flew at night. I flew shorter legs and on cross-country trips quit around midafternoon. I was doing fewer business trips, only flying about half the time on business. So, Anita and I decided to acquire another plane while N4696T was being repaired, but no more retractable gear. We enjoyed our 182RG so decided to get a fixed gear 182. This would also make our insurance company happy. So far with my annual hours flown, all my safety training, and slowly, over time downsizing my aircraft, insurance was never a concern. Obtaining the coverage I wanted was never questioned by my insurance company.

A friend in Oklahoma had a friend who had too many planes, one being a Cessna 182 in excellent condition. My friend, a commercial pilot as well as an A&P mechanic with inspection authorization, ran a large maintenance shop in Lawton. He had worked on the plane and flown it. He said it was in great shape, had a new overhauled engine, Garmin 430 GPS, and S-Tec autopilot. An excellent cross-country airplane.

I contacted the owner; he flew the plane to Las Cruces, and I sat in the right seat while the owner flew the plane. It flew nicely, and I tested every piece of equipment on the plane. Everything worked perfectly. I wrote a contract for the plane provided it passed the pre-buy. My friend in Lawton did the pre-buy: nothing wrong, no surprises, so I bought the plane.

The plane cost me $79,925 plus $500 for the pre-buy inspection. With so much money tied up in N4696T, I took out a line of credit to buy the 182, which would be paid off when I sold the 182RG. On the afternoon of November 1, 2013, I flew N9277G home. My last flight as a medically certified pilot was on April 18, 2015, practicing instrument approaches.

In July 2015 I underwent open-heart surgery to keep me alive by replacing a faulty aortic heart value with an artificial tissue valve. Heart valve replacement is an automatic medical disqualifier for flying a plane. Agent Orange, from 24 months of combat in Vietnam, destroyed my heart.

I got back in the left seat on September 26 with a good friend, a CFII. For the next four months the two of us would periodically fly the plane. At

78 years old and with my new physical disabilities, I knew I would never receive a special issuance medical, so I decided to sell N9277G. I placed an ad in the Cessna Pilots Association magazine. It attracted a few lookers. None were serious about buying a plane except the last person. He wanted a cross-country plane, and mine was excellent for him. He paid $77,000 for it.

During the 26 months I owned the 182, I put 81.4 hours on it. Most of those hours were in 2014.

## Forty Years in the Sky

Forty years owning and flying nine different airplanes resulted in a total of 7,050.4 logged hours with 1,054.4 hours being in actual instrument conditions. My planes have landed in 49 states (missed Hawaii in my plane but visited there several times, by commercial air) and three foreign countries (Mexico, the Bahamas, and Canada). On most flights, in the right seat next to me was my partner and wife, Anita. She was as passionate about flying as I was. Not too shabby for a nonprofessional general aviation private pilot.

# Six

# Financing

## *The Army Paid Me to Fly My Plane*

As previously described, I learned to fly because of my travel requirements for the Army. The CFI at Fort Sam Houston in San Antonio who guided me through my private pilot examination and check ride used to be an Army recruiting sergeant in Yuma, Arizona. At that time, he was also a pilot and flight instructor. Traveling around southwestern Arizona and southeastern California on recruiting business, he flew himself. The Army would issue orders for him to visit smaller towns throughout his recruiting area. Most of his colleagues would drive to their destinations in their own cars, and the Army would reimburse them for using their vehicles.

The Army issues travel orders specifying where the military person is authorized to go and when. Typically, the orders could also state: "Travel by POV authorized." POV means "privately owned vehicle," referring to the person's automobile. But examination of the Army's regulations on travel shows that it also includes private aircraft, either owned by the traveler or leased/rented. The Army, though, did not reimburse the full cost of the aircraft. It could pay the amount authorized per mile for driving one's car or pay the traveler what a commercial airline ticket would cost the Army.

In the 1970s and '80s, the IRS allowed travel costs beyond any reimbursements to be declared as a deduction on federal tax returns. Today, some travel expenses may be deductible as an employee expense—see IRS Publication 463 ("Travel, Gift, and Car Expenses").

The cost for an employee to travel to conduct business for an employer is a business expense for the employer. Sometimes, though, the amount paid to the employee for travel is less than what it costs the employee. In certain cases, the IRS may allow the employee to claim the amount not reimbursed as an expense on the employee's federal tax return. To ensure compliance with the federal tax codes, seeking advice from a certified public accountant (CPA) is suggested.

While this section discusses what applies for a plane owned by the pilot, it can still relate to aircraft expenses of leased or rented aircraft. If the plane is leased or rented, the pilot pays a fee for the use of the plane. Leased or owned, tax-wise, the costs of flying a plane would most likely be treated the same.

I would keep a record of every penny spent on my airplanes. This would include insurance, maintenance, parts, gas, oil, hangar rent, away-from-home overnight parking, debt service costs, charts, iPad aviation-related subscriptions, GPS data discs/downloads, windshield cleaner, etc. At the end of the year, I would total up all costs. I would also calculate all hours flown and then split them between hours flown for business (for my employer, the Army, and later universities I worked for) and nonbusiness or personal hours flown for me. If the business flights were 70 percent of all my flying, then 70 percent of all aircraft costs were employee-business related. For example, if the annual costs of owning and operating your plane were $50,000, then 70 percent—or $35,000—could be tax deductible. But from this sum, you would have to subtract whatever reimbursements you received from your employer over the year.

Today's tax laws may not include employee travel expenses as a deduction. Therefore, reimbursements will reduce your aircraft expenses, but costs beyond reimbursements are probably not deductible.

The year after I retired from the Army, the IRS notified my wife and me that we were to be audited by a local IRS office. The audit was initiated because of an erroneous report by a university where I taught part-time.

When the agent saw the airplane deductions, she questioned us on the airplane ownership. She asked, "Did the Army require you to own a plane for travel?"

I considered this for a moment, then replied: "No, the Army did not require me to own an airplane, but then, it did not require me to own Amtrak, American Airlines, or Greyhound. It just orders me to go from point A to point B. How I get there is my choice, my decision."

She asked, "The Army ordered you to travel? Do you have copies of those orders?"

I produced a two-inch-thick stack of my travel orders, along with copies of all my reimbursements. The agent glanced at them, asked an aide to make copies, and that was the last time the IRS ever questioned my tax returns for my airplanes.

## Flying Records

There are several key points regarding my flying experience and the IRS. First is to understand both the IRS regs regarding employee and travel expenses and the FAA FARs related to flying costs and reimbursements. Second is to document all paperwork regarding employee travel. Then perfect records should be kept on travels, costs, reimbursements, and of course on the plane (pilot logbook, airplane logbook, and aircraft expense records).

After the Army, I would travel to university-sponsored conferences, educational conventions, symposiums to present research papers, and teaching seminars, all paid for by the school where I taught. All the documents showing that the university authorized me to be away from my teaching duties and reimbursement papers were retained.

Of course, if your flying is to support your own business, flying expenses are part of doing business, thus deductible if necessary and ordinary to your business. If you use your plane for travel as an employee, then other tax regulations will apply.

Other forms of aircraft deductions may be relevant if you fly for a charitable organization such as Pilots N Paws, Angel Flight, Civil Air Patrol, or other aviation volunteer groups that rely on pilots to donate flight time for the association. To determine what costs may be tax deductible, the organization will probably have documents outlining their understanding of the FAA's regs and IRS tax laws. The FAA supports humanitarian efforts, and since many flight organizations are charities, aircraft out-of-pocket costs may be allowed as a charity donation. Again, see your CPA for advice.

There are many ways to receive some reimbursement for flying and/or to record your flying expenses as a charitable or business or employee deduction. The correct way to do this is to understand what the organization's position is, what the FAA says, and how to properly file your tax return. In the case of larger charity organizations that use donated flight time, the organization will probably have all the tax answers.

## *More Considerations: You and the IRS*

Employee deductions today are different from what I did as described above. IRS rules regarding deductions change often. Navigating IRS rules and regulations can be confusing and frustrating. What was an allowable itemized deduction last year may be prohibited this year. Also, certain employees of specific professions or categories of employees may have different allowable exemptions. Therefore, the service of an experienced tax person is recommended.

The IRS has a Large Business and International Division Concept Unit that provides its staff with guidance and explanations on general tax concepts. Their document titled *Allocation Methods of Personal Use of*

*Aircraft* is most helpful to airplane owners. It explains how aircraft owners should record aircraft expenses to support expense claims.

Because different flights (charitable flights, employee travel, or flights by business owners) may be justified as a deduction under different rules, pilots and aircraft owners should be aware of these diverse types of flights for both IRS and FAA purposes. Thankfully, today, both the FAA and the IRS recognize that the use of personal aircraft for business travel is no longer viewed as for the rich and famous only. Experienced tax preparers and accountants understand that the use of a small plane for business travel is an accepted and customary practice in today's business environment.

Using your flying and your plane as a tax deduction can become complicated as rules and interpretations are subject to change. Therefore, I suggest one use a tax preparer who understands business usage of equipment and especially aviation-related business travel with a personal plane. The following sections will explain ways to have others pay your flying costs or how to claim your flying as a tax deduction.

## Other Ways to Support "MY" Flying

Retiring from the Army in 1981, I moved with my wife, Anita, and two of our daughters to Canyon, Texas, a college town of about 11 thousand people. I was newly hired as a management professor in the School of Business at West Texas State University (today West Texas A&M University), part of the Texas state university system with an enrollment of just around 6,500 students.

Anita was president of Worthington and Worthington Management Consultants, the business we kept from San Antonio. I taught at WTSU, and Anita managed the consulting contracts we had. I had traveled quite often for the Army, mostly flying my own plane. Once retired, all aircraft costs were now ours. I needed to find other ways to support our aircraft expenses.

Amarillo, Texas, is 17 miles north of Canyon, with two major airports. One is Amarillo International Airport, a controlled airport with two runways and multiple instrument approaches. The second is Tradewind, a non-controlled general aviation airport with two runways, hangars, maintenance facilities, a restaurant, a Beech dealership, and a flight school. It was also home to the Amarillo composite Civil Air Patrol (CAP) squadron. This unit's adult members ran aircraft search and rescue (SAR) missions throughout western Texas and northeastern New Mexico. The cadets participated in a variety of aerospace education and flight programs and provided ground support to SAR missions.

Our Cessna 172 was based at Tradewind because it could be hangared, and the airport had several instrument approaches. Canyon had a single dirt strip airport, but it was VFR only. While arranging to base my plane at Tradewind, I heard about the CAP unit. I learned that if I belonged to the CAP unit, I could use my plane for CAP missions and get reimbursed.

*Above and opposite right:* **Bob in his Civil Air Patrol flight uniform.**

## Civil Air Patrol

CAP is a national organization of pilots and planes. As an auxiliary of the U.S. Air Force, CAP is a congressionally chartered, federally funded, 501(c)(3) charitable organization. It is comprised of volunteers who participate in airborne search and rescue operations directed by the Air Force, other emergency services, and aerospace education for both cadets and adults. The CAP units follow military customs and wear modified USAF uniforms or specific nonmilitary civilian dress. Adult members wear military rank. Progression in rank is based on advanced training and experience. Membership is open to U.S. citizens; those aged 12 to 18 join as cadets.

Adult members are trained for specific CAP positions such as communications, logistics, SAR pilot, and others. Most efforts of a CAP unit involve emergency services like SAR missions, humanitarian assignments, and disaster relief operations. The purpose of CAP is to provide planes and pilots to support these three areas of operations or missions. There are CAP units in all 50 states, Puerto Rico, and Washington, D.C. Operational units have CAP-owned Cessna 172s and 182s for training and flight missions. Members may also use their own planes for CAP missions or training and get reimbursed for their expenses.

When I learned that I could fly my plane for the CAP and get reimbursed, I asked how to do this. First, I had to join the CAP. Then I had to

be trained and certified as a SAR pilot. This meant studying, taking tests, and being checked out by a CAP check pilot and participating in regional or statewide training mission operations. Upon satisfactory completion, I was certified as a SAR pilot, flying my C-172. By the time I was certified as a SAR pilot, though, I had traded my C-172 for a C-182.

This was one way to fly and have someone else help pay the cost of flying my plane. During my time as a CAP pilot, I flew all three kinds of missions. Most missions were searching for downed aircraft.

If a plane went missing or a locater beacon went off, the USAF is notified, and the CAP units in the area the plane is suspected of being are contacted to begin a search. The Amarillo unit, during my time in it, probably received four to six SAR missions a year. I went on most of them. The search planes held two to three members consisting of the pilot, a ground observer, and a mission observer who navigated, communicated, and coordinated the mission. Our unit had one CAP 172; most mission aircraft were privately owned.

One thing I learned is that unless the plane survived intact, a crash site mostly resembles a small garbage dump with burned debris scattered around rather than the form of an aircraft.

I flew one humanitarian mission in my five years with the CAP. In the fall of one year, a hurricane hit Texas between Houston and Galveston. The following day a baby boy was in a bathtub in Amarillo when a sister turned on the hot water. The baby, severely burned, and his mother were immediately flown by a local corporate jet to the Shriners Children's Texas burn hospital in Galveston. The entire island was closed, and the airport closed to traffic, due to the severe hurricane damage. The airport allowed the jet to land.

By that night, two-thirds of southern and eastern Texas was IFR weather with considerable rain. I was contacted around 11 p.m. and asked if I would fly the father to Galveston as the baby was in serious condition. I would be provided an instrument rated copilot and the father. We departed at midnight.

The distance to Galveston was 504 nautical miles or 3.6 hours flying time. About an hour into our flight, we hit rain. I was flying my 182, N96551, so my call sign became Angel flight 551. Center set me up on my instrument approach to the Galveston airport about an hour out. We were cleared for a direct ILS approach to runway 14. The control tower would not be operating, but the airport would function for my approach and landing.

We made a very wet but uneventful landing and were met by local CAP members. We first took the father to the hospital, and then my copilot and I were taken to the sole hotel open for hurricane first responders.

## Six. Financing

We went to sleep around 4:30 a.m., slept a few hours, ate breakfast, and went to the airport and departed back to Amarillo. Unfortunately, the baby died shortly after we delivered the father.

I also flew one natural disaster flight. Late one night a tornado hit the Texas Panhandle, doing considerable damage to a couple of towns just northeast of Amarillo. The state needed an assessment of damage, so I was asked to fly a tornado damage expert on an aerial recon of the area.

Tornadoes and hail go together like bread and butter. I flew normal search patterns where asked by the expert in my right seat. Wanting more fuel, I landed at a small airport. It was uncontrolled, with a small FBO, few hangars, one fuel truck, and tie-down parking next to the FBO. Parking in front of the FBO, we got out, used the restroom, and stretched our legs. Tied down next to the FBO was a brand-new Cessna 172. Unfortunately, the hail from the tornado had completely destroyed the plane. I asked the fuel guy what happened. He replied that a couple from out west had flown commercially to Wichita, Kansas, the previous day to pick up their new 172 from the factory. They arrived at this airport around dusk, stopping to spend the night. Parked in the open, the plane was unprotected. Both front and rear windscreens were totally shattered. All wings and fuselage had half-inch pockmarks throughout. The instrument panel was soaked and shredded as well as both front and back seats. This brand-new plane was a total disaster. I felt for the owners, picking up their dream plane, only to have it destroyed after a few hours' ownership.

I was assigned as the coordinator of the cadet flight training. They had a textbook outlining what needed to be done. I taught classes on flight planning, preflighting the plane, and navigation. After the classes, the cadets planned a flight with two stops. The flights were to be conducted on a nice VFR day. Each leg would last around 30 minutes. I would take three cadets; for each leg a cadet would occupy the right seat and tell me where to fly as the navigator. The flights would introduce the cadet to flying, and I would allow them to manipulate the controls. Each cadet was allowed up to five such flights. Most became very good at flight planning and navigating. For me the enjoyment was watching young people, who had never been in a small plane before, eagerly inhale their classes, and then successfully guide the plane from one airport to another. Sharing my passion for aviation with them never became dull or boring. It was fun for all of us.

But flying for the CAP was infrequent and unpredictable. Once I ended a cadet flight orientation training, I was done for a year or more. We did not get that many new cadets to do this training that often. SAR missions and SAR training missions did not come along that often, either. In a year I might fly a couple hundred hours or more but maybe only 70 to 100 hours for CAP. Less than half my flights would receive some reimbursement. Clearly, I had to find another way to pay for more of my flying.

## Becoming an Aviation Writer

As we moved into 1983, we needed more ways to fly the plane as a business expense. At that time, I was a subscriber to several aviation periodicals such as the *AOPA Pilot, Private Pilot, Plane and Pilot,* and *General Aviation News*. A weekly newspaper all about general aviation, it was referred to as GAN or the Green Sheet; its masthead on the top of the front page was printed in green ink. Its editorial offices were on the airport in Snyder, Texas.

In my aviation magazines, I would read articles about the writer flying somewhere to test fly a plane for an article. I would also read articles about air shows, aviation conventions, airplane travel stories. All these stories required flying somewhere to gather the information to author the article. I considered doing the same. If I could get a part-time job writing aviation articles, I could use my plane as a tax deduction by flying to do the stories.

I was a good writer. I was an instrument rated pilot with about 1,200 hours, and I was the owner of my second plane. I was a business professor and management consultant. I could write aviation business articles. I wrote to the editor of GAN offering my services. I received a reply that my services were not needed as there were no openings for another aviation writer.

I called the editor, almost begging to be heard. Finally, he surrendered and said that on Friday afternoon, April 15, 1983, from 1 p.m. to 2 p.m., he would meet with me and my wife. He cautioned that at two o'clock, our visit would cease, and we would leave. Snyder is 180 miles south of Amarillo, so the trip was short. We landed and parked in front of the editor's office, arriving a little early. He was waiting for us. We must have hit it off with the editor as he seemed very interested in my background, as both a pilot and a business expert. Two o'clock arrived, but he continued to ask questions. Finally, at 5 p.m., he said he had to leave. When Anita and I departed Snyder, I was the new GAN business editor. The man I replaced was a pilot who wrote about business, but he did not have a background in business.

I became the author of a column titled Aero Consultant. My first column appeared in the fourth issue of May 1983 on page 4. Initially I was contracted for one column a month at $50 a column for around 1,500 words. In four months, I was also doing other articles. By January 1984, I became a staff writer covering all aspects of general aviation. My wife and I began doing travel articles for other aviation magazines.

In 1985 I created The Left Seat column for a Cessna owners organization magazine, and Anita created and wrote her column, The Right Seat. I also began writing for aviation business magazines. reporting on the status of general aviation businesses in the United States such as FBOs, aircraft dealers, maintenance shops, flight schools, and airport managers.

The freelance writing became so busy that Anita and I shut down our management consulting business (although, a major revision of federal tax laws initiated the decision to close it). I resigned my tenured faculty position, and we moved to milder Las Cruces to write full-time. Upon moving, I resigned from the CAP. Because of my writing assignments and frequent trips, I would not be around enough to be relied on as a SAR pilot for the local CAP unit.

What does it take to become an aviation writer? While this is covered in detail in Chapter 7, I will say that one must be an excellent writer and very knowledgeable in aviation and flying. And the writer should be agreeable to editorial suggestions. If the editor is paying you, you need to write what they want and need. I get paid to keep editors happy. I do what they want. If they want something other than what I have submitted, I redo it to their specifications. Difficult writers do not get repeat jobs. Writers who satisfy editorial needs get more work.

Aviation writers get to test new products and, in some cases, keep them, to test fly new planes, and to meet great and famous people in aviation. At age 86, I no longer fly, but I am still writing about aviation, and still enjoying it.

## Ways to Support "YOUR" Flying

Throughout my 40 years as a pilot, my wife and I owned nine different airplanes. Every plane became a tool for business travel. I was never a professional pilot. I did not possess a commercial certificate. I could not use my plane for hire with me as the pilot. But there are numerous ways a private pilot can use a plane for business purposes and receive compensation or reimbursement or declare expenses as a tax deduction. But the pilot/aircraft owner must realize that both the FAA and the IRS have specific laws or regulations detailing what can or cannot be done.

Often, the sage advice of a certified public account or tax attorney before engaging in practices involving you, your plane, and money, can prevent future problems. Additionally, pilots should be aware of IRS Topic No. 511 ("Business travel expenses"), FAR Part 61.101 ("Recreational pilot privileges and limitations"), FAR Part 61.113 ("Private pilot privileges and limitations: Pilot in command"), and FAA Advisory Circular 61-142 ("Sharing Aircraft Operating Expenses in Accordance...").

As a private pilot and/or an employee, what the FAA and the IRS allow as legitimate expenses, tax deductions, and allowable reimbursements can seem complicated. Additionally federal tax laws seem to change often such that an allowable deduction this year becomes forbidden next year. Therefore, I strongly suggest that a CPA be consulted. For some complicated business arrangements, even an aviation tax attorney may be needed.

During my 40 years I would use my planes as both an employee and as a business owner. Over the 40 years, tax laws regarding what were legitimate expenses came and went. Here is how you might use your plane as a business expense or be compensated for its use as an employee. Because IRS and FAA regulations are always subject to change and what I describe I did in the past, it may not be allowed today. Seek expert tax advice.

## As an Employee

I became a pilot because my Army assignment required considerable cross-country travel. A four-hour trip by a general aviation plane could take an entire day by commercial air. Flying myself, I could often save two days of travel.

Initially I would rent a plane, but when I became a plane owner, I flew my own plane. The Army reimbursement would never cover all operating costs, but still, I got to fly and part of the costs were borne by the Army.

After I retired and became a university professor, I learned that the schools would fund travel to present research papers, attend professional conferences, and participate in educational seminars and courses. Because most colleges and universities award tenure, partially based on scholarly research presented and published, conducting research and presenting the results at professional conferences was encouraged and financially supported. Again, I flew myself and was reimbursed part of the aircraft costs. Sometimes, another faculty member flew with me, and I also pocketed their travel reimbursements within FAA guidelines.

## As a Business Owner

The tax regulations regarding aircraft usage and expenses as a business owner are less complicated than for an employee. But some words of wisdom. Expense claims for any business tool including aircraft must be ordinary and necessary. That means the use of an aircraft should complement the operation of a business. To justify aircraft usage the business should require travel of some distance such as a company whose sales region encompasses an entire state. This is an ordinary usage. And the travel is required for face-to-face interaction with customers and clients, making the travel necessary.

## Six. Financing

Two more words the IRS appreciates are that business expenses should not be extravagant or lavish. Claiming that a $15-million, six-passenger jet is needed to cover a 100-mile sales area for a single person may appear too extravagant when an $80,000 used Cessna could also do the job.

Be careful about submitting expense claims. Earning $500 in a year as a writer, while claiming $20,000 for your airplane expenses may wave a red flag in front of the IRS. There are no federal laws proclaiming that a business must operate at a profit. But a business must function with a profit motive. Your business must be organized and managed to make money. The IRS realizes that companies can struggle financially for years before the ledger turns from red to black. Your CPA can explain what may amount to justifiable expenses and those bordering on lavish or extravagant.

My wife and I owned rental properties scattered around different states where we once lived. Sometimes we would fly to inspect the properties or conduct other business related to our investments. Because the properties generated a substantial amount of income, the expense of an occasional visit represented a small percentage of revenues.

Our management consulting firm had contracts across the nation. We established a two-year management training program for a series of banks in Alabama, where we would spend a few weeks each year conducting evaluations and leading training programs. In Louisiana, we had a three-year contract to create a special education program for an entire parish school district. This required several visits each year conducting training and evaluating progress. On both these contracts we flew to do the consulting.

As aviation journalists, my wife and I created several aviation research programs for several aviation business magazines. One such report was the quarterly publication of the status of the general aviation industry across America. Initially we flew across the United States interviewing FBOs, aircraft sales dealers, maintenance shops, flight schools, and other aviation-related businesses. Our task was to understand their business and get them to agree to accept a faxed questionnaire every quarter asking about the health of their business, problems faced, challenges, and their solutions or responses.

All this data was tabulated, analyzed, and summarized by my wife and me and a report article written for the magazine. Occasionally, on our business travels around the country we would conduct more interviews for our reports.

As we flew around the country we would encounter, learn about, or find interesting aviation stories. Once on a stop in an Idaho airport we found out how the airport prepared the runway for safe landings during heavy fog. An ag plane would load its hopper with chopped dry ice and fly down the runway, just above the fog, immediately prior to the arrival of a commercial jet. The dry ice dissipated the fog on the runway, allowing the jet to land visually.

Another time I was covering an air show that also had tables for vendors. Two tables, side by side, were manned by two World War II pilots who had written books about their adventures as fighter pilots. At one table was retired USMC Colonel Greg "Pappy" Boyington, a Medal of Honor awardee, selling his books, one which described his being shot down and becoming a POW. At the table next to him was Masajiro (Mike) Kawato, selling his books describing how he was the Japanese pilot who shot down Boyington. Interviewing each of them made an interesting story, although it was later discovered that Kawato was not the pilot who shot down Boyington.

Another trip, resulting in a major tragedy, began the year before. I was covering the Confederate Air Force (CAF) annual air show at Harlingen, Texas, in the fall of 1983. Because I was an editor of *General Aviation News*, I was allowed to fly in a World War II warbird as part of the show. My steed was N16KL, a USN World War II PBY-6A Catalina bomber and the only World War II bomber in the CAF inventory that had flown World War II missions. I flew in the air show, and on December 19, 1983, my article, "CAF's Catalina Evokes Memories," was published.

I was scheduled to fly in the CAF air show the next fall, on October 16, 1984. After the 1983 air show the crew gave me a color photo of N16KL, in flight. On the back, each crew member had signed it. But I never received my second flight in N16KL. On October 14, two days before the show, the plane was on a photo mission at Harlingen when it crashed. Six onboard were killed, and four survived, including the two pilots who flew me the year prior. N16KL was destroyed. I still have the color photograph on my desk as I type this section.

Often, specific trips such as covering air shows, aviation conventions, or interviewing people, would also yield other, totally unexpected stories. The more I wrote, the more acceptable my expense claims for my plane.

## *Other Ways to Cover Aircraft Expenses*

One friend worked for a company in the Midwest that manufactured screen doors and windows. These products were sold to stores that sold doors and window screens. My friend was a pilot who interacted with the stores. The manufacturer authorized my friend to rent a plane to travel to the companies with the manufacturer covering the rental costs.

Another friend sold rural real estate in western Oklahoma, specializing in farms and ranches. He had a reputation as an expert in evaluating rural property. He used a Cessna 182 to travel to rural locations as a realtor and also used his plane to recon rural lands to arrive at a price for the property. All his aircraft expenses were a business deduction.

Another friend is paid to teach aviation ground school classes around the state. When he flies to the airport to teach the class, his aircraft costs are a business expense.

Another friend is the president of a statewide aviation organization, a 501(c)(3) nonprofit. His flights as a speaker to state chapters become charitable donations.

## Get a Partner

One way to reduce the costs of owning and operating a plane is to share expenses by having one or more partners. One partner can cut costs considerably as the fixed costs for annual inspections, hangar, debt service, insurance, etc., are split and the variable costs of operation are then determined by how much each partner flies.

Because of the economic value of this relationship, it should be carefully conceived and completely thought out. Financial risks are shared, flight decisions decided equally, and management resolutions made together.

Partners should think alike, tend to agree on how a plane should be treated, and share safety values equally. Major differences can lead to trouble. If one partner believes every small quirk should be remedied immediately while the other prefers to put off spending any money on a plane until necessary, arguments may mar the partnership.

A difference in flying skills, experience, and ratings can also lead to disaster. If one pilot is a low-time, VFR-only flyer and the other prefers long, often IFR cross-country flights, opinions about equipment needed can differ greatly.

A proper partnership should be a legal, written contract, with clearly defined concepts of how to share ownership and usage. The sharing of costs should also be understood and agreed upon. Decision-making must be shared and parameters for required annual training for each partner agreed upon. The importance of safety should be mutually agreed upon without compromise.

The partnership contract should include provisions for how to dissolve the relationship for any reason. Situations could change, making it impossible for the partnership to continue, such as losing a medical, having a job transfer, losing a job, divorce, death in a family, or some form of financial difficulty.

The potential financial risks involved with shared ownership should dictate that legal advice be sought to properly draw up a partnership contract. AOPA has information pertaining to the formation of shared aircraft ownership that is readily available.

I was never interested in sharing my plane with anyone for several reasons. Primarily I wanted a plane available to me 100 percent of the time. I also wanted total control of decisions regarding how the plane would be used, what equipment would be in the plane, and maintenance considerations. I did not want to share any of this with anyone else. Of course, financial decisions would have to be shared with my wife, and we never ever encountered any differences regarding our financial support of our planes. Certainly, compromises were made, but safety always was the most important consideration when spending money on our planes.

Sharing aircraft ownership is not for everyone. But for the right pilots, it is a way to reduce costs to make flying much more affordable. It is not a relationship suitable for all, but executed properly it can provide the opportunity to afford flying.

## Rent Out Your Airplane

Another way to reduce the costs of flying is to rent out your airplane. There are several ways to do this. The plane can be placed with a local flying club, an FBO, a flight school, an aviation company, or any business requiring a plane for travel purposes, or rented to others by you directly. Essentially you are creating a business that leases your plane to another business or individual. As such you should have commercial insurance to protect both yourself and your aircraft. You also need legal advice on how to properly establish your rental business and contracts for who will rent your plane. Another consideration is how you will vet whoever will be leasing your plane.

If you create a business to rent or lease your plane, some words of advice. Consider some form of incorporation to shield you. The corporation owns the plane and if something happens and the plane's owner (your corporation, not you) is sued, your loss will only be what you have invested in the corporation. But, if criminal activity is involved, that can be another matter. Being incorporated does protect you personally under normal business operations.

Do as much as possible to know who or what business is using your plane. During the lease period keep track of the business (flight school, charter service, FBO, private company, or individual). Markets can vary, businesses can have their ups and downs. Your plane is a healthy financial investment; keep watch on whoever is using your plane. If the lessee is facing economic difficulty, that may not bode well for the welfare of your plane. If you retain responsibility for maintenance, you will know if your plane is being abused. If the lessee assumes that responsibility, just keep watch. Consider a clause in the lease contract allowing you annual inspections of the plane and logbooks.

You should ensure that you are in full compliance with FAA regulations and those of the IRS. Additionally, your state and local government will also have rules and regulations you must meet as you are creating a business.

Sometimes the aviation business acquiring the use of your plane such as a flight school may have legal documents already in place for you. Again, because of the potentially high financial risks involved, legal advice and proper insurance coverage are a must.

You will probably need advice on how much to charge. Renting a plane is not unlike placing real estate for lease. Over time the plane depreciates in value. Normal maintenance and needed repairs should be planned on. Parts will wear out, and inspections are required. Your rental income should cover all operating costs, future maintenance expenses, and make you some profit. If you charge too much, no one will rent your plane. If you charge too little, you may lose money.

Contracts can be prepared allowing you use of your plane. But keep in mind that often, the pilot flying your plane will want to maximize speed and thus will fly your plane as fast as possible. Your plane will not be babied. Renting your plane to a flight school or flying club that has its own maintenance facilities may be best for you.

Many aircraft owners have been very satisfied renting out their planes. Their arrangements have been profitable for them, allowing them to reduce their own flying costs. At the same time, some rental contracts have caused the aircraft owner to lose money and go into debt. Inspect any rental agreement carefully; ensure that you will be in compliance with both the FAA and the IRS. Unless you are experienced in this venture, seek proper legal advice before signing any papers. Renting could prove to be a financial boon for you or a financial disaster. Do your due diligence.

## These Suggestions Are Not for Every Pilot

Most of my pilot friends are not interested in creating ways for their flying to generate income or using it for tax deduction flights. To claim aircraft expenses as a tax deduction requires tax law knowledge and additional records and filing more than a standard tax return. It can become complicated, and many pilots aren't interested in dipping into legal waters.

Using the plane as a business expense requires one to own and operate a business. For most pilots, this endeavor exceeds what they want to do.

But if you are interested in at least examining what it takes to claim your plane as a business deduction, then read the next section.

## *Making Your Plane a Business Deduction*

### Why Create a Business for Your Plane?

I fell in love with flying, then owning planes, then loving everything about general aviation. Finally, I became an aviation writer. I was totally enmeshed in the aviation business.

Essentially Anita and I already owned a business. Our consulting business was a sole proprietorship owned by me, and Anita was an employee. The firm also wrote training manuals for management contracts we had with our consulting clients. When I began writing for *General Aviation News* as the business editor, this income became another aspect of our consulting business. Obviously writing was becoming a larger part of the consulting business.

Each airplane was the property of my wife and myself. All business flying became an expense of the sole proprietorship. When we moved to New Mexico, we closed the management consulting portion of my sole proprietorship. Now our business income was from our rental property and writing. All our businesses were operated out of our home. We never claimed any part of our home expenses as part of the business for two reasons. The recordkeeping was not worth the tax deduction, and doing so could raise a red flag with the IRS.

Basically, for tax purposes we claimed all income from writing and rental property as business income from my small sole proprietorship. Once we moved to New Mexico Anita was no longer an employee of the business, although she did contribute to my writing efforts. We claimed the usual expenses for writing and rental income such as the on-site rental managers, computer costs, postage, paper, etc., but the largest expense was travel, mostly the cost of owning and operating the plane for business usage. I did have full-time employment outside of aviation as a university professor. This meant that items like tax withholding, social security payments, and other aspects of operating a business were not required of me. If your sole source of income is from your business, then both federal and state business requirements must be met. Your accountant, business attorney, or a consultant from a federal or state organization may be able to help you.

The U.S. Small Business Administration has a national network of organizations created to help small businesses. These include Service

Corps of Retired Executives (SCORE) and Small Business Development Centers (SBDC), as well as some Veterans' Outreach Centers and Women's Business Centers. The U.S. Veterans Affairs offers veterans help in starting a business, and most states have offices to help create businesses. There are more than 380 SCORE chapters across our nation.

Eventually, over eight years, we sold all our rental property, and the sole proprietorship income came from writing.

## Creating Your Business

Having a plane as a tax deduction is not a complex matter. To be safe, an aircraft owner should understand applicable IRS and FAA rules that regulate what you want to do. One must also be very adept at record-keeping as that fact often separates winners from losers when justifying what you do to the federal government. To me, the biggest part of claiming an aircraft as a tax/business deduction is to be honest. Declaring your plane as a business expense when it is not is just looking for trouble. Additionally, defending your business tax claims can be time-consuming and expensive.

Here are some fast IRS rules. To claim your plane as a business expense, then obviously, one must have a business. It can be full-time or part-time. A business should be created to earn a profit; this differentiates it from a hobby.

Now there is no federal law requiring any business to be profitable, but the assumption is that the owner is doing everything possible to be profitable. For many businesses, the path to making money may take years. For example, *USA Today* operated for almost five years before income exceeded expenses.

What is an acceptable expense? The IRS says ordinary and necessary. Ordinary means common to managing the business. If one makes shoes, purchasing leather is an ordinary expense. Necessary refers to the cost of something that is helpful or appropriate to run the business. If one delivers fuel to gas stations, having a tanker truck is necessary. Being necessary does not mandate it to be indispensable or requisite for the business. An example is a business that has a shaded patio outside the office. This is not related to what the business does. But indirectly it can be a business expense as it provides a safe place for employees to eat lunch and keeps them out of the hot sun while taking a break outside.

What constitutes a business? For tax purposes there are several types, such as sole proprietorship where you are the only owner, partnership, and different types of corporations. For me, I was always a sole proprietor, requiring me only to say, "I am in business." States and municipalities may have their own regulations to follow, however. If protection of personal assets is a concern, consider a limited liability company (LLC). The structure of an LLC is governed by state statutes.

## To Incorporate or Not to Incorporate? That Is the Question!

Another question for pilots is if it is worthwhile to create a corporation or LLC for your plane. Occasionally one may see an ad in an aviation magazine advising aircraft owners to create a corporation or LLC, usually in Delaware because of state tax laws, as a means for liability protection or for tax purposes. Some tax advisors or attorneys may suggest that there might be other, less complex, and less expensive ways to create and protect a business.

Yes, being incorporated does offer protection for owners beyond the investment in the corporation. And there can be certain tax advantages to being incorporated. But there can be disadvantages. For example, if a plane is in a corporation, then ownership is not with you, but the company. This can change the FAA determination of the plane from private ownership and usage to commercial ownership and usage because it is no longer a personal aircraft but now a business aircraft.

The move of your plane to an LLC or type of corporation should be based on how the plane would be used and liability risks. For me all my businesses were sole proprietorships, and all planes were owned by me and my wife. My business did not involve a high degree of risk. I was covered with several different insurance policies for the plane and personal liability. My flying was under FAR Part 91. The decision to become incorporated should be discussed with an aviation-experienced accountant or attorney. Becoming incorporated costs money, requires reporting and paperwork, and may not be financially advantageous. On the other hand, being incorporated may provide advantages and safety that you and your plane may need. Expert advice in this area is suggested.

## Business Operations

I keep a file on every article or book written, another file on income earned, and a third file on expenses. This last file can become tricky as the IRS may change what can qualify as a tax-deductible expense. For the plane, though, the expenses are easy to justify. Insurance, maintenance, parts, hangar rent, gas and oil, and away overnight parking fees are all collected in my expense file. For flying I used a separate pilot logbook every year. At the end of the year, I would total the hours flown and then note those hours flown for business. If I flew 300 hours and 250 were for business, then 83.3 percent of all my flying costs would become a business expense.

The calculations of expenses, depreciation, etc., can be complex. That is why I always used an accounting firm and a CPA to do my taxes.

The IRS does not view a plane much differently from other equipment or vehicles a business needs to earn a dollar. Owning a Cessna Citation for a business whose sales area is confined to a 100-mile radius may be a stretch by the IRS. Owning a Cessna 182 for a contractor who builds throughout the state will most likely be accepted without question by the IRS. Documents such as a business plan or corporate minutes may prove helpful with the IRS.

In all cases travel was a necessary aspect of my business as a writer, so I needed a means to get there, therefore using a private aircraft was considered by the IRS as an acceptable form of transportation.

Some words of caution: Using an accountant familiar with the business use of vehicles and IRS regulations governing such usage can be vital, as opposed to doing your own taxes. Using an aircraft as a business expense can be complex in that other rules apply. If a plane is used more than or less than 50 percent of the time, different accounting procedures must be followed. If the value of a plane is depreciated over time, surprises may arise when the aircraft is sold or traded. If the sales value of the plane is more than its depreciated value, then the owner may have to pay taxes on the gain. Recovery from depreciation is ordinary income. I have found that there are other depreciation concerns involved when selling or significantly changing the business use of the plane. Also keep in mind that every year the tax code may have changes that impact you.

I have covered how I used my planes as a business deduction. All my part-time business endeavors were created to make extra money, and the tax returns were honest. I maintained extensive files on every transaction involving my work and the use of the plane. I possessed incontrovertible evidence to support every claim presented in my returns. This is the honest part.

Since I was always a sole proprietorship, all business taxes were filed using a Schedule C as part of my personal tax return. Another suggestion: the IRS provides ample resources on how to create and manage a small business. But more information specific to aviation business may be found through various industry-related associations, such as AOPA and National Business Aviation Association.

## What Can You Do?

So, what kind of part-time work can you do that makes money, is fun, and requires a plane to accomplish? What kind of part-time endeavor can you invest in that will require travel using your plane? Remember that it must have a profit motive, i.e., be created to make money; it should be honest; and you should maintain meticulous records. Having a CPA can go a long way in keeping the IRS away. One last reminder: two federal government agencies regulate your business usage of your plane, the IRS and the FAA. For some businesses, state and local statutes may also apply. One must comply with all.

## *Suggested References for a Pilot Wanting to Use a Plane for Business*

All of the following are available on the internet.

AOPA: "The Pilots Guide to Taxes"
CFR Title 14 Part 61.113, "Private Pilot Privileges & Limitations: Pilot in Command"
FAA AC 61-142, "Sharing Aircraft Operating Expenses"
IRS Publication 334, "Tax Guide for Small Businesses"
IRS Publication 463, "Travel, Entertainment, Gift, and Car Expenses"
IRS Publication 535, "Business Expenses"
IRS Publication 583, "Business Start-up"

The following guides are for IRS examiners to use during an audit to ensure that the business owner has proper documentation to support compliance with IRS rules and regulations. It is a helpful guide for business and tax planning.

IRS "Allocation Methods of Personal Use of Aircraft" and next line IRS "Audit Techniques Guides (ATGs)

## Seven

# Aviation Journalism

An aviation journalist is a person who presents reports on a segment of the aviation industry. This person does research, gathers information, and reviews facts. Then this person prepares or writes about what was learned in some form to be presented to an interested audience. This process consists of two main parts. One is the aviation background of the journalist. The second is the method of presenting the aviation news or story, meaning the medium used, such as print (newspapers, books, magazines), radio, TV, or social media (podcasts, blogs, YouTube, websites, or streaming).

Aviation journalists can cover any aviation category, such as airlines, military, or general aviation; they can specialize in the aviation industry, reporting on business, travel, or aeronautical engineering and aircraft design or personal use. There are no limits to what an aviation journalist may decide to specialize in or focus on.

## For Whom Do Aviation Journalists Work?

Aviation journalists come in assorted flavors. Those who write for major newspapers such as the *Wall Street Journal*, *New York Times*, or the *Washington Post* tend to focus on the big picture, such as the aviation industry as a business, the airline business, or aircraft manufacturers. They report on the business aspects of aviation, the leaders who make news, or the industry's business difficulties. Radio and TV news programs use reporters like these as experts when covering aviation news. These writers are usually paid staff, but some are hired to focus on a specific event or situation, typically for TV news shows.

Aviation trade magazines tend to focus on a specific aspect of aviation, such as professional pilots, aircraft maintenance, FBOs, airports, commercial aviation, and so forth. These include magazines such as *Professional Pilot*, *Aircraft Maintenance Technology*, *Ground Support Worldwide*,

*Airport Business, Business and Corporate Aviation Management, Business and Commercial Aviation,* or *Aviation Week & Space Technology.* These periodicals have their own staff but may also accept freelance submissions. Early in my career as an aviation journalist I wrote for aviation business magazines. One series I wrote discussed the aviation industry in the Pacific Rim; it received a national writing award for an aviation business series.

There are also magazines that cater to specific parts of aviation such as military, airlines, or general aviation. These magazines include *Air Line Pilot, Air & Space Force Magazine,* or *Combat Aircraft Journal.* These magazines have paid staff but accept freelance submissions.

Now we come to my area of expertise: general aviation. Being the largest segment of aviation in the United States, it has the greatest number of publications. These are consumer magazines. Some are printed by publishing companies to include *Flying, Midwest Flyer, General Aviation News,* or *Plane and Pilot.* Others are published by aviation organizations like AOPA (*Pilot*) or EAA (*Sport Aviation, Warbirds,* and others) or owner organizations of specific aircraft manufacturers such as Cessna, Piper, Mooney, Cirrus, Diamond, and others. All these magazines have paid staff but accept freelance submissions.

Then we get to smaller aviation organizations such as the New Mexico Pilots Association or the Florida Aero Club. They may publish print or digital newsletters, but all have a presence on the internet, and some may accept freelance submissions. Most do not pay for what they use, but this is a way for writers to garner credibility for aviation articles.

## *Today's Technology*

When I began my career as a professional writer in 1967, I handwrote everything on yellow legal pads. My wife would type my draft and then, together, we would edit and rewrite what she had typed. Then she would type the final draft with a typed carbon copy. The original was sent to the editor. In the mid-1970s we moved to word processors, machines that would display what was typed on a screen before it was printed out. Two decades later, in the mid-1990s, home computers with word processing programs were common.

Until the advent of digital cameras in the mid-1990s, photographs accompanying my articles were taken by me using film. Using a home darkroom, I developed my own black and white or color photos. Most editors preferred black and white negatives or the developed Kodachrome film. When digital cameras became readily available, I gave up film and developing and transferred photos from camera to computer and emailed them to my editors, along with an attached article. Now, smartphones have excellent camera resolution capability.

Digital and electronic technology today allows multiple opportunities for people to pursue aviation reporting for free. All aviation media that used to be primarily print present their information in a variety of ways. The major publications are still print magazines but are into digital and electronic technology, big-time. For example, *Midwest Flyer* was a bimonthly regional print aviation magazine until 2021, when it went online. Today subscriptions to some digital magazines are free. Going online removed expensive printing and mailing costs and increased subscribers.

Another common business practice is to use email to send information to clients, customers, or subscribers. An additional digital form of communication is the creation of a website. Information can be distributed using print and photos, sound, or visual video. Since most are used by aviation reporting media, there are additional opportunities for aviation journalists.

One format consists of using online blogs, a written journal published via the internet. The term "blog" is a derivative of a web log. Another digital medium is a podcast, a digital audio file or program presented via the internet. In this case voices and sounds are presented to the audience through the internet.

Another concept for delivering both audio and visual presentations is by web streaming, and the most popular (and free) platform is YouTube. The only cost in acquiring a YouTube channel is the equipment necessary to create the material and post it on YouTube.

## What It Takes to Be an Aviation Journalist

Two primary skills are required to be an aviation journalist. One must be a good writer, able to effectively and efficiently use words to connect with readers. The second skill is knowledge of aviation. The writer must understand the industry and the users who are the readers. Writers should recognize what the readers want and be able to deliver just that, using words.

From here on I will focus on general aviation, but first a caveat. I do not know any aviation journalists who became rich by their writing. The ones I personally know make a decent living. Those who have made a career as an aviation journalist and have moved up the ladder from writer to editor to even senior vice president of publications or media will make more money. And as you rise in titles and responsibilities, if you become an expert in the new forms of media technology you become more desirable and useful. Being an aviation journalist is not the best vocational avenue to become rich. That said, let us move on.

All general aviation writers I know are pilots. Some are private and instrument rated, which allows them to fly anywhere, anytime, while others are commercial or airline transport pilots. Many are also flight instructors and ground instructors. They may also work in aviation as managers, business owners, school operators, salespeople, maintenance personnel, or consultants. My background, in addition to being a pilot, is as an aviation psychologist, a businessperson, and a safety and survival instructor. My point being that all my aviation writer friends and acquaintances do have a deep connection to general aviation.

Many aviation writers have college degrees in subjects where writing was necessary. I do not recall any whose education was in journalism, but that is an excellent choice (I say as a retired journalism professor). Most became involved in aviation first and aviation writing second, although there are aviation writers who started in journalism, then became involved in aviation reporting areas, and only then became pilots. There is no single way to become an aviation writer. Physicians must go to medical school, attorneys must go to law school, but aviation writers can come from anywhere.

My colleagues include an oncology surgeon, a Harvard English major, and a screenwriter. Several have been airline pilots with a passion for general aviation. We come from all occupations (I used to be a career infantry officer in the Army). But all can write and love aviation.

## *Why Be an Aviation Journalist?*

As I said, aviation journalism is not the road to riches, not in the financial realm. But my career in this field has allowed me to meet people, fly planes, evaluate equipment, and view new aircraft before introduction to the public. If one is a writer for a respected aviation publication or news outlet, managers and leaders admire you and your employer. This opens doors for opportunities and experiences most pilots will never know. You may be invited to events as a guest, whereas the public must pay hundreds to thousands of dollars to participate. Being a member of the aviation press allows access to backstage information, introduction to movers and shakers in the aviation industry, and special tours to provide background information and details on what you write.

In air shows I accepted the opportunity to fly in-show aircraft during performances as a writer for *General Aviation News*. As aviation travel writers, my wife and I have been guests at prestigious vacation locations around the United States. We attended inaugural ceremonies introducing new and different aircraft to the world. I met and spent time with big names in aviation such as Richard Branson (Virgin Group), Bob Hoover (air show pilot), Colonel Gregory Boyington (USMC Ace), Herb Kelleher (cofounder Southwest Airlines), Edna Gardner Whyte (air racer and flight instructor), Patty Wagstaff (aerobatic and air show pilot), and others. All were willing to sit and discuss aviation with me.

An advantageous part of being an aviation writer is being able to fly planes. Covering aviation stories usually involves airplanes. On occasion I have been able to fly a plane for a story. Once I flew in a World War II warbird during an air show performance. Another time I had the opportunity to fly a World War II North American T-6 trainer. Recorded in my logbook is the 45-minute flight.

One year covering an AOPA annual aviation expo, I met the sales manager of an aircraft dealer who brought a brand-new 1992 American General Tiger for display. I flew the plane and authored an article on the "new" Tiger. Several months later I bought that plane.

These are some adventures I experienced as an aviation writer. The people I have met, the planes I have flown, and the events and air shows I have covered will remain with me always. And the best part is that everything has been recorded and published, so I will always have these memories.

## *How Does One Become an Aviation Journalist/Writer?*

If you already have published articles in another area, then all you need to do is use your credibility in aviation to sell your stories. If you are not published, where does one start? Search the internet for books on how to write articles that get published. Obtain a copy of the book *Writer's Market*. These options will provide valuable information on writing articles that will sell.

Go to places that publish either print or online, such as state pilot associations, local aero clubs, or magazines of smaller aviation organizations. Although they do not pay for what they print, if sent good copy they will publish it.

I suggest that you get several issues of the publication you want to write for. Read them and understand what they publish. It is not productive to submit queries for articles that are not their areas of focus; that reveals that you do not understand the publication or its readers. Do not submit ideas already published. Letters to the editor may suggest what readers liked or what they want to read. Story ideas may come from there. Bottom line: know the publication before pitching an idea.

Okay, you have read a year's worth of publications, what now? Based on your reviews of past issues, you have ideas for the publication. You contact the editor by email if you have an address. First introduce yourself, providing your credentials and experience in writing. Then do the same with your aviation background. You need to convince the editor that you can write and that you know aviation. Then you present your article ideas. At this point I suggest you also present your market research data to show why what you are proposing is of value to their readers.

For example, I pitched a story idea this way. I discovered an exercise machine that provided both cardio and strength exercise. I wanted to do an article for pilots on this machine. It was both compact and not expensive. Pilots could place it in a bedroom or den or office, and they could afford it. But I had to convince the editor that this was a story of interest to pilots. So, in my email to pitch the story, I cited this data: "Most people in the U.S. are physically unfit. Physical fitness experts say we should exercise at least 150 minutes a week, both cardio and strength exercises. To retain the privilege to fly, pilots must remain physically fit. Most are examined by the FAA every six, 12, or 24 months to ensure they are healthy. Thirty minutes a day with this machine would keep pilots healthy to pass their medicals." The pitch was accepted and the article published.

I write for editors. What they want, I write. The editor may suggest a different slant to one of your ideas. You now have a choice. You can say that you will not alter your idea, or you can embrace what the editor wants and become published.

Over time you can develop a résumé of publications and seek bigger media outlets.

## Eight

# Aviation Psychology

Aviation psychologists are found throughout the aviation industry. Their subspecialty helps the FAA in a variety of ways, from certifying pilots, to designing cockpits, to assisting in aviation-related mental health issues and accident investigations, to designing aviation training materials. But, ironically, unless you are a professional pilot, you probably will never meet one.

## *Psychologists*

What is an aviation psychologist? First, I should define a psychologist. A psychologist is a professional trained in the study of human behavior. A bachelor's college degree is the minimum education required to work in the field. Most jobs require at least a master's degree. To practice independently as a psychologist, most positions call for a doctoral degree, certification, and state licensing.

Psychologists typically serve in one of three capacities: clinical/counseling, consulting/teaching, or research. All deal with how humans behave within certain vocational, family, educational, or social frameworks. Clinicians or counselors collaborate directly with people in a variety of settings in hospitals, mental health clinics, businesses or organizations, or specific settings such as education, professional or collegiate sports, law enforcement or legal endeavors or even aviation. Consulting psychologists serve as advisors to organizations or industries regarding the utilization of people. Research psychologists use their expertise studying human behavior under distinct settings such as examining human performance in specific situations, how to best match people with concepts of new equipment or machines, or analyzing human responses under certain conditions.

Psychologists observe human behavior and make predictions regarding future human responses or advise groups, organizations, or businesses on how people will behave. Psychologists use their knowledge of the behavioral sciences to provide their expertise and skills in a wide variety of fields. While most psychologists serve in mental health areas as counselors and clinicians, they may work in most endeavors involving people.

## *Aviation Psychologists*

Psychologists serve in a variety of functions in aviation. I am an aviation psychologist. As a PhD psychologist I was educated to understand how to observe human behavior and to predict how humans will respond to specific stimuli. As a veteran pilot, I have experienced most stressors, demands, and challenges that can occur while flying or being in an aircraft, including combat and crash landings.

My specialty is to examine how pilots behave—and why they behave the way they do—in specific situations in flight such as losing an engine, having equipment failure, facing emergency situations, severe weather, or experiencing personal issues. I then strive to understand which behaviors lead to successful performance and which result in failure. Using this knowledge, I can create educational seminars or lessons explaining what is happening and why, then teach pilots how they can either avoid bad situations or how to effectively control what is happening.

My work as an aviation psychologist began in the military (see *The Making of an Army Psychologist*, 2023). I would teach Army aviators about such topics as managing stress in the cockpit or the psychology of survival after a crash.

The airlines use psychologists to select pilot candidates to hire. Pilot applicants complete computerized psychology instruments measuring personality characteristics to best match those of successful pilots. Psychologists assess these tests and interviews to best match a candidate's personality characteristics with those of effective pilots. The military also use aviation psychologists to assist in their selection of pilot candidates.

For example, pilots should tend to follow rules and regulations. If the tests reveal high scores in these areas, that is good. But a candidate with low scores could be a poor selection. On the other hand, airlines do not want "high-risk" pilots, those who will cut corners or compromise safety to complete a mission. Psychological tests can identify candidates with these undesirable personality traits. Airline and military aviation psychologists also support the mental health of aviation support staff like air traffic controllers and flight crews, who constantly deal with the demands of time, weather, passengers, schedules, and potential flight hazards.

Family and personal pressures likewise affect behaviors while flying. Airlines and the military have specially trained aviation psychologists

# Eight. Aviation Psychology

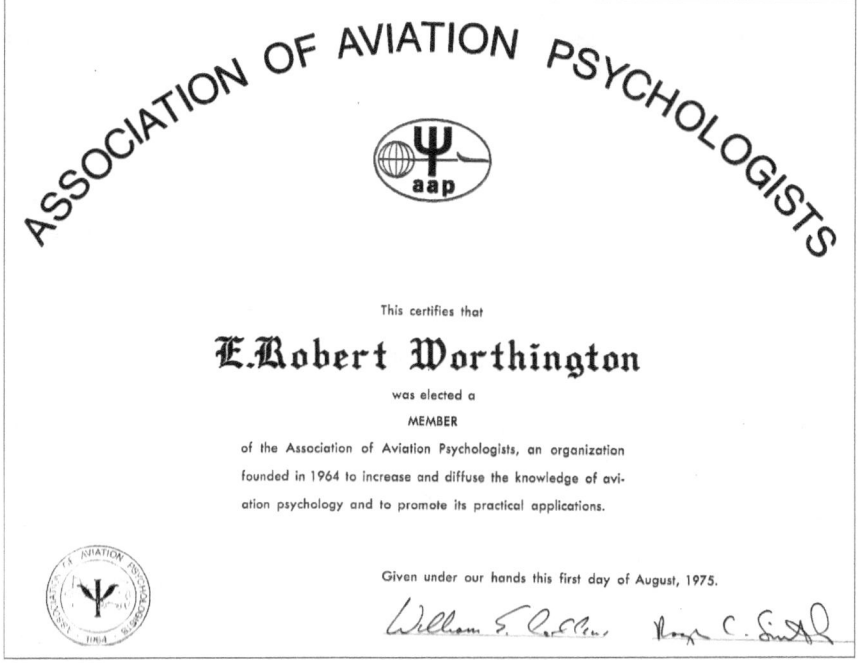

Bob's certification as an aviation psychologist in the membership of the Association of Aviation Psychologists.

available to help flight crew effectively deal with personal issues or difficulties ranging from family and marital problems to depression or anxiety to substance and alcohol abuse or addictions such as gambling.

The airlines recognize the pressures and demands on pilots and flight crew members that may affect their behavior and flight performance. Additionally, the FAA has strict regulations regarding pilot mental health issues and treatment. And family members are not immune either. The airlines and professional pilot organizations have made available to employees (and their family members) professional help from behavioral scientists (psychologists, psychiatrists, social workers, and mental health counselors), as well as volunteer peer-to-peer counselors.

Aviation research psychologists are trained to understand in-flight stressors to assist in the design of aircraft cockpits or equipment to make utilization or manipulation easiest for humans to accommodate.

Flying can be a taxing endeavor. Learning to be a pilot can be both financially and emotionally demanding. Aviation clinical psychologists understand the stressors found in flight training and piloting performance and therefore can help aviators more effectively overcome behaviors that interfere with safe flying. Several colleges and universities and major flight schools have psychologists on staff or on contract to assist students with personal crises that inhibit learning.

Aviation psychologists are like aviation accident investigators; most pilots will never meet one. National Transportation Safety Board data show that up to 80 percent of aviation accidents are attributed to human error; the data also reveal that 78 percent of aviation accidents involve general aviation aircraft. Thus, someone has failed to do something or did something wrong that led to an incident or accident. This is human factors, the study of interactions of people with technology, equipment, devices, or systems, usually in the workplace. The goal of human factors is to make the work environment more efficient and safer through research and application of what has been learned. Human factors investigators examine links between what went wrong and human responses. Aviation psychologists examine the decision-making processes leading up to accidents to understand why pilots make mistakes in judgment. Within the National Transportation Safety Board aviation investigations, human factors issues are examined by the Human Performance Group, which contains aviation psychologists as well as other human factors scientists to include industrial designers, engineers, and medical experts. The military also uses human factors experts.

And because most aviation accidents are due to human error, aviation psychologists often become a part of the investigation. Along with other human factors scientists, all attempt to determine why a person made a mistake. Learning "why" leads to training to prevent this from happening in the future. An excellent example of human factors and an aircraft accident is depicted in Ernest Gann's 1961 best-selling memoir, *Fate Is the Hunter*. The late captain of the airliner that crashed was blamed for causing the accident, but a recreation of the accident revealed that the culprit was a spilled cup of coffee, not human error flying the plane.

Many aviation training programs are designed and conducted by aviation psychologists. Safety seminars are created and taught by aviation psychologists. Engineers and research psychologists design instrument panel gauges, screens, and switches to obtain the optimum placement for easy use by pilots and to avoid misuse of controls by mistake.

In 1964 the Association of Aviation Psychologists was founded to create a professional organization for those psychologists involved in aviation. In the early 1970s, every aviation psychologist I knew was a researcher involved in studying the interaction between pilots and cockpits. By the mid–1970s, several clinical psychologists, most of whom were military psychologists who, like me, either were previously military pilots or now civilian pilots, began to discuss how and why pilots made correct or incorrect decisions while flying. We were using our behavioral science skills to add another dimension to the field of aviation psychology.

The military has a three-week course at the Army Aviation Center of Excellence at Fort Novosel (formerly Fort Rucker), Alabama, for military aviation psychologists. This Aeromedical Psychology (the military term for aviation psychology) Training Course teaches Department of Defense doctoral-level clinical, counseling, and research psychologists about the demands and stressors facing military aircrew to help them retain their flight status.

## Mental Health Issues and Aviation

Consider this: The National Institute of Mental Health states that 19 percent of Americans experience mental illness issues. The Hope for Depression Research Foundation says that depression is the number one cause of disability worldwide. Mental illness is defined as mental, behavioral, or emotional disorder. Severe mental illness is where vocational or social life activities are functionally impaired.

Several studies find that pilots are not immune to mental health issues. The challenges and demands on professional pilots can be fierce. The responsibilities of commercial aviators and pressures placed on them by their superiors seldom diminish. One study found that up to 12 percent of commercial pilots encounter mental health disorders with up to 27 percent of those pilots experiencing heavy workloads being affected. See "Common Mental Disorders Among Civil Aviation Pilots" in *Aviation, Space, and Environmental Medicine* 83, no. 5 (May 2012) and "Assessing Pilots with 'The Wrong Stuff': A Call for Research on Emotional Health Factors in Commercial Aviation" in *International Journal of Selection and Assessment*, April 16, 2003.

Despite the excellent physical condition of pilots, they experience mental health issues the same as the rest of our nation. While workers in professional institutions, retail operations, construction sites, or any other workplace may seek help with little fear of becoming unemployed, it is different for pilots.

Yes, times are changing, but to remain a pilot and exercise the privilege of flying, one must comply with FAA medical regulations. Herein lies some problems. The FAA prohibits piloting if certain mental illnesses are present such as psychosis, bipolar disorder, some personality disorders, or substance abuse. Some diagnoses prohibit flying, while others may allow flying if there is proof of absence of the disorder, but sometimes there must be a grace period of up to 24 months.

Therapy and medicinal treatment protocols have been successful at curbing mental illness disorders, especially anxiety and depression. Unfortunately, medical and behavioral clinicians believe the FAA's regulations are lagging behind medical science, and some treatment programs are still not allowed by the FAA.

Many treatment programs include both therapy and psychotropic medicines, but not all are authorized by the FAA. The FAA clearly states that it encourages pilots with mental health issues to seek help, emphasizing that if properly treated, pilots are not disqualified from flying. For many pilots, though, noting on a medical exam any hint of a mental illness is perceived as the kiss of death. A study published by the *Journal of Occupational and Environmental Medicine* ("Healthcare Avoidance in Aircraft Pilots Due to Concern for Aeromedical Certificate Loss: A survey of 3,765 pilots," April 2022) reveals that 56 percent of the pilots surveyed did not seek health care to avoid any negative aspects of their medical exam.

Mental health care for aviators is a topic best hidden as viewed by pilots, especially professionals. Because of this prevalent feeling, the industry has taken steps to remedy the situation. American Airlines, Delta, and other airlines have programs for all employees to aid with mental health issues. American Airlines has its peer-to-peer care using trained volunteers for its Project Wingman, where pilots provide support to other pilots and their families. The Air Line Pilots Association has its Pilot Peer Support program, where peer pilots provide counseling and broad medical advice to pilots and their families. Delta has an Employee Assistance Program where a master's level mental health counselor can provide immediate help to employees and their families. Other airlines offer similar programs to assist employees and family members dealing with mental health issues.

Around the country are a variety of private medical and mental health clinics that specifically cater to the aviation industry. Some—such as Emerald Mental Health, Aviation Medicine Advisory Service, or Bradford Health Services—are designed to treat air crew members with mental health disorders and get them back in the cockpit. While these programs are not cheap, insurance may cover some costs. Other non-clinic programs such as HIMS (Human Intervention Motivation Study) combine a network of professionals specifically put together to detect and treat substance abuse problems to place pilots back on the flight deck.

Despite these dire comments on pilots and mental health issues, mental health breakdowns in the cockpit are extremely rare. Yes, this topic is the aviation elephant in the room, but mental health issues should not be self-treated or ignored. Feelings of depression, anxiety, panic attacks, or other emotional states are best treated by professionals. As this section has pointed out, there are numerous options specifically for pilots to seek help from mental health professionals trained to offer support, counseling, or medical intervention.

Most programs, as mentioned, are created for professional pilots seeking mental health help to retain their jobs flying. The situation for the nonprofessional private pilot is considerably different. In most instances a career is not at stake, but the same FAA regulations apply. A private pilot holding a third-class medical certificate faces the identical scrutiny whether declaring a mental health challenge at a medical exam or having sought mental health care. The FAA has programs to expand mental health training for aviation medical examiners. The FAA strongly encourages all pilots with mental health issues to seek care, stating that under certain conditions pilots can fly while taking prescribed mental health medication.

## The Future for Aviation Psychology

As aircraft operating systems become more complex, the potential for mistakes increases. Add to this the complexity of life today and the risk of experiencing some form of mental health challenge. For these reasons, despite more automation, piloting skills still depend on human responses. The experts in these areas are aviation behavioral scientists. Yes, the military fly aircraft without human pilots inside the aircraft for unmanned aerial systems or drones; however, humans still do the flying in another cockpit, but on the ground, not in the air. And they face demands and challenges similar to those experienced by pilots in the sky. As flying and the aviation industry continue to expand, more aviation psychologists will be needed. This is a profession that is expanding and becoming more valuable to aviation.

# NINE

# FAA Investigations

## *What Is an FAA Investigation?*

The FAA is charged with conducting investigations involving aircraft airworthiness, airmen competency, medical qualifications, and potential violations of the federal aviation regulations. The FAA has a special organization to investigate events concerning aviation safety, the Office of Accident Investigation and Prevention, staffed by highly trained personnel. For details see FAA Order 8020.11D with Change 1: "Aircraft Accident and Incident Notification, Investigation, and Reporting" (September 17, 2021).

Per the FAA: An accident is an occurrence associated with the operation of an aircraft from the time anyone boards intending to fly, until all have disembarked in which people have suffered death, serious injury, or the aircraft has been substantially damaged.

And an incident is an occurrence, other than an accident, associated with the operation of an aircraft that does or could affect safe operations.

Another aspect of aviation accidents involves the National Transportation Safety Board (NTSB), an independent federal agency responsible for investigating all civil aircraft accidents in the United States, or outside the United States if the aircraft was U.S. operated, U.S. manufactured, or U.S. registered. See CFR Title 49 Part 831.2. If the accident concerned a crime against the aircraft or air travel, the appropriate federal agency, typically the FBI, would also become part of the investigation.

Sometimes an investigation could be simple, lasting only a few days until the cause of the accident was determined and the pilot was determined not to be the cause of the accident. Other times the investigation could take several months to determine what happened, why and how, and if the pilot violated any FARs.

## My FAA Investigations

During my 40 years in the left seat, I was the subject of three investigations, one by the NTSB/FAA and two by just the FAA. In all three cases, I knew I had done nothing wrong. I was the victim, not the cause of the reason for the investigations. Two were aircraft accidents where my aircraft received substantial damage; one was totaled, the other nearly totaled. One was an incident, an alleged pilot deviation involving the air defense identification zone around Washington, D.C., where I was being investigated for possible violation of the federal aviation regulations.

One last point. Enforcement actions by the FAA against pilots are few. Therefore, the chance of any pilot being investigated is slim. The chance of the FAA taking legal action against a pilot is even slimmer. But if it happens to you, this chapter may prove to be helpful.

This chapter describes, in detail, three events that occurred while I was piloting a plane that resulted in investigations by the FAA and NTSB. It includes an FAA investigation from the investigator's viewpoint and my suggestions for what a pilot should do, if investigated.

### My First Airplane Off-Airport Landing, 1996

The local newspaper called it a crash. I called it an off-airport, unscheduled landing. Whatever, it totaled my Mooney.

**Plane crashes in cotton field west of Lubbock**

Newspaper article about the crash of Bob's Mooney 201, N4538H.

It was late August on a Sunday afternoon. That morning my wife and I, in our 17-year-old Mooney 201, departed Dayton, Ohio, en route home to Las Cruces, New Mexico, a distance of about 1,500 miles. We first landed at Springfield, Missouri, then landed at Lubbock, Texas, around 4 p.m. local time.

After refueling and getting some snacks, I preflighted N4538H. Everything looked fine. We departed a few minutes before 5 p.m. for the last leg home, a flight of about one hour and 45 minutes. We were on an IFR flight plan, even though the weather was VFR.

Departing runway 17, we climbed to 10 thousand feet MSL. About nine minutes after departure, the engine began to lose power. I was between 1,700 feet AGL and 2,700 feet MSL. I had been turned over to departure control, so I declared an emergency as we had loss of power, low RPMs and little manifold pressure. Lubbock was now 8.5 miles east of me, but I could see Reese Air Force Base to my right front. My GPS stated that it was 5.2 miles away at 220 degrees, so I announced my intentions to land there. I realized that, due to our sink rate, I could not make Reese, so I told control I was going to have to land where I was. Now less than two thousand feet above the ground, I realized I had zero power. The prop was turning, and there was noise in the air, so initially I thought I had a partial power loss and therefore had some ability to stay in the air. But I did not. Restarting procedures did nothing. I was now committed to land, somewhere.

I knew that at this low altitude my selection choices were limited, and I had to fly the plane until it stopped. For much of my life I had encountered life-threatening situations as a cop, a combat infantryman, three combat tours, and now as a pilot, so I was trained not to panic. The land below me was flat with almost no trees but made up of fenced crop fields and dirt roads.

I noted a dirt road but upon closer inspection realized it was a muddy ditch, not a road. Immediately I saw a real dirt road and turned there, only to see that right along one side were very thick fence posts. Not good.

Off to my right was a north-south hard-surface farm-to-market road. The wind was from the south, and I was on a 45-degree heading toward the road. I radioed control I was going to land on the road. About 150 to 200 feet away from the road I realized that the only way I could reach it was to stretch the glide. I also knew that lifting the nose could result in a stall and most likely a deadly spin into the ground.

Beneath me was a cotton field with growth about 24 inches high, which I could not tell until after I landed. Just before reaching the road, I lowered my landing gear, expecting to land on the road. Knowing I would not make the road, I turned to parallel the road and told Anita to hang on for landing. She grabbed a pillow for her face, tightened her seat belt, and said nothing. She was ready and not panicked, and she placed her faith in my ability to save us.

The wheels grazed the tops of the cotton plants, I flared, and we sat down at around 60 miles per hour. Unknown to me (not visible from above) were 18-inch furrows. I landed on the two main gears, and when the nose gear touched the ground, it was ripped off. Next the right main collapsed, and the right wing hit the dirt and was ripped almost off. The plane swung 90 degrees to the right and stopped within 55 feet of touchdown. I flew the plane until it stopped, and both of us were alive.

For a split-second as I was landing, I noticed a car coming north on the road. It was driven by an older lady whose attention was totally focused on the road directly in front of her. We crashed 20 feet to her front, and she never saw us, driving away from the smashed plane. It was good we didn't land on the road because she would have crashed into us.

Shutting down the plane, I asked Anita how she was. She replied okay, so I told her to unbuckle and exit the plane and move away. The Mooney only had the one door on the passenger side. I could smell avgas as the wing tank was ruptured and gas was flowing out of the full tank. We both exited and I had her sit down on the side of the road.

Cars stopped, cell phones called for help, and a driver who happened to be a nurse sat with Anita, who was sore because of her bruises, until an ambulance took her away to a local hospital ER, where she was later released. I stayed with the plane, waiting for NTSB and FAA officials to arrive.

Out of everything that happened, one aspect of the crash I will never forget. During a normal landing at an airport, the visual image is one of your plane slowly descending to touch the runway. You see the plane dropping to meet the runway. Not so with a crash landing. Here the image is not of the plane descending but of the ground rushing up to hit you. The sensation is one of the plane being suspended and the ground rapidly moving toward you. You know that when the ground hits you, it will hurt.

The right wing was crumpled and almost separated from the fuselage. The gears either collapsed or broke off. Both prop blades were bent (almost 90 degrees), but no undercarriage destruction was visible.

The police and a deputy sheriff arrived, as did two ambulances, a fire truck, and crews from local TV stations and the *Lubbock Advocate Journal*. We made the 10, 11, and 12 o'clock news that night and the front page—with a color photograph—of the Monday newspaper.

A man who identified himself as an FAA aviation safety inspector and an NTSB investigator approached me about an hour after the crash. He stuck out his hand and congratulated me. I asked why, and he replied,

The Mooney 201 after it was removed from the crash site.

"Most times when a pilot loses his engine this close to the ground, I do not have any live pilot to talk to." He asked what happened and I told him. He said he suspected a mechanical failure but would know in a couple of days. He said he listened to all my radio calls to Lubbock control, and I was calm, not excited, so he did not believe the crash was due to any pilot error.

Knowing that the NTSB investigated aircraft accidents, I asked why the NTSB investigator was actually an FAA employee. He responded that staffing shortages would not allow NTSB officials to investigate every aviation accident. In this case both pilot and passenger were alive with no serious injuries. This FAA safety inspector was trained to comply with NTSB investigation regulations, so he responded. He said that if there were bodily injuries or any deaths, the NTSB would have arrived, not him.

The NTSB/FAA investigator had called a nationally known plane recovery service, which was based in Lubbock, to retrieve the plane. He stayed there until the company arrived to secure the plane. I was given an eight-page NTSB accident form to fill out.

Anita and I reunited at a local hotel. The next day, the hotel drove us to the airport, where we met the investigator at the aircraft recovery office. I handed the completed report to the man, and he read it. He commented on how the narrative read just like an accident being written up in an aviation magazine. I told him I was an aviation journalist.

I asked how this accident would look for me as a pilot. He said, "Don't worry. If anyone reads my report [see NTSB identification FTW96LA357] they will see that you saved two lives." He also commented that I did not land very hard. I asked what he meant, and he replied, "Your ELT or emergency locator transmitter, a device that is activated when a plane crashes, never went off."

Two days later the investigator called me at home, explaining that he had found out why the engine quit. In the Mooney 201, the engine has two magnetos but only one drive shaft. The magneto had been overhauled four months previously and properly replaced. But the retention nuts had come loose, allowing the single shaft to disengage from its drive gear. I learned that this was not an uncommon problem with 201s, but most were discovered on the ground due to oil spills from the loose magneto. The Mooney was totaled, so the insurance company paid me for the plane, which was fully insured. Anita vowed never to fly in another 201. It was replaced with a Mooney 231, which did not have magneto issues.

When my engine quit, the engine noise and spinning propeller did not. While the engine instruments said the engine was not working, the noise suggested otherwise. I was not fully aware of the engine loss until we began to sink. Picking a single landing spot and committing to land there also did not work out.

Being close to the ground doesn't give a pilot time to make many decisions, especially when also trying to restart the plane. But essential takeaways are that practicing emergency protocols is very important and that not quitting but flying the plane until it stops does make a difference.

My interactions with the investigator were cordial and very pleasant, as were my dealings with my insurance company. In just under seven weeks, I had purchased another plane, paying cash.

## FAA Investigation for Illegal Entry into an ADIZ, 2007

One day, I received a certified letter from an East Coast FAA Flight Standards District Office, which stated: "Personnel of this office are investigating an incident that involved a C182 aircraft, N4696T ... observed operating in the Washington, DC Air Defense Identification Zone on a 1200 transponder code. Operations of this type may be contrary to Federal Aviation Regulations."

After reading this letter I thought, well, yeah, that's exactly what happened.

Pilots are aware of the rules and regulations defined in the federal aviation regulations and the *Aeronautical Information Manual*. If you have devoted much time to reading them, you understand that for every regulation stipulating what to do, there seems to be another regulation stipulating the opposite. Now a conflict may arise; which regulation should you follow? This investigation came about because I complied with one regulation while the FAA believes I should have obeyed a different one.

The question becomes, which has priority?

The evening before this flight I obtained an FAA weather briefing and filed an IFR flight plan from St Mary's County Regional Airport (K2W6) in Maryland, 40 nautical miles southeast of downtown Washington, D.C., and six miles west of Patuxent Naval Air Station (KNHK). My destination was Zanesville, Ohio (KZZV). My flight path would cross the southwestern edge of the Washington, D.C., ADIZ. This should have presented no problem as my flight through the ADIZ would be on an IFR flight plan.

The next morning, I called for another briefing and was told, again, "Yes sir, your flight plan is in the system."

St. Mary's airport is under control of Patuxent NAS for instrument approaches and departures. For 20 years I have been flying IFR in and out of St. Mary's, seldom experiencing problems. But that morning I faced unbelievable difficulties. It was VFR under a solid overcast, six thousand to eight thousand AGL. On the ground I radioed Patuxent Approach—who answered—and requested my IFR clearance. But they never gave it to me. Three or four times I called, requesting my clearance. Nothing. I departed VFR, contacted Patuxent Approach again while in the air requesting my clearance but was told that there was nothing on file and they were too busy to help.

Climbing to three thousand feet flying my filed flight plan, I contacted the Lockheed Martin Flight Service Station (FSS) at Leesburg, Virginia, explained my lost flight plan, and asked for my clearance. I was keeping my eye on the GPS outline of the ADIZ perimeter, south of the ADIZ. Leesburg said my plan was in the system, so they issued my clearance less the transponder (squawk) code. The FSS said to return to the Navy for my code.

Contacting Patuxent again, I explained that I had my clearance and was told to get my transponder code from them since I was about to enter the ADIZ. The Navy controller said he had no information on me and could not help, but in the background, I heard, "I found it, I've got it." I immediately received my transponder code. The rest of this trip was uneventful.

Upon returning home, three days later, I received the warning from the FAA. Since this was my first FAR violation investigation, I needed help.

I spoke with three good friends, all experienced pilots, whose opinions I regarded highly. All suggested that I file a NASA report. This Aviation

## Nine. FAA Investigations

Safety Reporting System protects pilots from any fine or certificate suspension, even if an FAA violation was determined, provided no criminal offense or accident was committed. The NASA report is a means of describing an incident or accident that impacts safety. The purpose is to allow pilots and other aviation-related personnel to report a safety issue yet not be punished for the report. It goes through NASA as a third-party agency, not part of the FAA.

The FAA letter also invited me to submit evidence or statements I might want regarding this matter, but within 10 days. If I declined to do so, the FAA would proceed without my statement. I had a little over a week to respond.

My friends suggested my letter to the FAA not cite any incompetence or stupidity but be nice, calm, and leave room for the FAA to find fault with the system as the cause of my problem. Don't blame the FAA but point out how the system failed me.

I had the AOPA Legal Services Plan. I spoke to an aviation legal advisor. She knew the FAA investigator and said that he played by the book but was fair and easy to talk to. She listened to my story and explained the investigation process. Again, the question: should I submit my NASA report?

In her experience, no one violated the FAA regs on the ADIZ without being punished, usually by a certificate suspension, which in my case she believed would be a loss of flying privileges for five to 30 days. She was convinced that I would be found guilty of the ADIZ incursion. She suggested that I write my version of what happened and request under the Freedom of Information Act (FOIA) recordings of all my radio and telephone conversations prior to, during, and after my flight through the ADIZ. I needed evidence to support my version of what happened.

She explained that I should simplistically describe what happened, being factual rather than emotional. She added that I should end my letter with information on how experienced and safe I was as a pilot and my background as an FAA safety counselor and educator. She reviewed my letter draft and made some comments, and I mailed it to the investigator.

Before mailing the letter to the FAA investigator, I called him. He was friendly and was not adversarial at all. He was pleasant and sounded like he understood the position I was in. I asked how he would learn what happened. He explained that he would obtain the same tapes I requested and speak to the Navy, FSS, and FAA people I had contact with. He would study the radar tapes and consider whatever I sent him. He said he would do an impartial investigation and then report his findings. It would take about six months to complete. Asking about the tapes, he said whatever he had would also be available to me. When finished, his recommendations would go to his FAA region headquarters, then the FAA legal office for final approval. He said I could call any time to see how the investigation was proceeding or if I had any questions.

Briefly, here was the situation. From my perspective everything I did was legal. I filed an IFR flight plan and was informed it was in the FAA system. While the Navy controllers refused to give me my clearance, I did receive it from the Leesburg FSS, minus the transponder code. I was told to go back to the Navy to get the proper code as I was squawking the VFR code 1200. It is not legal to operate in the Washington, D.C., ADIZ without a specific code. Again, the Navy initially refused to provide me with a discrete code. Finally, they gave me a code about the time I entered the ADIZ.

From the FAA's viewpoint, their radar showed that at the time I entered the ADIZ I was on the 1200 transponder code. Thus, I was violating the FARs.

My defense was to show via recordings of all my radio transmissions that I had done everything possible to remain legal, that the air traffic control system was at fault, not me. Therefore, I needed copies of all my radio calls.

I received a response from the FAA acknowledging my FOIA request, eventually receiving copies of everything I requested from the FAA, although I had to pay for them. I was told that the Navy and Lockheed Martin are not part of the FAA and therefore that I should contact them directly.

I contacted the officer who was responsible for the safeguarding of the Navy Air Traffic Control tapes. He said all the tapes were not available. They had been deleted, although they should have been kept for several weeks and still be available.

The Lockheed Martin legal department advised me that they are not subject to the FOIA and do not release any information regarding their business operations. There would be no tapes of my radio contact with the Leesburg FSS proving that I had received my IFR clearance.

The foundation of my defense was based on two FAA requirements. First is in the *Aeronautical Information Manual*, Chapter 4. Air Traffic Control, Section 4. ATC Clearances and Aircraft Separations, paragraph 4-4-3. Clearance Items. This states that ATC clearances normally contain the following: clearance limit, departure procedure, route of flight, altitude data, and holding instructions if needed. Note that a transponder code is not on this list. Second is FAR Part 91.123 ("Compliance with ATC clearances and instructions"). Paragraph (a) states: "When an ATC clearance has been obtained, no pilot in command may deviate from that clearance unless an amended clearance is obtained, an emergency exists, or the deviation is to a traffic alert." I had the clearance, and unless Patuxent controllers amended that, I should fly the clearance received, which I did.

The AOPA legal team pointed out that two FARs say otherwise. Part 91.139 states that when an emergency NOTAM has been issued the operator of an aircraft must abide by the NOTAM emergency procedures. Part 99.7 states that each person operating an aircraft in an ADIZ must comply with the special security instructions issued by the administrator. Essentially these regulations mean that a discrete transponder code is required to operate in the ADIZ and without such a code you can't fly in the ADIZ.

In six months, the investigator called. The Navy refused to help him, but he was able to interview Navy personnel who were on duty when I called, and they confirmed what I had told the investigator. Lockheed Martin would not share anything.

He had completed his investigation and concluded that I did everything possible to avoid entering the ADIZ without the code. He also said that it was possible that I did not enter the ADIZ before I received my code but that due to my low altitude the radar returns were not accurate enough to prevail in court. The investigator said that the investigation would terminate with no action being taken, declaring the incursion a "nonevent," meaning that nothing happened.

To tell the truth, I was worried about the outcome of this investigation. I was an FAA safety counselor and an aviation journalist. If I was found guilty of violating a FAR and lost my flying privileges, it would crush my credibility. I prided myself on my knowledge of the FARs and my knowledge of aviation. Losing my ability to fly would be so embarrassing, but I believed in the system. I knew what I did was right, but the Navy for whatever reason failed me, and apparently they did not care what they did. Deleting the tapes told me that they knew they were wrong so they hid their mistakes. I believe the FAA investigator also realized this.

The AOPA legal people were a significant help, as were my pilot friends. My knowledge of the FAA regulations was certainly very important. I believed I was right and responded in a calm and collected manner. I also know that the FAA investigator was as fair and impartial as the AOPA legal advisor said he was. In the end I was not found guilty of violating any FARs.

## My Third Aircraft Incident, 2013

Anita and I had departed the Washington, D.C., area the morning of Saturday, April 20, after almost a week of business. The day was VFR, clear and sunny with some winds. Our first stop was in South Carolina, with the next stop in Birmingham, Alabama. One more stop in east Texas, and then home in Las Cruces, New Mexico. Our plane for this trip was a completely rebuilt Cessna 182 with retractable gear. It was fast flying—between 150 and 160 knots—and could carry quite a load. The day was perfect for a lengthy, cross-country flight.

As we crossed into Alabama, the winds began picking up. Approaching Birmingham-Shuttlesworth International Airport (KBHM) the winds were from the north 350 to 360 degrees at 11 knots, gusting to 15, so runway 6 was the active. Of the two runways, 6-24 was the longest at 12,007 feet. Cleared to land on 6, I used the localizer on final, being on both the glideslope and localizer.

On the base leg, I lowered the gear and on short final both Anita and I confirmed that the gears were down and locked by the green light. Upon landing I always have my left hand on the yoke and my right on the throttle in case I have an emergency go-around, which has happened. Because of the gusty winds off my left, I landed with some power at 87 miles per hour, about 12 miles per hour faster than normal. The landing was typical, as was the roll-out. My destination was Atlantic Aviation Services West off to my left. Slowing down to exit the runway to my left, the nose gear collapsed, and the plane slid to a halt. Both main gears remained down and locked.

The tower called me asking where I had parked, so I replied, "On runway 6." Confused, he asked what I meant, so I explained how the nose gear collapsed and I was stranded on the main runway. He called for an emergency vehicle to remove the plane, but the FAA said to leave it there until an accident investigator could arrive. The plane stayed where it was, but a car took Anita and me to the FBO, where I began to think about what I had to do next.

The prop was bent, so I knew the engine had to be torn down. The underside of the cowling was torn up and the nose gear was crumpled. The front-end damage was serious. I realized that the damage was major, requiring several weeks, maybe months to repair. I needed an airframe and power plant facility capable of doing the repairs. I also needed an alternate way to get home.

I was told that Constant Aviation was a reliable shop and that they had the ability to fix my plane. I was able on a Saturday afternoon to contact a manager, who said they could recover the plane and repair it.

About an hour later an FAA investigator arrived, so we went to the plane where he inspected the sorry-looking aircraft. He asked what happened, and I told him. He asked if I could have accidentally retracted the gear, thinking I was raising the flaps. I explained no. My left hand was on the yoke and my right on the throttle, preparing to make a left turn, off the runway. I also pointed out that while the flaps could readily be moved up or down, to raise or lower the gear, the gear handle, a large, flat, circular knob, had to be pulled out and then moved up or down. Not an effortless process. Additionally, only the front gear collapsed, not the main gears, which should have happened if I had retracted the gears. All three tires were on the ground as I was at the end of my landing roll-out. What happened was a mechanical error, not a pilot error. For some unknown reason, the nose gear failed and went down.

The investigator agreed, requested I complete an accident report, and said he would confer with the maintenance people on Monday. The plane was moved to Constant Aviation. The FBO arranged for me to rent a Jeep SUV. In addition to our baggage, the plane had charts, items in the glove box and the center console, pillows, and a blanket, as well as a tow bar and survival gear—way too much gear to take on a commercial flight home. Loading the Jeep, we spent the night in a local hotel and departed for Las Cruces Sunday morning.

The FAA investigator said that no one could determine why the front gear collapsed. Throughout the repair process, the best maintenance minds for Cessna aircraft were asked for their opinions. Several specific inspections were conducted with no answers. Even today, no one knows why the gear collapsed.

Lesson learned: Anything made by man can fail for no apparent reason.

The plane was almost impossible to fix because required parts were no longer available. Halfway through the repairs, another aviation company bought the unfinished plane, completed the repairs, and sold the plane. Since there was no loan on the plane, the purchaser paid me for the plane and the insurance company paid me for the repairs yet to be made.

The investigator found that the collapsed gear was not due to pilot error but an unknown mechanical malfunction.

## My Investigation Results

In all three cases I was cleared of causing the accidents and incident. All three required written statements from me describing what had happened. Also, several times each of the investigators asked me verbally what happened. If you choose, you may remain silent, which I do not recommend. If you decide not to say anything, the FAA/NTSB will continue their investigation without your input.

In all three of my investigations, I knew that I did nothing wrong; what happened was through no fault of mine. I wanted the investigators to understand this, so I answered all questions as thoroughly as I could. Obtaining legal assistance is also a wise move because lawyers understand what the process is. My actions were based on my belief that I was not to blame. I did learn about the investigation process and how the FARs come into play. I also learned how to approach an investigation and some things to do and not do. The next two sections will cover what I think will help you if you are ever the subject of an FAA or NTSB investigation (which, remember, is unlikely).

## *The Investigator*

An investigator will get a text message from the Regional Operations Center once notified of an accident by an air traffic facility, airport, flight service, or anyone aware of a crash. And with today's technology, they may never need to leave the office to complete an investigation. The investigator can contact local police and emergency responders and can ask for and receive all the pictures of the accident site needed. Utilizing the computer, data and certifications of the pilot and the aircraft are readily available to the investigator without having to contact the pilot directly.

Before going further, understand what an aviation accident is by examining CFR Title 49 Part 830. Here we find the definition of an *accident* and an *occurrence* (other than an accident) associated with the operation of an aircraft, which affects or could affect the safety of operations. These definitions lead the investigator to determine what happens.

After gathering the initial data an investigator has up to 30 days to contact the pilot. Technically, the first person who contacts the pilot could be a National Transportation Safety Board (NTSB) member since that agency—not the FAA—is charged by Congress to investigate all aviation accidents. However, due to NTSB staffing, it may often be an FAA investigator initiating the investigation depending on the severity of the accident as they have their own set of statutes they must investigate. It could be that the pilot is interviewed by both agencies. Bottom line: regardless of who initiates the investigation, the pilot should respond professionally.

Any radar data plots or radio recordings with air traffic control are collected. Weather data is gathered. Maintenance logbooks and pilot certificates and pilot logbooks are retrieved. Interviews with eyewitnesses, refuelers, family, and friends are completed, if warranted. In the best-case scenario, the pilot and passengers who survive the accident are interviewed.

As much material as possible is gathered before the scientific investigation begins. No preconceived ideas as to what caused the accident are taken into consideration until the data, the evidence, and the documentation lead the investigator to the most obvious conclusion. Occasionally, no conclusion presents itself. But the primary goal is to find the cause so a future accident can be prevented. This can take the shape of a rule change, an airworthiness directive, or safety bulletins and notifications to the public highlighting accident trends.

It should be noted that general aviation pilots are getting much better at avoiding accidents. Unfortunately, they still run out of fuel short of the runway, fly VFR into IFR conditions, and crash perfectly good aircraft, but they are getting better. Education is a big part of improving our accident trends.

To aid the investigator, as the survivor of an accident, write down as soon as possible the sequence of events as you remember them. Numbers, such as altitude, heading, and airspeed, engine noises, audio transmissions, anything and everything recalled about the accident will guide the detectives—that would be the pilot and the investigator—to a conclusion about what caused the accident. Ultimately, it is the investigator who makes the final call, but the pilot is an integral part of the conclusion, having had a front seat at the event.

The FAA investigator, again working in conjunction with the NTSB, is looking at nine areas covered in FAA Order 8020.11 to see if these areas of FAA-specific responsibilities were factors in the accident. Mentioned earlier were the obvious items of the airworthiness of the aircraft, certifications, and medical status. But also, they will be looking at the adequacy of the Code of Federal Regulations (CFR) and if there was an apparent violation of said CFRs. The performance of FAA facilities or functions is listed as the number one factor an FAA investigator examines. Number two is the performance of any non–FAA facility or navigational aids. To round out the nine factors specifically listed for the FAA investigator to inspect are airport certification safety standards and airport security.

Those nine areas of FAA responsibility are led by the FAA's general duty, "to ensure that all facts and circumstances leading to the accident are recorded and evaluated, and that action is taken to prevent similar accidents," per FAA 8900.1, volume 7, chapter 1, section 1.

Although the pilot may feel they have done something incorrect, often it is one of these areas completely out of the pilot's control that led to the incident. The bottom line here is to not hide anything. Give the facts as best as remembered; do not try to bury something.

And even after that, the investigator's report is reviewed by other investigators to ensure that no clue was missed and any rules that may have been broken are documented properly. All this can take considerable time. Patience and legal counsel should assist with the investigation.

A caveat on "lawyering up." A lawyer becomes an intermediary between the pilot and the investigator, possibly causing prolonged delays in answering the questions, and thus delays in getting the investigation completed. The FAA is not out to hang the pilot; it is out to prevent future accidents. If the pilot is open and up front with any errors perhaps made versus trying to hide the obvious, they may receive a letter requiring some flight training and a check ride, not a bad solution considering a worse-case scenario. Or the pilot may receive a "thank you," case closed.

Legal counseling is definitely a good idea. Legal services provided by such organizations as AOPA should be sought out just to ensure that the pilot does not make things worse during an investigation. Legal assistance can provide information on how an investigation is conducted or advise pilots on how to draft their details of what happened. Talking to those who have "been there, done that" is another worthwhile suggestion. Just be prudent and professional during interactions with investigators.

The FAA has a "Compliance Philosophy" defined in a two-page Order 8000.373, paragraph 4.c., stating, "When deviations from regulatory standards do occur, the FAA's goal is to use the most effective means to return an individual or entity that holds an FAA certificate, approval, authorization, permit or license to full compliance and to prevent recurrence."

This philosophy is further expanded in Order 8900.1, volume 14, chapter 1, with the statement, "If the deviation does not involve intentional, reckless, or criminal behavior and the airman/organization is qualified and willing to cooperate, FS [Flight Standards] should resolve the issue through use of compliance tools, techniques, concepts and programs."

The bottom line here is for the pilot to work with the investigator to uncover what caused the accident or incident, to prevent a similar event from happening again, and to not hide anything.

## *How to Survive FAA Investigations*

The previous section was written to reflect the investigator's point of view. This section is from my point of view as the pilot. Here are my suggestions for what a pilot should do pending an investigation.

### **An FAA Investigation**

The FAA becomes involved upon the belief that a federal aviation regulation has been violated. The investigator works for the FAA, and the investigation assignment is to determine what happened and whether the pilot did something wrong. Having been the subject of three FAA investigations, I can say I never felt threatened by the investigator, nor did I ever feel he was "out to get me." All three times I believed that I, as a pilot, did nothing wrong. I believed that the investigator was seeking the truth, and I was committed to help as much as I could. But because this is an area of aviation most pilots have never experienced before, legal help should be sought.

## What Initiates an Investigation

There is one prime reason the FAA may initiate an investigation. While the NTSB investigates accidents, the FAA investigates if they believe the pilot violated a FAR. It may result from an aircraft accident or an alleged violation of an FAA regulation. The FAA may appear at the site of an accident, or the pilot may receive a letter explaining the investigation. Either way, the pilot may respond or not. Regardless, the FAA investigation will continue.

## Do This Immediately

First, if appropriate, file the NASA ASRS (Aviation Safety Reporting System) Pilot's Form ARC 227B (see Advisory Circular 00-46F, ASRS Program Briefing, and FAR Part 91.25). Pilots and aircrew members use this form to report, within 10 days, perceived safety issues or concerns. Then respond to the investigator after seeking legal counsel. Review every facet of the flight and write what you believe happened. Ensure that what you state is correct and honest. It is difficult to take back mistakes or defend errors later. Understand the rules and regulations as they apply to your alleged violation. This is where a firm understanding of the FARs applicable to the investigation becomes especially important. The purpose of the investigation is to determine if you violated a specific FAR.

Under the Freedom of Information Act request any appropriate FAA tapes immediately due to the time constraints. Do not be belligerent or antagonistic when interacting with the FAA investigator. You want them to be on your side. Do not project blame or fault. Be honest with the investigator and be honest with yourself. I think one must have faith in the FAA investigation process.

If a violation of the FARs is involved, the FAA must investigate; provided certain qualifications are met, civil penalties or certificate suspensions may be waived.

## How to Respond to an FAA/NTSB Investigation

I did not assume an adversarial role with the investigators; instead, I provided as much help as I could. If I could provide information regarding my behavior during the two accidents and single incident, it should help the investigator. That is exactly what I did. Nothing was withheld. At the end of each inquiry the investigators confirmed that my honesty was quite helpful arriving at their decisions.

I am not an attorney, so I am not providing legal advice. Rather I am sharing with you my response each time I was investigated because of something that happened when I was piloting my plane.

Shortly after the first and last incident, I was approached by an FAA/NTSB investigator in person. The second incident began with the air traffic controller (ATC) asking me to call a phone number at my next landing. Three days after the phone call I received a letter from the FAA. In all three incidents I was asked to provide a written account of what happened.

Let me intercede to voice two very important assumptions necessary for how to proceed in an FAA or NTSB investigation. First is the fact that you, as the pilot, did nothing wrong. That is, whatever happened, you were performing the duties of pilot in command in an accepted manner. If you did violate a FAR, my only recommendation is to immediately seek aviation legal advice.

If the incident was not your fault, then next assume that the investigator is not out to get you but is an expert charged with the sole responsibility of determining what happened and finding the truth. The investigator is an independent individual tasked with finding what happened, how it happened, and why. I saw all my investigators as colleagues, not as cops out to arrest me. As such, we both desired the same outcome, and it was in my best interest to work with the investigator not against him.

The investigation has several purposes. Did the pilot do something wrong, or were they the victim of an accident? Are there any safety lessons to be learned or safety issues that need addressing? What happened, and how can it be prevented from occurring again? This all begins with what transpired and your written description of what you believe happened.

First, everyone who flies a plane is regulated by the FARs. I believe that legal assistance and advice should always be readily available. If you are rich enough, you could have your own aviation attorney on retainer. Since this is beyond the pocketbook of most of us general aviation pilots, I highly recommend the legal services of the Aircraft Owners and Pilots Association (AOPA). This service is very affordable and provides excellent legal assistance.

Another resource I have found helpful to me is fellow pilots who have had experience in this matter or in dealing with the FAA. I contacted these friends when I was being investigated and explained what happened and asked them what I should do. We discussed the incident and what choices I had in how to respond to the investigation. Just talking with my friends made me more cognizant of what the FAA wants/needs to know or understand regarding what occurred. In my case this review with friends always provided clarity to me about what to do, how to do it, or what not to do.

In every accident and incident I was involved in, I believed that I had done nothing wrong, that I was not the person who initiated the cause of the incidents, that I was a victim of what happened. This means that in the investigations, I had to provide proof or evidence that I did everything possible to avoid the incident.

Now comes the time when you need to write your version of what happened. I do believe that at this point I have an advantage most pilots do not. As an aviation writer I am used to employing words to help readers to understand issues about aviation. Therefore, I can utilize these skills to expertly describe what happened and try to convince the investigator that what ensued was not any fault of mine.

An initial suggestion is to go to the FARs and find out what the rules and regulations state. Determine what guidelines define the parameters of the incident; what policies cover what is allowed, authorized, required, or perhaps prohibited; and how these directives specifically relate to or control the incident being investigated. Understanding the pertinent regulations governing what happened allows you to better understand the legal ramifications of what occurred and what the investigator will focus on.

If the regs clearly state that you cannot do what you did, then you should know why it was necessary to ignore this regulation. Understanding the law helps to better describe what you did and why. For example, you are flying over an abandoned airport and on both ends of the runway are painted a bright yellow "X." This means you cannot land there, and if you do, then you are subject to an FAA investigation as to why you violated the law—see *Aeronautical Information Manual* (AIM) 2-3-22. The fact that you did not know what the "X" meant and you just decided to land is probably not a good defense. On the other hand, if an engine went out above the airport forcing you to land, this is allowed by another FAR, permitting the landing in an emergency. Sometimes the FARs may seem to contradict each other. In this case the "X" means you cannot land there, while another FAR may allow the pilot to ignore the "X" in an emergency.

Here is the advice I received from both my friends and the AOPA legal team regarding how to write my report of what happened. Stick to the facts. Describe what happened but do not place blame or state your belief that someone else screwed up. Stick to just describing what happened, what you did, and why. In my ADIZ incursion, it was suggested that at the end of my report, I indicate my aviation background as an FAA safety counselor (today called a FAAS team representative), all the safety seminars I have created and taught, and my background as a senior officer and search and rescue pilot in the Civil Air Patrol, as well as my ratings, certificates, and flight hours, and to indicate that I was an aviation journalist with hundreds of published articles. This was to emphasize my extensive safe experience in aviation and as a pilot.

Two incidents, the crash and the collapsed nose gear, did not require help in my reports. But the airspace incursion did. I sent my draft to the AOPA legal team, suggestions were made and returned to me, and I completed the edited report. In all three investigations I was honest and reported everything that happened. Some aviation writers have suggested that a pilot being investigated not talk to an investigator without legal representation present. In my case, I knew that what I did was not the cause of the incidents, so I did not fear any reprisals and explained everything.

In all three incidents and subsequent investigations, I am convinced that by being honest and being able to provide in writing my version of what happened along with receiving expert legal advice in the case of the incursion, all served me well. In all three incidents, the investigations concluded that I was not guilty of any wrongdoing.

# Ten

# Advanced Proficiency Training

## *Complacency Can Kill You!*

Aviation safety has different meanings for different people.

According to the FAA, 70 to 80 percent of aviation accidents are pilot-related. Therefore, most of the noncommercial, fixed-wing general aviation flights that ended up badly went awry because of the pilot. Why? Because the pilot did something wrong, made some bad decisions, or failed to do something right.

So why do so many smart pilots do so many dumb things? As an aviation psychologist I have been studying this enigma for almost 50 years. And I get it. I understand why smart people do dumb things. It is called complacency, the state of being satisfied with the status quo. Essentially the pilot takes shortcuts, believing that nothing bad will happen. Previous efforts at cutting corners never produced unpleasant results. Therefore, these bad behaviors become more frequent habits.

How am I so familiar with this complacency? I fell victim to it during a war in the Middle East in the 1950s, and lived to write about it.

In 1958, I was a U.S. Marine private first class and at the bottom of the military food chain when it came to supplying labor for work details. I was a member of a reinforced marine infantry battalion, fighting in a small war in Lebanon. Combat ensued for a few weeks, then things settled down, and after a few months we got word that as the first unit to go in, we would be the first to leave. But prior to leaving, 90-millimeter point detonating shells for our supporting tanks had to be collected and turned into an ammo salvage dump. The tanks were positioned all over the mountains, reachable by dirt roads and trails. So, a bunch of privates and a 2½-ton truck were detailed to pick them up.

We were instructed in the dangers of point detonating rounds and told to be cautious, to protect every round completely by surrounding it with sandbags, to drive very slowly and carefully around the mountains.

Early in the morning we began. The tanks were spread out quite a bit.

The mountain roads and trails were in poor condition and very treacherous. It was hot and dusty in the mountains. We began being super vigilant. The bottom of the deuce-and-a-half was covered with sandbags. Then double-bagged coffins were made for each round. This took a lot of time, and we could not get many shells in the truck bed. Also, the driver never went over 15 to 20 miles per hour to minimize bumping. By noon we had hardly dented our recovery process. We could envision days of hot, sweaty, backbreaking labor ahead unless we did it differently.

We knew what we were doing was safe, after all; we did not blow anything up. So maybe we could increase our load a little and drive faster. By the end of the day, we had quadrupled the number of rounds in the truck: we used only one sandbag to protect the pointed end of each round, there were no more elaborate coffins, and the driver drove as fast as he could without tipping over. We increased our risks because nothing bad happened. We became complacent.

That is why pilots who fly known distances with a minimal amount of fuel believe it is a safe practice because they always make it. The fact that there is no reserve doesn't matter because it is never needed. The fact that a slight headwind or a small diversion around weather may empty the tanks before landing is not considered because it has never happened. One becomes complacent.

Poor decision-making comes about because of a need to be expeditious, a lack of appreciation for potential risks involved, and the fact that nothing bad has happened before doing the same thing. But pilots should be prepared for the worse scenario, not the ideal.

The aviation insurance industry knows how to beat complacency. Fly often, attend safety seminars frequently, and fly with a CFI regularly to have someone evaluate your habits and provide feedback.

When flying, always have a backup plan. In combat I would always plan different options in case plan A didn't work. The idea was to automatically switch into plan B or C without missing a step, without having to stop and think, "What should I do next?" Just do it. Pilots should have the same frame of mind. I am getting tired, I should stop. I am not comfortable with this weather, so I should stop. The air is rough up here; I should land.

The best way to fight complacency is to recognize it and make plans to avoid it. Don't take shortcuts. Think hard about decisions that will make a flight "more efficient." Engage in constantly training. Practice for all sorts of emergencies. Do not become complacent.

# Ten. Advanced Proficiency Training

## Combating Complacency

One way to stave off becoming complacent is to become involved in unique types of proficiency training. Learn how to fly different ways. Gain expertise in specific kinds of flight that add new skills, increase aeronautical awareness, and make you a better and safer pilot. How do you expand your flying skills and become proficient in a totally different realm of flight?

Learn backcountry flying in and out of rugged dirt or grass short strips. Learn mountain flying. Acquire a seaplane (or float plane) rating. Pursue acrobatic training or receive upset training. Consider a form of high-altitude training. Take glider training. All of these require adding different aeronautical skills to your repertoire as a pilot. All increase your awareness and enhance your skills in flying a plane. The training discourages complacency and places more very useful equipment in your personal aviation toolbox.

## Backcountry Aircraft Landing Strips

In 1975 I became a pilot. I was in the Army and stationed in San Antonio, Texas. In 1977 I bought a 12-year-old 145-horsepower Cessna 172. By 1978 I decided to use my plane to go trout fishing in the mountains of New Mexico as Texas wasn't known for its trout streams.

I knew that the closest trout streams were in southwestern New Mexico, but they were in the mountains, and I had no experience flying into any mountains. Therefore, I located a local CFI with mountain flying experience and at an elevation of 550 feet, I learned mountain flying and landing. South of San Antonio were several small dirt strips surrounded by tall trees where I was taught how to land and take off as in mountains. While we did not have the actual high density altitude environment, the instructor would use partial power training to teach me how the plane would perform at nine thousand feet. Books on mountain flying completed my education.

My first trip was into a short 3,500-foot, rough dirt strip at 5,400 feet elevation used by the U.S. Forest Service for aerial support of fighting forest fires. I flew in at the end of the day and it was early morning when I departed. This dirt strip was high enough in the mountains that people using vehicles would not be fishing up this high. With my backpack, I had the rest of the 10,000-foot mountain and its excellent trout streams all to myself. Over the next few decades my planes transported me to many dirt mountain strips and trout streams higher than most people visit. My mountain flying has encompassed all of the Rockies, Canada, and much of Alaska.

Backcountry and mountain flying can be two separate types of flying yet can also be the same. Why? Not all backcountry strips are in the mountains. So, dirt or grass landing strips at lower elevations become a challenge due to their surface being rough and short and their potential to be surrounded by tall trees. Landing requires remaining high until over the obstacles and then diving down to land quickly. If in the mountains, altitude (elevation) can add density altitude challenges to the landing because the plane has less power. But with proper training, pilots can learn how to properly handle an airplane in both landing and departing backcountry strips at sea level or high in the mountains.

Today flying into backcountry airstrips has generated a great deal of interest in pilots with a desire to use their planes for recreational flying into out-of-the-way places. Camping, fishing, hunting, hiking, and other outdoor activities have encouraged pilots to learn how to locate and safely use backcountry airstrips.

Unfortunately, over the past several decades, backcountry airstrips have fallen into disrepair, or governments have forbidden their use, or public use has been disallowed by owners due to liability concerns. Thus, the number of usable backcountry airstrips has decreased significantly.

Six backcountry pilots were discussing the loss of wilderness strips to fly into. In 2003, they decided to do something about it and formed the Recreational Aviation Foundation (www.theraf.org). Its mission is to halt the demise of backcountry airstrips. It has worked to protect, create, or rehab backcountry airstrips from New England to the Pacific, between the borders of Mexico and Canada and in Alaska. There are RAF liaison members working with 40 state and federal government agencies and policymakers as well as private landowners.

Several western states have found that having backcountry airstrips that are open to the public increases recreational activity revenues for the state and promotes aviation tourism for the state.

Where does one obtain backcountry or mountain flying training? Use the internet to seek information on "mountain flying training" or "backcountry flight training." Each fall the New Mexico Pilots Association (NMPA) hosts a two-day program with classroom teaching and actual flying in and out of small mountain strips. I have attended this program several times to train with experienced mountain CFIs and to retain my backcountry and mountain flying skills. As president of the NMPA in the 1990s, I was one of the creators of this training program. More information is at www.nmpilots.org.

## *Seaplane or Floatplane Rating*

Obtaining this rating involves a totally separate set of landing and departure skills. There is no written exam and no required flight review.

One just takes the training, which is typically six to eight hours depending on the plane used and flight experience, and then demonstrates their ability to fly in a one-hour check ride. If a sport pilot flying a light sport airplane, you will receive an endorsement, not a rating.

A floatplane lands on water on pontoons or floats like wheels on water. Seaplanes land on the water on their bellies or the bottom of their fuselage. Some floatplanes are also amphibious because they have wheels that are below the floats so they can also land on a runway.

Probably the major learning areas for a seaplane rating are understanding the water conditions (smooth, calm, some waves, or stormy whitecaps) and wind speed and direction. You will learn the three departure modes: idle, plow, and step taxiing.

Flying a floatplane requires experience handling increased drag. Landings must be precise to avoid flipping the plane by not utilizing the appropriate flare relative to the long floats. Passing the check ride is not difficult for most pilots. But as with the private pilot certificate, it becomes a license to learn. More training and more practice are required to become a competent seaplane pilot. But as with mountain flying, you are introduced to a different area of aviation and must master the judicial usage of a unique skill set to be competent and safe.

## *Aerobatic Training*

Aerobatic (or acrobatic) flying does not require any rating, certification, endorsements, or exams. The FAA defines aerobatic flight as the intentional maneuver involving an abrupt change in an aircraft's attitude, an abnormal attitude, or abnormal acceleration, not necessary for normal flight (FAR Part 91.303). While the FAA regulations on aerobatic flying are sparse, it does place a variety of restrictions on where aerobatic flying can be done. It also requires that each person in a plane performing certain maneuvers wear a parachute.

Two more tidbits regarding aerobatic flight. While the pilot does not need to be certified, the airplane does need to be approved for aerobatics. If the pilot is to be paid for performing aerobatics, one must possess a commercial certificate and a second class medical.

What is the purpose of aerobatic training? There are several. For many pilots, it is just plain fun. They enjoy it. There are also competition events involving aerobatic flight. But being a competent aerobatic pilot also makes one a safer, more experienced pilot. Learning to make precise moves with the plane and be comfortable and confident performing flight at the outer edges of a plane's flight envelope is what aerobatic training can do for you.

There is no required amount of classroom or flight training for aerobatics. It all depends on what the student hopes to accomplish. The pilot will spend time in class as well as in the sky. The training involves unusual attitudes, spins, stalls, and the various aerobatic maneuvers seen in most aerobatic shows.

Aerobatic training is another way for pilots to get a different type of flight training and to increase their skills at piloting a plane.

## *Upset Prevention and Recovery Training*

Another phase of aerobatic training some schools offer is upset training, teaching pilots how to recognize and properly respond to conditions leading to losing control of the aircraft. Causes may be inappropriate control inputs by the pilot, an out-of-control autopilot, or wind shear. Often these events occur close to the ground, requiring instant recognition of what is happening and immediate corrective action by the pilot.

This training involves classroom time as well as flight training. Class sessions teach theory and the dynamics of aeronautically inappropriate maneuvers and situations and what the appropriate response should be. The flight training teaches what happens and what the appropriate response should be. Prevention techniques are also taught. This is another very valuable safety instrument for the pilot's toolbox.

## *Glider Training*

Training in a non-powered aircraft such as a glider really introduces a powered aircraft pilot to how winds, hot air currents, and atmospheric conditions affect flight. One does not need to add a glider rating to learn about gliding or soaring. Introduction flights and training in a glider offer pilots the ability to understand how the forces of nature impact flight decisions. Details on glider training are found in Chapter 15.

Powered aircraft pilots will find some differences flying gliders. For example, gliders have a single landing gear in the center of the bottom of the fuselage and a wheel below the tip of a wing. Additionally, the wings are much longer and narrow for lift. Because of these longer wings, maneuvering is slower in a glider than a powered plane.

A powered aircraft pilot does not need to obtain the glider rating to benefit from glider training. Participating in some introduction flights, reading books on glider flying, or even flying some glider computer simulator programs will increase a powered aircraft pilot's situational awareness and impart how winds and air currents impact flight dynamics of even powered aircraft. Check out the Soaring Society of America (www.ssa.org).

# Ten. Advanced Proficiency Training

On January 15, 2009, a U.S. Airways airliner, an Airbus A320, departed New York City's LaGuardia. Just under three thousand feet, the plane flew into a flock of Canada geese, and both engines shut down. Captain Chesley "Sully" Sullenberger took control of his plane, now a glider. Unable to reach any nearby airport, he safely landed it in the Hudson River, without a single life lost. The National Transportation Safety Board declared the landing "the most successful ditching in aviation history."

Captain Sullenberger is also a glider pilot.

## Tailwheel Training

Most planes made today have two main gears under the wings and a single gear called tricycle gear under the nose. When aviation began, the main gears were under the wings, but the plane also landed on its tail. Early aircraft, from Piper Cubs to DC-3s or military C-47s and most World War II fighters, were tailwheel aircraft. Landing a tailwheel plane takes a bit of stick (control column) and rudder skills, because if the approach to landing is not right, dreadful things can happen, such as a ground loop (where the tail wants to swap ends with the front of the plane). Tailwheel training teaches pilots precise landing techniques required to safely place a conventional plane (a tailwheel) on the runway or a grass or dirt strip. This training improves any pilot's skill set and enhances their landing behaviors, regardless of what landing gear the plane has.

The FAA (see FAR Part 61.31[i]) allows the requirement to be tailwheel trained and competent as an endorsement. It is a proficiency-based regime, usually with a pilot undergoing seven to 12 hours of training to obtain the endorsement. The training required depends on the skill and experience of the pilot.

## High-Altitude Physiology Training

While not skill training for flying, this instruction makes pilots aware of what happens as we fly higher. As a plane climbs higher in the sky, the percentage of oxygen in the air remains the same, but the reduced air pressure means that a person receives less oxygen, resulting in hypoxia, a very bad physical condition due to reduced oxygen consumed by the body. A reduction in oxygen results in a decrease in a person's performance; if continued, it can lead to death, which is why I recommend that all pilots carry a pulse oximeter in their plane to test for the percentage of oxygen in their blood. High-altitude training can teach pilots what they need to know and understand to avoid becoming hypoxic.

The Code of Federal Regulations Title 14 Part 61.31(g) (1-3) covers what training and certification pilots are required to have for flying pressurized aircraft. FAR Part 91.211 defines the oxygen requirements for aircraft and flight altitudes. The legal requirements tend to be higher than what is medically recommended. For example, the FAA does not require pilots to have supplemental oxygen until above 12,500 feet above sea level and then only if above that altitude for over 30 minutes. Above 14 thousand feet MSL, oxygen is always required for crew members. Above 15 thousand feet (MSL) everyone in the plane must be on oxygen.

It is medically recommended that pilots flying at night go on oxygen above six thousand feet MSL and during the day above 10 thousand. What I have found is that these suggestions are dependent on where one lives. While these may be most applicable to residents of Florida or Connecticut where there are no mountains and people live near sea level, people living in the mountains—say in Denver, which has an elevation of a mile, or anywhere in the Rocky Mountains—are already acclimated to the air at five thousand to 10 thousand feet MSL, so their oxygen tolerances may vary.

There are a variety of training courses to teach pilots about high-altitude physiology and to allow them to become certified or receive the high-altitude endorsement. The FAA Civil Aerospace Medical Institute in Oklahoma City provides information on locations where chamber training may be available. It also has a mobile unit that travels around the country. Colleges or universities such as Arizona State or Embry-Riddle in Florida offer various trainings. Some aviation flight schools like King offer online courses. Sometimes state or national aviation organizations can make arrangements with local military bases to allow training for FAA civilian pilots in their facilities.

If you are a pilot, high-altitude classes and experiencing the chamber training is a very valuable resource. As a nonmilitary pilot but being an Army officer, I was able to arrange to attend the U.S. Air Force two-day high-altitude course, which included academic classes as well as time in the high-altitude chamber. Mental exercises without oxygen masks revealed how much personal performance is lost due to reduced oxygen. For most pilots in my class, what they learned became an eye-opening experience for them. It is highly recommended.

## *My First Experience Becoming Hypoxic*

Early in my flying career, my Army job required me to travel from my home base in San Antonio, Texas, to the U.S. Army Medical Center

## Ten. Advanced Proficiency Training

located in El Paso, Texas, for consultation visits. East of El Paso, the Hueco Mountains range from 6,787 feet (MSL) to 8,749 feet (Guadalupe Peak). El Paso sits at 3,710 feet, while San Antonio is at 550. Flying west I would fly VFR sometimes at 10,500 feet MSL.

The flying time in a Cessna 172 would usually take four and a half to five hours. I would usually stop about halfway—at Fort Stockton—for fuel. My flights would mostly be in the afternoon, arriving at El Paso in late afternoon. But after supper in the early evening, I would get headaches. The next morning, I would still feel woozy and sickish. I did not know why. Typically, I would return to San Antonio that evening, having spent an entire day in El Paso.

By my second flight I believed my headaches were somehow the result of flying to El Paso. The only difference in those flights was how high I flew. Assigned to a major Army medical facility, I discussed my conditions with our pulmonary specialists and was told that my condition was caused by hypoxia. I was told I needed supplemental oxygen to stop it.

I began reading what the FAA said about hypoxia and found an FAA chart describing how much supplemental oxygen was needed at what altitudes defined by liters per minute. Returning to my pulmonary experts, I borrowed some bottles of hospital oxygen with a flow meter and the small plastic masks; later I used nasal cannulas. For my next flight, using the FAA oxygen chart, I flew sipping the supplemental hospital oxygen. No headache. Problem solved.

I knew I needed supplemental oxygen, but the FAA-approved aircraft portable oxygen systems are expensive. At an aviation convention I met the owner of a national company that produced aviation portable oxygen systems. Previously, he was a pulmonary specialist. He said he sold the necessary equipment to convert a medical oxygen system for aviation usage. My wife discovered a complete medical oxygen system for sale by a widow for under $50. She bought it. The FAA said my converted system would meet the FAA definition for approved supplemental oxygen. That experience convinced me to sign up for the Air Force high-altitude chamber class.

With the Mooney 231s I owned, which had a service ceiling of 24 thousand feet MSL, we were required to wear full oxygen masks. The planes had onboard, built-in supplemental oxygen systems, but for every other plane I owned, my converted oxygen system was always in the back seat. I ended up with several oxygen tanks, so we always had full tanks on hand.

I never had any ill effects from hypoxia after my second El Paso flight. The highest my wife and I have flown using supplemental was around 25 thousand feet (MSL), and we always returned to earth feeling well.

## Aircraft Specific Pilot Proficiency Training

Several aircraft brand membership organizations offer a variety of training in a pilot's airplane. This is a way to learn more about your plane from an instructor who is an expert on your plane. I attended several Mooney Pilot Proficiency Programs sponsored by the Mooney Aircraft Pilots Association (MAPA). Many were one-day events providing credit for the FAA Wings program, an instrument check ride, and a flight review, as well as other flight training. Once, at a MAPA event in Colorado Springs, Colorado, I participated in an all-day mountain flying program. Another time, after I purchased a used Mooney 231, I attended a Flight Safety International multiday training course that included academic ground school classes, training in a Mooney full-motion simulator, and then flight training in my plane.

Other aviation organizations have also provided sponsored aviation training such as instrument proficiency check rides and flight reviews as well as multiday mountain flying courses. Check the internet to locate an organization for your plane, join it, and sign up for their training programs.

## Summary

This section lists several ways for pilots to increase their aeronautical skills and to become proficient in other ways of flying. All these suggestions will make a pilot better and create different challenges for the pilot. The training should also help erase the bad habit of becoming complacent. The training will add new flying skills to the pilot's current repertoire, making them a better and safer pilot.

My quest to become a better and safer pilot saw me using a variety of ways to achieve this goal. I never did everything listed above. Several times I experienced aerobatic training. I took spin training in the aerobatic Cessna 150. I also did aerobatics in a World War II T-6 trainer. I have enjoyed numerous two-day mountain flying courses that involved a day of ground school and a day of flying and landing in the mountains. I completed an Air Force high-altitude course. I participated in several plane-specific courses sponsored by a Mooney aircraft organization. Every six months I would receive an instrument proficiency check ride with a CFII, and every year I would complete a flight review. On my own I would practice emergency procedures and instrument approaches at my home base and nearby airports.

One can purchase apps, online courses, videos, and books from pilot schools and aviation vendors such as Sporty's Pilot Shops or King Schools or go to YouTube to download videos on all diverse ways of flying. Most YouTube videos I have watched pertaining to aviation have been valid, reliable, and honest depictions of appropriate ways to fly. If in doubt, ask your favorite flight instructor how applicable the video is.

Another option, depending on your bank account, is a flight simulator. While this has been better described in Chapter 2, a flight simulator that is either part of your computer system or a stand-alone simulator and various apps can also challenge pilots and allow one to experience difficult flight regimes safely. Just another way to train and become safer.

This constant training should always increase a pilot's aeronautical proficiency. This training should enhance a pilot's awareness regarding becoming complacent. Constantly challenging one's skills (in any area, not just aviation) prepares one for surprises and emergencies, which may or may not ever arise. I can personally state that I have experienced aeronautical emergencies where my extensive training has made the difference between walking away or becoming a fatality statistic. Additionally, insurance companies reward this kind of training with reduced premiums.

# Eleven

# Nontraditional Landings and Survival

## *Successful Handling of Off-Airport Landings*

### Panic: How to Understand It and How to Avoid It

Human beings do make mistakes. But we can learn from them. And pilots are no different. Like when we note that our cruise speed during a flight is less than expected. Then we realize we forgot to raise the flaps. Sometimes a mistake can lead to becoming panicky. Good training and reliable equipment can prevent errors and prepare pilots on how to handle emergencies and not panic.

*Merriam-Webster* defines panic as a sudden overpowering fright, acute extreme anxiety. I define it as an emotional, physical, and psychological state of hopelessness such that an individual feels unable to do anything to avoid the situation. A panicked person can be so paralyzed that while they may respond emotionally they are unable to do anything appropriate or productive.

I have spent a lifetime as a behavioral scientist studying the performance of people in high-stress and risky or dangerous endeavors. Specifically, I have focused on the actions of soldiers in combat; how professional athletes respond to world-class competition for the Olympics; and the behavior of pilots in the cockpit when something goes very wrong.

Typically, panic in the cockpit occurs when two things arise simultaneously. First the pilot encounters a risky or potentially dangerous situation. It may be an engine failure or an instrument landing when visibility is impossible or any other event where the pilot must respond appropriately and instantaneously to remedy the situation. Second the pilot believes they are unable to do anything to remove the risk and be safe again. This is a physical and behavioral state where the pilot has no confidence in being able to rectify the situation.

The resulting panic can be a state of paralysis where the pilot is unable to do anything but freeze or the pilot initiates a frenzy of very ineffective and futile behaviors that only exacerbate what is happening, hastening the inevitable.

Consider this example. A pilot is at a business meeting planning to leave after lunch, but the meeting isn't concluded until after dark. Now the pilot is worn out and so eager to fly home that he skips supper and finally launches in mild IFR weather. As he approaches his home base the weather deteriorates, winds increase, and visibility dwindles.

Now at night he must make an instrument approach to land. He is tired and hungry. It is pitch black and raining hard, and both the ceiling and visibility are down to minimums. He is vectored for an ILS approach—a piece of cake, he surmises.

As he flies to intercept the glideslope, the winds change enough to require landing on another runway. He is told about the wind shift and instructed to fly to a waypoint to use the RNAV (GPS) approach to land. Frustration and confusion arise as now he has too many things to do at the same time. Reprogram the GPS, change the heading bug, grab his tablet and find the proper approach plate to check what is now required for the new approach. And fly the plane.

In his rush he pushes the wrong button, the autopilot is deactivated by mistake, and he can't find the RNAV approach on his GPS. He fumbles his tablet, and the plane drifts to his left and down. It is dark and windy, and rain is pounding the plane like small bullets. He is losing control of both the plane and himself. He becomes scared, blunders around his instrument panel, and can't focus on what to do. He panics, and the plane goes down. What will the NTSB report say?

## What Can Be Done

There are things a pilot can do to avoid panic in the cockpit. The simple response is to not exceed the limitations of the aircraft or the pilot. First, fly the plane as it was designed to be flown. This can be as simple as not attempting a four-hour flight with three hours of fuel. Or it can be as complicated as knowing how to reprogram your GPS, change radio frequencies, and set up a new heading, all at the same time and while still flying the plane.

For the pilot, this becomes a dual-bladed sword. First the pilot must be fully cognizant of their limits or piloting skills and then establish personal limits to avoid encountering a situation where those skills are insufficient to safely fly.

Continual training is the key to improved confidence. Every six months take an instrument check ride with an instructor. If not instrument rated, still fly with a CFI to practice emergency procedures. This is a safe way to understand your limitations or deficiencies and train to become better. Fly with a friend who can voice emergency commands such as "abort" on short final to see how quickly and well you respond.

Another aspect of flying that causes problems is the pilot's level of competence with the equipment in the aircraft. Very few general aviation pilots are completely trained in every aspect of what their equipment can do. Additionally, multitasking is a myth. The human brain is not designed to focus on multiple complex undertakings simultaneously. Serious complications may arise if, for example, on an IFR flight at night and in bad weather the controller amends a pilot's clearance to provide a different route, and a different frequency, and the pilot is not totally familiar with the navigation equipment on the panel. Several accidents have happened because the pilot became too fixated on trying to figure out how to reprogram the equipment to simultaneously fly the plane. Practice, practice, practice with the equipment in your plane and employ computer-based training programs for that equipment. This takes a lot of time and effort, but your life may depend on your level of competency using your equipment.

In the mid–1980s I bought an almost new IFR-equipped Mooney 231. It took me 25 hours of flying with a CFII to master the navigation gear in the plane, and this was before GPS and glass cockpits. Twenty years later I rebuilt a plane and had the latest GPS navigation tools and connected autopilot installed. This time it took 100 hours of training and practice to become proficient and safe in its operation.

Early on, I purchased an analogue, desktop simulator to practice instrument flying. I could set up all kinds of instrument approaches on the simulator. At that time my job required me to travel quite a bit, and I elected to fly myself. A day or two before a flight I would set up instrument approaches similar to my destination and practice for a few hours. When landing at my destination I was very confident even if it was IFR weather since I was just repeating something I had done numerous times on my simulator. Today computer simulators can serve the same purpose.

Additionally, YouTube and tutorials can add to the pilot's repertoire on handling emergencies.

Another great confidence builder for cross-country trips is to begin collecting en route and destination weather data a few days before your flight. This way the pilot can begin to understand what the weather is doing and better predict what the weather should be during their flight. The analysis might even suggest that the flight be done another time.

## Eleven. Nontraditional Landings and Survival

As a new VFR-only pilot I had a business flight planned. The day of the flight the weather was iffy, especially to a neophyte aviator. I was on the phone with an FAA weather briefer, and he could tell I was a very low-time pilot. FAA regs prohibited him from telling me I could not/should not fly due to weather. Here is what he said, "If you do not fly today, you will always be around to fly tomorrow, but if you fly today, you may not be around to fly tomorrow." That has been my standard throughout my flying days. I have never had second thoughts or regrets canceling a flight due to weather or anything else that would have made the flight suspect such as my health or aircraft issues. I have abandoned my plane and taken an airline flight home several times, to retrieve my plane another day in better weather.

A pilot should establish personal limits that will reduce the opportunities for their flying skills to be uncomfortably tested. Usually this relates to weather and what the pilot can accept as safe. Avoid flights where your skills or the limitations of your plane will be sorely tried beyond what you can handle.

In concept, avoiding panic in the cockpit is very simple. Become very skilled in the operation of your plane, flying it, and operating all its equipment. Secondly, fully understand your expertise and limitations and shun flights that may exceed the limitations of you or your plane. Finally, practice, train, and challenge your capabilities. Become more proficient at receiving and initiating abrupt changes in your flights by flying with another pilot or instructor.

Thus far this section has focused on being proactive in avoiding panic while flying. The question arises on what to do if you do become panicky when flying. Fly the airplane and ask for help. The stress created by a flying issue, concern, or serious problem only increases your anxiety. So, don't try to do everything at once. First control the plane, then call for help.

If IFR, most likely you are talking to a controller. Explain that you can't locate the amended waypoint, or you are having difficulty reprogramming your GPS, or you are having problems controlling the plane and at the same time complying with the changes received. Let the controller deal with any airspace problems your noncompliance initiates. Once when I was IFR and lost some of my primary instruments, I told the controller what had happened and that I needed to land quickly. I was given a new heading and instructed to descend. I radioed back that I could descend or I could turn to a new heading, but I could not do both at the same time. I was told to first fly the new heading, then descend.

If you encounter a situation where you are not in radio contact with anyone, your primary responsibility is to fly the plane. Fly straight and level, avoiding any obstacles. Think through what must be done, then plan how to do it. Avoid complications, keep your plan simple.

The better trained you are as a pilot and the better you understand your levels of expertise and personal limitations, the better prepared you will be to avoid panic in the cockpit. Never stop training, and do not overestimate what you are capable of as a pilot. If you do become anxious when flying, remember that your priority is to fly the plane, then solve the problem.

## How to Handle an Engine Failure

Student pilots are taught about dangers associated with flight such as weather, aircraft performance limitations, pilot frailties, and poor decision-making skills. Enriched training and knowing when to say no go a long way toward lowering the potential danger of flying.

Yet, since aircraft are designed and made by man, the opportunity for failure without any rhyme or reason is always present. The chance of this happening is very, very rare. But, if your engine fails in flight, you know that you are going down and that, sooner than later, the plane will impact the land beneath it. How that connection between plane and earth is made depends on your skills, your training, and how well you deal with stress. Pilots with minimum training, poor flying skills, and the tendency to handle stress ineffectively typically end up as statistics on what not to do during an engine-out encounter.

Having experienced an engine failure in flight, I will share with you some tips on how to improve your chances of surviving an unscheduled, off-airport landing.

First, let me share some myths of engine stoppage in flight. Occasionally I read about how quiet it gets in a plane when the engine quits. Not so. The prop may continue to turn, there is noise, and instruments suggest that the engine is still running. The best clue to recognizing that you have no power is that the plane starts going down. It will still have plenty of forward movement and speed, but you are getting closer to the ground.

Another trickery of engine stoppage is illusion. During a normal landing at an airport, the pilot observes descending to a point on the runway. Instinctively you are aware of the plane going toward the ground. When you lose an engine and are going to land where there is no airport or runway, the visual image is totally reversed. You do not see the plane descending but instead you see the ground rushing up to impact you. Landing on a runway, you are focused on gliding onto the surface with a very smooth "chirp, chirp" as two tires gently touch down. An off-airport landing resembles a very violent, rapid upward movement of the ground and may result in very badly damaged people and plane.

Often, though, in-flight engine failures do not have to be catastrophic if the pilot remains calm and flies the plane until it stops.

## Some Tips to Be Prepared for an Emergency Landing

Train, train, train. Many aircraft accidents come about due to pilot panic. Training for dealing with emergency situations should be conducted regularly, not just for a two-year CFI flight review. Training instills in us the ability to quickly respond appropriately to challenging conditions. Training allows us to respond instinctively, without thinking. Driving a car when a child or animal runs in front, we instinctively move our foot from accelerator to brake. No thinking but an immediate reaction to change the outcome. Training allows the pilot to respond instinctively and positively.

An excellent way to understand powerless flight is to experience flying a glider. Spend some time in a glider with an instructor. For details see Chapter 15.

Recognize that piloting an engineless plane requires multiple actions simultaneously. First, accept that the plane is descending. The pilot should try to determine why the engine has quit and try to restart it but also survey the ground to find a place to land. This is where your superior emergency training pays off. It is very important to know how far you can glide and how long before you meet the ground. Losing your engine at 10 thousand feet AGL offers many more options than at one thousand feet. A clear understanding of time and distance sets up what your priorities should be. Practicing emergency procedures at altitude with a CFI hones your ability to know what to do.

Gear up or gear down? If you have retractable gear, the only way to determine what is best is after the plane stops. In water or rocks, extended landing gear may prove more dangerous than skidding on the belly. On the other hand, landing wheels down may absorb energy and speed, resulting in a safer landing. Of course, with a fixed gear plane, the question is moot.

Never ever stretch the glide. When the NTSB investigator arrived at the scene of my unscheduled, off-airport landing, which totaled the plane, he congratulated me. I asked why. He replied that almost every time he investigated an emergency landing with engine failure this close to the ground, he seldom had a live pilot to talk to. I inquired why, and he said that most tried to stretch their glide, ultimately stalling and crashing. Enough said!

Prepare for a rough landing. Check the tightness of the seat belts to impede any body movement upon impact. If a gear and or a wing strikes the ground, the plane will quickly and violently be tossed in that direction. The person on that side can be smacked into the door or side of the plane, potentially causing severe injury. Just before landing remove any glasses, as they can cut the face or cause black eyes. Grab a pillow, blanket, or loose clothing to put in front of your face. Just before impact shut down the plane, pull out the mixture, and turn off the ignition. Then exit. Upwind! If there is a fire, you are out of its path.

This is my take on the best way to survive losing your engine in the air. It worked for me, yet keep in mind that most pilots will never experience this.

## *Survival Training and Equipment*

### Not Being Prepared

One event that happened in my early twenties made an indelible impression. In the early spring of 1959, I had returned to Dartmouth College after a two-year tour in the Marine Corps. The campus was abuzz regarding the disappearance of two respected physicians, faculty members of the college medical school.

On Saturday, February 21, 1959, two medical doctors departed the Lebanon, New Hampshire, airport (KLEB) in a Piper Comanche for trips into northern New Hampshire towns to see patients and perform an autopsy. The weather was not good—icy and snowy. The work completed, the plane departed for home around 3:30 p.m. into snow squalls with deteriorating weather and low ceilings. By 9 p.m. that night, because the plane never returned home, Civil Aeronautics Authority, the predecessor of the FAA, was notified. Unfortunately for several days the severe weather prevented any search. When the weather cleared, the hunt was intense, but the effort lacked coherent leadership and the plane was not found.

On May 5, 1959, a plane sighted the wreckage, and a ground search party was able to reach the Piper crash site. The pilot and passenger survived the crash but died from exposure and lack of food. They lived for four days and left short notes. The plane crashed because of carburetor icing, which impeded the flow of gas, causing the engine to lose power. Also, the crash site was not on their designated flight path.

Typically, aviation accidents have a chain of little events or circumstances that add up to causing a bigger problem. In this case, while the pilot had 20 years of flying experience, he was not instrument rated. He was also known to take risks, especially with weather. Unfortunately, a survival kit had been removed from the plane for a previous flight and never replaced. The pilot began a flight home at the end of a winter day into snow squalls and subfreezing temperatures with low fuel. Additionally, the passenger only wore street clothes, no winter gear. This is a perfect example of "get-home-itis," a human condition where the desire to get home surpasses common sense and overrides the fact that continued flight is risky.

In my early teens growing up in a rural small town, camping, fishing, and hunting were favorite pastimes, summer or winter. My parents had faith in my ability to survive, camping out by myself. I would construct a shelter and augment my meager stock of food with fish or small game I would kill. Over time I became very adept at living in the wilderness, depending solely on my ability to care for myself. I understood what it took to endure in harsh environments.

I was not a pilot that spring, but my winter camping experience and my recently completed first combat tour (Beirut, Lebanon, 1958) told me that these two men took unnecessary risks, were unprepared, and paid with their lives. When I became a pilot, I could never forget this winter crash and how the two men died because they were not equipped for the elements. My planes always had survival gear appropriate for the season and the terrain I would fly over.

## What Is Survival?

Survival, with regard to flying, is the process in the event of a crash of staying alive and well until rescued. This process should begin the moment one decides to become a pilot. What I am referring to is the fact that flying an aircraft does have risks, but most risks can be mitigated by common sense, training, and being prepared.

In the accident described above, the fact that the pilot safely crash-landed his plane indicated that he was experienced and did not panic. But he left his survival equipment home and departed in very dangerous weather. He was not fully prepared for the flight. Survival is initiated when the pilot has aboard the equipment needed for the pilot and passengers to safely persist in the weather, medical supplies to treat crash injuries, and food and water to sustain everyone until rescued. I always add a paperback book or two to fight boredom until help arrives. I understand that this sounds like a pilot must pack half the camping section of Walmart in the back of the plane to be prepared. No! What is needed can be packed in small duffel bags or backpacks. This becomes a compromise between passengers, personal baggage, fuel, and what survival gear is needed.

Of course, the terrain being flown over and the time of year dictates what survival equipment is needed. Winter requires less water, more food, and warm clothing. Hot summers call for less clothing but more liquids.

## Survival Preparation

Aviation accident studies reveal that 70 to 80 percent of the time the reason for an accident is a pilot making a wrong decision. Failing to recognize a potential problem or ignoring what could happen is common. Running out of fuel always makes me wonder. Why does a pilot, knowing that they only have one hour of fuel in the plane, initiate a one-hour flight? As an aviation psychologist, I know why. The pilot is convinced that they can make that flight successfully. After all, nothing bad has ever happened before, so it will not happen this time. They become complacent.

General aviation survival consists of two parts. First is what has been done before going down, and the second deals with what you do once on the ground. File a flight plan. When in flight, if deviating from your filed plan for harsh weather or extra sightseeing, let the area air traffic controller know about your deviation. Train enough so that if the engine fails you can quickly and instinctively respond. If not IFR use flight following. In the sky, I love it when I know that I am more than a blip on a radar screen, that I am a real person talking on the radio with another real person who knows who that blip is. I feel secure. Let friends or family know where and when you will be flying. At the very least, if you do not arrive at your destination airport, someone will know where to start a search for you because they know your flight path.

If you lose an engine and do make an unscheduled, off-airport landing and your emergency locator transmitter (ELT) is on and armed, it should transmit a signal letting the proper authorities know where you are. When properly configured it will automatically send a distress signal. A second source of security is found in a personal locator beacon (PLB), a personal ELT. This device, carried on your person, transmits a signal when activated just like your plane's ELT, showing where you are on the ground.

There are many different types of PLBs, with differing capabilities. Some work alone, while others may require a cell phone. Essentially the PLB transmits a signal from you to a satellite. That signal is relayed to response agencies; the National Oceanic and Atmospheric Administration monitors distress signals in the United States. The response agencies notify local search and rescue (SAR) authorities to initiate a rescue operation.

Which unit is the best to buy? That depends on where you might fly, your pocketbook, and the degree of reliability you expect. I suggest that you do an internet search and go from there. Also consider extra power, carrying either a solar charger or some form of extended power equipment.

On January 1, 2020, the FAA required all planes flying in the United States to have Automatic Dependent Surveillance—Broadcast Out (ADS-B) equipment on board. ADS-B is a satellite-based global positioning system technology designed to eventually replace ground-based radar monitoring of aircraft. The "Out" version reports individual aircraft position, altitude, and speed, and tracks aircraft movement. This tracking data can also be used to locate downed aircraft.

Survival on the ground depends on your training, your physical condition, your current state of mind, and having the appropriate survival gear in the plane.

## Survival Psychology

In a previous section I described panic as a psychological response to a person's belief that in a dangerous situation they lack the ability to persevere and come out okay. Panic results in fear, the inability to act appropriately, and doing nothing right. Panic can be as simple as having a 10 a.m. doctor's appointment and feeling anxious because you know you will be 10 minutes late. Or it can be as difficult as driving on an icy road and skidding into oncoming traffic despite attempts at evasive action.

Panic is the by-product of being in a dangerous situation in which you have no confidence in your ability to correct what is happening. It is the inability to act because you don't know what to do and the result will be very, very harmful to you. You will be hurt very badly.

But if you understand what to do and believe in your ability to correct the circumstances, you should not panic.

In aviation training, we practice emergency procedures constantly with instructors. The better pilots continue to practice emergency procedures to the point where if something goes wrong their responses are correct and instinctive, flying the plane until it stops on the ground. But this is only half the battle. Once you're on the ground, what comes next?

This is where your survival training and equipment come into play. Injured? You have a first aid kit. Thirsty? You have water. Hungry? You have food. Cold? You have a coat and sleeping bag. Wet, rainy, or snowing? You have a small camping tent. Thus, you are prepared. Your PLB sends out a distress signal so a local SAR unit can then seek you out. So, you treat any injuries and make yourself and passengers comfortable until help arrives.

## What Now?

You are now on the ground, and the plane has stopped, so what is the next move? Shut down everything, and if there is no fire danger, you can assess the situation. If there is fire or smoke, vacate immediately. Treat injuries, activate your personal locater beacon, and relax if possible, knowing you are down, safe, and have your survival gear.

As an experienced Civil Air Patrol SAR pilot, I have been involved in searches for lost planes throughout the Southwest. One thing I have learned is that downed aircraft are very hard to see from the air. In several years of search missions, I have never seen a downed plane that looked like a plane. Most were either hidden in brush or trees or so destroyed that they were no longer visibly identifiable as a plane.

What does this mean? If a single-engine four-seat plane is almost impossible to see, how difficult would it be to see people? GPS technology and accuracy can pinpoint an ELT or PLB position most of the time. But malfunctions or failure to activate could render the equipment useless.

Wisdom and experience clearly suggest that pilots and passengers should remain at the crash site. There are several reasons why. SAR units will be looking for the plane. If people are not there and the plane is located, another search must prevail. Besides, the plane itself can prove useful for survival. Avgas and/or oil produces dark smoke if burned, creating a signal readily viewed from the air. An intact interior provides shelter.

If (and that is a big if) you know exactly where you are, and if you know exactly where civilization and help is, and if you are physically capable of getting there, you could leave the plane. But all three conditions should be confirmed and doable.

The two doctors described above constructed snowshoes out of branches and surgical tape from their medical bags. They departed the plane but, not knowing where they were or where they were going, just wandered around for a while and returned to the plane, only to succumb due to the lack of nourishment and the elements.

Best option? Stay with the plane.

## What Is in the Back of Your Plane?

Survival equipment in the back of a plane varies depending on when and where you fly. I place all my survival gear in a backpack so that if I left the plane, all my gear would be with me. What I carried flying across Alaska was totally different from what I carried flying across the deserts of the Southwest. Also, survival gear is a compromise between weight and the worst conditions you think you may need protection from. In summer deserts one needs fluids, while in Midwest winters the primary need is protection from cold.

Cell phones are not viewed as ideal for survival usage. Cell phones require towers to operate. Your phone is both a radio receiver and a transmitter. When calling, the phone sends an electromagnetic radio wave to a cell tower where it is received and sent to another tower at its destination. When your phone receives a call, the process is reversed. Survival issues are related to the accessibility of a tower in the vicinity of your plane and

## Eleven. Nontraditional Landings and Survival

the potential masking of available towers due to mountains, hills, or other terrain features. While cell phones are useful in developed areas, they may not be so good in the wilderness.

There are research and prototype cell phone systems that can be used without towers, using other ground-based devices. Again, this employment would be helpful only in developed areas.

A satellite phone is a mobile radio-transmitter sending and receiving signals off satellites instead of towers. They are expensive, and the price per minute of usage is also costly. There are two types of phones based on their satellite usage. There is a geostationary orbit, which has a stationary location very high above Earth. This may limit some usage, depending on where you are and where the satellite is. The other version is low Earth orbit, where the orbit range is greater but the satellite is only a few hundred miles above Earth and there is a risk of connection interruptions.

Additionally, your airplane transponder should also alert authorities that you are on the ground somewhere. If you were on an IFR flight plan or using flight following, then you were talking to a controller somewhere who could know what was happening. When on an extended VFR flight plan, I would periodically call in my location to a controller so that if I went down, they would have a better indication of where I was and where I had already flown.

When flying cross-country, monitor the emergency frequency, 121.5 MHz, so you can immediately call Mayday if an emergency arises. Better yet is to have the Air Traffic Control (ATC) frequency for where you are flying as they are controlling and monitoring air traffic where you are. Either frequency may be monitored by other aircraft who can help you.

Based on my training and experience in survival, I assembled my own survival gear. This included weather protection, fluids, and food for energy. Flying over the eastern United States reveals plenty of streams, rivers, ponds, and lakes. These are of no use to you, though, if your crash site is one-eighth of a mile away from a source of water and you flew solo and now have a broken leg.

Since most of my flying consisted of long, cross-country flights, my baggage contained plenty of clothing, shirts, pants, coats, etc. Therefore, extra weather protection was already at hand. Survival gear in the back of a plane is not designed to be used over and over again for a long period of time. It is for (hopefully) a one-episode event, and, until needed, it is handled with care. Mummy sleeping bags can be purchased for between $20 and $60, weighing two to three pounds and good for temperatures down to freezing. In 40 years of flying, I never used my survival gear.

Food should be high in calories and nutrients. I would pack myself dried fruits and nuts, dried meats, and protein bars. I would package them in assorted ziplock plastic bags, which could also be used for other purposes. A caution on fluids: they are most necessary but also heavy. I do not recommend energy drinks because of their contents. Sports drinks such as Gatorade were designed for a specific purpose, to maintain the body's ionic balance after a vigorous workout. High in sugar and sodium, they were not designed as an alternative to plain water. My survival gear contained plain bottled water.

All my survival gear fit inside a backpack that also contained several heavy-duty, large, plastic garbage bags. My sleeping bag was in another small bag, next to my backpack. In the plane I had a comprehensive medical kit with an excellent book on first aid. As a combat infantryman, I had quite a bit of training and experience treating combat injuries. My medical kit contained supplies to treat broken bones, serious cuts, infection, and pain. If you have never done so, avail yourself of lessons and seminars in practical first aid. I would also have a couple of bottles of water purification tablets, just in case.

Other items I deemed important included a lightweight foil emergency blanket, lightweight waterproof ponchos, a Swiss Army knife or Leatherman-type tool, a lightweight collapsible shovel and small hatchet, several feet of parachute cord (or get a parachute cord bracelet with six to 20 feet of nylon cord), waterproof matches (I would take "strike anywhere" table matches, dip them in melted candle wax, and store them in a small medicine bottle), small flashlights with extra batteries, and heat tabs (chemical tabs that burn providing heat to cook with), and assorted spices. Freeze-dried foods for camping are excellent, but one must have water and a source of heat. My survival pack would also contain a cooking pot with a cup inside, both lightweight aluminum, and a sheath knife (I prefer the USAF survival knife issued to pilots).

Most of my survival equipment is available in sporting goods stores catering to hikers and campers and Army surplus stores.

When flying over extended water areas such as the Caribbean, water flotation equipment becomes most vital. My wife and I would slip on U.S. Coast Guard–approved life vests, and behind us, readily reachable, there was an approved two-person life raft, stowed in a small bag with grab handles. One would remove the collapsed raft, pull it out, and in the water pull on a handle filling the sides of the raft with air. This equipment could be rented, but I owned the vests. They had to be periodically inspected and certified. FAR Part 91.509 mandates what overwater survival equipment is required if flying over 50 nautical miles from shore.

We all carry insurance on our cars, planes, RVs, and homes. But how many of us have submitted a claim for a tornado-destroyed car or a burned-down house? We don't assume we will lose a home or vehicle, but we are insured. So, when flying, don't be complacent: carry survival gear.

Next is an item that in today's "politically correct" environment can lead to trouble, legally or otherwise. On my cross-country flights I carried a handgun. In Alaska I carried a high-caliber rifle. In northwest Canada I used to carry a high-caliber rifle, but today's firearms laws make that very difficult. First, I am an expert with handguns (I competed as a full-time professional athlete in bullseye pistol matches) and carried as both a police officer and a combat infantryman. Second, I was a certified instructor in pistols, rifles, and shotguns. The handgun would be used as protection against wild animals, signaling, or for food. A nine-millimeter hollow-point round fired into a pool of water in a stream can stun enough fish for several meals.

I had concealed carry permits good for several states. The decision to have a firearm in your plane is a personal one, and I do not advocate either way. I am only sharing with you what I would do and my rationale. But one word of advice: if you are not totally competent with a firearm, don't carry one!

## Can I Legally Fly with a Firearm?

Can you legally carry a gun in your private aircraft? The correct answer is: maybe, sometimes, it depends. This confusing response is because of the multiple jurisdictions that control the possession and usage of firearms in the United States.

If you are not experienced using a handgun, don't fly with one. Now, assuming you are an expert with a handgun and safety is a primary concern, let me continue with the question: can you carry a pistol in your general aviation aircraft?

Suppose you plan a flight from Tennessee to Texas and you have a handgun in your airplane. What laws apply to your flight? First, the Bureau of Alcohol, Tobacco, Firearms, and Explosives defines which weapons are legal to possess. Each state you fly over has its own firearms laws. Each airport also has laws regarding the possession of firearms, and some airports come under the Department of Homeland Security's Transportation Security Administration (TSA). What happens if you run into harsh weather, run low on fuel, or encounter another situation requiring you to land en route? More state, local, and airport gun laws to comply with. Now you can understand why flying legally with a handgun can be quite complicated.

While an ideal solution may be to possess a concealed carry permit for every state one flies into or over, that may be impractical or impossible. For some places having a firearm in your plane may be illegal; that is why knowledge of state firearms laws is important. Flying out of the United States with firearms is not wise. Flying into Canada en route to

Alaska having hunting rifles or shotguns may be allowed by declaring the firearms upon landing in Canada and obtaining a permit allowing the transportation of firearms to Alaska. For firearms details see the Royal Canadian Mounted Police website.

Also, not everyone may possess a firearm. Federal law prohibits convicted felons from possessing a firearm (see the Gun Control Act of 1968 for more information on who cannot have firearms). State and local laws may also have restrictions as to who may possess firearms, such as age restrictions and which weapons are legal and illegal. One should contact the state agency that controls firearms possession for each state you intend to fly to, from, and over for details on the laws. This information is available in books and on the internet.

FAR Part 91 contains regulations for general aviation operations. Nowhere in this section of regulations can I locate any rule prohibiting a person in a private aircraft from possessing a weapon in flight. But there are other laws that may impact this privilege. The type of weapon (a fully automatic rifle) or the purpose of transporting a weapon for sale in your plane (interstate commerce laws on selling a firearm) are subject to other federal laws.

Who controls the possession of handguns at an airport? That depends on the airport. Small airports without commercial carriers may come under the authority of the municipality or county that operates the airport, or perhaps only the state.

Airports with commercial air carriers have both sterile areas and non-sterile areas. Sterile areas are that portion of an airport with commercial traffic that provides access to people boarding or exiting commercial aircraft. In most cases enforcement of sterile areas is done by personnel of the Transportation Security Administration. The TSA is responsible for the security of our traveling public. Some airports have private contractors for security, but they must be approved by the TSA. Firearms are prohibited in sterile areas except for authorized personnel.

The non-sterile areas, such as FBOs and GA parking areas, though, are governed by municipality and state firearms laws. One word of caution: if a business posts a sign prohibiting weapons inside their building, if you enter the business armed and you are asked to leave but do not, you can be arrested for trespassing. However, I have never seen such a sign at an FBO. So, if you land your private aircraft at an airport with commercial air service, avoid sterile areas!

One additional suggestion: review a book on state gun laws to ensure that you are not violating any regulations. For more information, search the internet for "carrying firearms in a private plane," and you will find all the information you are seeking regarding the legality of firearms in your plane.

## Survival Training

If you grew up in a camping family or discovered living outdoors on your own or spent some time in the infantry, you may already possess some survival skills. But if you spent your life in a city living in an apartment, you probably need training.

Where or how can you get the proper survival training? You can locate information or books on survival via the internet. I do suggest that you acquire a copy of the FAA's small, 142-page paperback *Basic Survival Skills for Aviation* (available from Amazon). It is an excellent guide written for aircraft crashes. Study it well before flying and ensure that it is a part of your survival equipment in your plane. Select your favorite survival book and add it to your survival gear.

Now that you have the books, buy the equipment and try it out. When it rains or snows, go outside in your backyard (try this during the night) to set up your equipment and spend the night. Learn what works for you and what does not before the real deal. Practice until everything becomes easy and natural.

There are several schools for survival as well as classes and videos. Local adult education classes or junior colleges sometimes offer wilderness survival classes, and videos are also available, especially on YouTube. Outdoor schools offer seven-day courses for over $2,000, while two-hour classes may cost only a few dollars. Go to the internet and search "wilderness survival training."

Chances are you will never ever have to see how good your survival skills are in real life. I urge you to train yourself and always carry appropriate survival gear whenever you fly. Never become complacent like the two physicians. Always be prepared for the worst and hope for the best. Take first aid courses and make sure your plane has appropriate medical items inside.

## Survival Equipment Means More Than Food, Water, and Shelter

What do you have in the back of your plane besides survival gear? I have seen planes in which the back looked pristine, void of anything, just like when it was new. Others look like a well-used toolbox, strewn with oily rags, half-empty oil bottles and odds and ends of junk. Each pilot decides what does or does not belong in the back of their plane.

When I started flying my own plane, a decade-old Cessna 172, it was usually on long, VFR, cross-country flights. One time, flying across the vast open spaces of western Texas, I encountered engine problems. I

**Packing the survival gear in the plane before a trip; (left to right): Anita; Bob's mother, Billie Worthington; and Bob.**

landed at a mostly abandoned country airport. After parking and searching for another human, I came upon a hangar where a mechanic was working on a plane.

He explained that he was too busy to be able to stop and fix my plane. He allowed me to use his tools, and under his guidance, the problem was fixed. Lesson one: carry tools on cross-country flights. If going on extended cross-country trips like flying to Alaska, consider carrying extras of smaller parts that might need replacing in the wilderness.

So, the back of my plane became the repository of key spare parts, tools, and survival equipment. Also included was a collapsible tow bar for moving the aircraft around, especially over rough terrain.

Yes, this "stuff" added weight to the plane, and weight is very important for those of us who fly over mountains and across deserts. So, compromises must be made.

Where I live means that mountains or deserts will be under my wings any time I fly. Heat and altitude are enemies of a pilot. Too often, pilots become accident statistics because they do not understand how density altitude and weight diminish the performance of an aircraft. Therefore, the weight of what is in the back of a plane, plus added luggage, must be considered in keeping the gross weight of the plane within acceptable limits.

Flying with less fuel, limiting luggage, or removing equipment not needed (like water if flying over a populated area) all reduce weight. In some of the planes I owned, I would remove the rear seat to reduce weight to carry more survival equipment. But check with your mechanic to ensure that removing something is not violating some FAA regulation, such as weight and balance. For my planes, rear seat removal was legal. And the freed-up space being occupied with survival gear and baggage did not alter the center of gravity.

Survival is a matter of training, expertise, and having the right equipment needed for where and when you will be flying. But doing this can become the difference between flying again or no more flights.

## Twelve

# Flying Warbirds

Most general aviation pilots are fascinated with former military aircraft. I am no exception. But I have a couple of advantages over most GA pilots: my age and my military background. You see, I entered the Marines at age 19, in early 1957. The Korean War was over, but the U.S. military was still flying several World War II aircraft. During my time in Vietnam (1966–69) the U.S. military was employing various World War II propeller-driven warbirds because jet aircraft were too fast or had limited loiter capabilities. My duties required flying in these aircraft. Now, well into the twenty-first century, these aircraft are found in aviation or military museums. Some, though, are still flying, and available for you to experience the thrill of also flying in them.

## *USMC R4D (World War II)*

My first flight in a warbird was in mid–October 1958. I was a corporal in the Marine Corps, having just returned to Camp Lejeune, North Carolina, from combat in the Middle East. My girlfriend (later my wife), Anita, lived in Washington, D.C., and we had been apart for six months, so I was very eager to see her. I secured a seat on a Marine R4D, a military C-47 but a civilian DC-3, for a two-hour flight to D.C.

This Douglas twin-engine utility/cargo tailwheel plane had a cruise speed of 160 miles per hour. Delivered to the military in October 1938, it was the greatest transport of all time. Over 80 years old today, around 150 are still flown all over the world. The aircraft remained in the active military inventory until 2008, flying with the U.S. Air Force 6th Special Operations Squadron (a modified version, the Basler BT-67). More than 10 thousand military versions were built for World War II, with some six thousand DC-3s built.

The canvas seats were not comfortable, the plane drafty and noisy, a very crude ride compared to a modern civilian airliner. What was most unique about this flight was what happened at the end. After we landed and parked, the two pilots stood up, removing their flight jackets. Both were enlisted, master sergeants, trained during World War II as part of the "Sergeant Pilots" program, where enlisted men were trained to fly combat aircraft. The last four Marine enlisted pilots retired in 1973. However, in 1958 all new military pilots had to be officers, so being flown by NCOs was a historic moment for me.

## USAF AC-47 (Vietnam)

My last flight in another military version of the DC-3 was in Vietnam in the fall of 1966. On the night of Sunday, October 17, the 300-man Vietnamese Army battalion to which I was assigned as a combat advisor made a night helicopter assault on a North Vietnamese regiment of 1,200 men. We did not know there were so many enemy soldiers. Pinned down and outnumbered, our unit survived because USAF AC-47s spent the night protecting us. Fifty-three World War II C-47s were configured as flying weapons platforms just for Vietnam. One circled over us all night long, dropping flares and placing 20-millimeter machine gun rounds around our outer defensive perimeters, keeping the bad guys at bay. When the sun came up the next morning, we had suffered a 30 percent casualty rate, but Spooky (its call sign) saved us from being overrun.

Throughout the eight-day battle, we persevered (but with 45 percent total casualties), thanks to Spooky keeping us alive every night. A week or so after the fight, I was invited to fly a mission in Spooky. Dubbed "Puff, the Magic Dragon" based on the 1963 song of the same name by Peter, Paul and Mary, the gunship entered Vietnam in 1965. Armed with three M-134 7.62-millimeter miniguns it would orbit at three thousand AGL, in a left-hand turn, at 138 miles per hour. The minigun could place one round in every 2½ yards of a 52-yard circle with one three-second burst. Every fifth round is a tracer, but because of its rapid rate of fire, it looks like a solid red-orange stream of fire. The AC-47 was replaced in 1970 with the AC-130, and by the end of 1969, most of the AC-47s were turned over to the Vietnamese Air Force.

On the ground in Vietnam, even at night, it was warm. With doors and windows open, Spooky got cold. The AC-47 can remain airborne for around seven hours. Depending on how long it took from departure to target, it would remain on station for hours, usually replaced with another Spooky. My flight was prepared to support a U.S. Marine unit in a night defensive position. Loaned a field jacket without the liner, I still froze my butt off. The entire night was very loud, noisy, and bitterly cold, with the wind whipping throughout the fuselage. The unit needed no support, so we helped a Vietnamese unit (I did the interpretations on the radio), but it was mostly a calm evening. Believe me, seeing the war at three thousand feet is so different from seeing it on the ground. I logged about seven hours of combat flight time as a crew member.

## USAF C-119 (Korean War Era)

In the summer of 1963, I flew three times in a Fairchild C-119 "Flying Boxcar" while attending the Army Airborne School for paratrooper training. The dollar nineteen was a twin-engine, high-wing cargo plane, with its unique twin-boom tail. Just under 1,200 were built between 1947 and 1955, with its Air Force service lasting until 1973. These were the only times in my life when I was not in the airplane I departed in upon landing. At the end of my third jump, I performed a perfect PLF (parachute landing fall); unfortunately, it was on a rock, which shattered my right hip, thus ending any more exits from aircraft in flight.

## USAF L-19 (Korea and Vietnam)

Vietnam, November 1966. I experienced a flight in an Air Force L-19, a Cessna single-engine tail-dragger observation plane. I needed to recon the mountains surrounding the old French fort where the Vietnamese unit I advised was based. We and the enemy shared the same terrain, often violently disputing ownership.

Introducing me to his tandem-seat plane, the pilot gave me a two-minute explanation on how to fly the plane if he was shot and incapacitated (at this time I was not a pilot). The plane was loud, breezy, and very agile, yet at the same time so very fragile. There was little between me in the rear seat of the plane and the entire world out there. We flew over North Vietnamese fortified trenches, sometimes only one thousand feet above them, turning, twisting, and banking so I could view them developing their defensive positions.

The pilot explained they seldom fired at his L-19 because they thought he was a FAC (Forward Air Controller) who would bring U.S. fighters down on them. If they did not shoot at him, he would not unleash his fighters. It was a symbiotic relationship, foreign to me. Even today, I find it hard to comprehend the sensation of observing the enemy, while they watch me, no one shooting at each other.

## USAF O-2 (Vietnam)

During my second tour (1968–69), I flew missions in Air Force Cessna O-2s, the "Oscar Deuce," a forward air controller aircraft also used for low-level reconnaissance missions, which I needed. The O-2 was a Cessna front and rear engine twin 337, modified for military combat flying.

During my first flight, the plane's windows would not open, so it was extremely hot in the plane. An hour of constant circles and steep banks so I could see the ground made me sick because I had consumed a big breakfast. Having no sick sacks, the pilot gave me his glove, which I promptly filled. He discarded it through a small opening in his window. Before our mission ended, I filled his other glove. On subsequent flights, I was prepared with extra plastic bags, but I never got sick again. I also never ate "big" again before a flight.

During two tours in Vietnam, I spent time in various aircraft, but most flights were in the ubiquitous UH-1B Huey helicopter. During my first tour I was not a huge fan of flying, but for some unknown reason during my second tour, I flew every chance I got. I ended my time in Vietnam with about 180 hours of flying. The most memorable flight was a special ops mission I was running the night of November 14, 1968, on the Cambodian border using a Huey. I was shot. For my combat flights I received the Purple Heart and an Air Medal.

My experiences in combat flying in Vietnam are described in my award-winning books, *Under Fire with ARVN Infantry* (McFarland, 2018) and *Fighting Viet Cong in the Rung Sat* (McFarland, 2021).

## USN PBY-6A (World War II)

In the fall of 1983 I was covering the Confederate Air Force (CAF) annual air show at Harlingen, Texas, as a journalist for the weekly aviation newspaper *General Aviation News*. Today the organization is known as the Commemorative Air Force and based in Dallas, Texas.

The CAF would allow aviation journalists to ride in World War II aircraft during the show. I was assigned to N16KL, PBY-6A Catalina, a high-wing, twin-engine, bomber/flying boat. It would depict the dive-bombing missions it flew in the Pacific, and then it would fly a rectangular pattern at 100 to 300 feet above the ground. This part of the show included one other PBY and single-engine dive bombers, all depicting the World War II air war against the Japanese.

Produced by Consolidated Aircraft from 1935 to 1945, more than 3,300 of these planes were built. Neither beautiful nor fast, the PBY was rugged and could stay aloft for 18 to 24 hours. Designed as a maritime bomber and for ocean search and rescue (SAR) missions, this twin-engine flying boat, cruising at 110 miles per hour, was not very maneuverable. For downed aircraft crew drifting in the ocean, the PBY rescuing them made it the most beautiful aircraft in the world.

One distinct aspect of this particular PBY was being the only World War II bomber in the CAF inventory that had flown combat missions in the war. During World War II in the Navy's Pacific bomber patrol squadron VPB-53, it flew 14 combat missions, including a SAR mission seeking USS *Indianapolis* survivors after their ship was sunk by a Japanese submarine. The ship had just delivered components for the atomic bomb Little Boy to the B-29 base at Tinian. The Navy declared this PBY-6A surplus in 1950.

Purchased by the Danish Navy, it served there for years. Declared surplus again in the 1970s, a private U.S. foundation bought it and used it in movies, one being *Midway*. In 1982 the Lone Star Wing of the CAF, located in Tyler, Texas, acquired the aircraft as a donation. Fourteen months and 1,700 person-hours later, the plane was restored to its military configuration of the 1940s. The 1983 CAF air show was the first for N16K.

With a crew of four we flew in the show going between 90 and 95 miles per hour. While the other six passengers watched the show from the

The World War II PBY-6A Bob flew in during an air show. This same plane was destroyed in a crash the next year, just before the air show.

plane's windows, I crouched between the two pilots. The plane was slow and very loud as it bounced and clattered following its scripted routine in the show. Being a pilot, I was in awe of the skill and ability of the crew to maneuver this awkward aircraft, remain aware of all the other planes in this performance, and fly in perfect formation during a sequence that to the spectators on the ground appeared very chaotic and unrehearsed. In nine minutes, our performance was completed, and we landed.

N16KL was slated to fly in the 1984 CAF air show, and I again was invited to participate. Early in the morning of Saturday, October 13, before the show, it flew a simulated water landing for photos over the open water between the Texas coastline and lower Padre Island.

Flying a pass over the lagoon, six feet above the water (it was prohibited from landing in the water), the copilot gradually descended to a foot or less above the water. Unfortunately, the PBY touched the water, decelerated violently, and broke up, killing seven of the 10 on board. This was the end of N16Kl as it was destroyed beyond repair.

## USN SNJ-6 (World War II)

In September 1998 I attended an aviation conference in Orlando, Florida. At Kissimmee airport (KISM) I visited Warbird Adventures, a new business, for a story. I was introduced to Thom Richards, CFI, founder and co-owner of this vintage flight school and museum, who said we would fly in a USN SNJ-6 (the Army Air Corps version was the AT-6 Texan) on a training flight. His company relocated to South Carolina in 2021 (warbirdadventures.com).

The North American SNJ-6/AT-6 advanced single-engine trainer has two tandem seats, student in front and instructor in the rear. The entire top of the plane is a completely glassed canopy. Military production began in 1937, with 15,495 built. This plane was both a trainer and combat aircraft into the early 1950s.

Before climbing into the front cockpit, I was given a World War II–style tan cloth helmet with ear receivers and a microphone. We departed KISM and flew at around 130 miles per hour to our practice area. My logbook of September 14, 1998, indicates that in 45 minutes we did rolls, loops, a Cuban 8, Immelmann, and split S, with one takeoff and landing. It was a fun, easy plane to maneuver and the only warbird I have flown as a pilot.

Near the approach of KISM I was still flying and was told to descend to 100 feet AGL. Now, to the right of the threshold, Thom asked if I could land. I replied that we were too far off the runway, too high, and too fast. I said that I would go around. Thom called, "I have the plane."

Releasing the stick to him, he made a 90-degree right turn, lining up flawlessly with the runway. Dropping the flaps, the T-6 dropped like a rock, and forward speed decreased. Lined up with the centerline, Thom made the perfect "three-point landing" as we decelerated down the runway, slowing for the turnoff to taxi to parking.

This was also my last flight in a warbird.

## Flying a Warbird

There are two kinds of flights in warbirds. One is as a passenger, where you get to sit and someone else does the flying. The other is where you get to fly the plane under the guidance of an experienced instructor. I have done both, and for me being the pilot is the most fun. The enjoyment of flying a warbird defies description. For this general aviation pilot, used to smaller single-engine aircraft, it is an experience never forgotten.

There are diverse ways to experience flight in a warbird. Some military aviation museums or foundations travel around the country in a World War II warbird, which is usually a bomber capable of accommodating more than one passenger, stopping at airports and offering rides to paying customers. Aviation museums may also allow visitors to pay to fly in their warbirds on special occasions.

Throughout the country there are flight schools that provide warbird orientation flights for either passengers or pilots (like Warbird Adventures). Many of these schools train pilots to fly warbirds. What does it take to fly a warbird solo? Just a pilot's certificate and a type rating to be legal. But from a practical side it takes much more.

It begins with what warbird you want to fly. A World War II fighter? A Korean War jet fighter? An L-19? A C-47? Or an O-2? Since most World War II trainers and combat aircraft have a tailwheel, you need to be proficient in flying tail draggers. Warbirds are powerful, complex aircraft, so extensive flying experience is a necessity. A few warbirds were modeled after civilian aircraft, like the Cessna 337 to the O-2, or Cessna 170 to the L-19, or the Cessna 172 XP to the T-41. Others may require jet experience or flying multi-engine heavy aircraft.

Flying warbirds is not cheap, so having money is a plus. Liability protection for warbird owners is necessary, but insurance can be costly and perhaps difficult to obtain. Numerous warbird pilots have extensive military or civilian flight experience. Usually, they begin their

*Opposite:* **Bob, flying a World War II T-6, is just entering the bottom of an inverted loop (where the top surfaces of the wings face outside the loop).**

warbird training by flying similar civilian aircraft such as a tailwheel, multi-engine, or jet aircraft, then progressing to World War II trainers and finally into the warbird they want to fly.

There are flight schools around the country that specialize in training civilian pilots to fly warbirds. The Commemorative Air Force has a need for qualified warbird pilots; therefore, some CAF state wings offer pilot training programs. To be eligible, one must be a CAF member and a pilot. If one is serious about becoming a warbird pilot, one must contact the CAF headquarters for more information. CAF wings may also provide lists of flight requirements to fly different CAF warbirds.

The concept of becoming a warbird pilot is not complicated. One must be serious and have ample flight experience. What follows will take dedication, money, and time. But around the United States are various flight schools (just Google "warbird flight schools") that train pilots to fly warbirds. To possess a logbook entry stating you spent $x$ minutes piloting a warbird is something most pilots, general aviation or professional, only dream about. I know as I have that entry in one of my logbooks.

THIRTEEN

# Flying Outside of the United States

There are three foreign countries immediately adjacent to the lower 48 states of the United States: Mexico, Canada, and the Bahamas. Your airplane allows pilots and passengers the opportunity to experience another country without the hassle of commercial airline travel. Use your magic carpet to enjoy the beauty of the land, its customs, and its culture.

It the 1970s through the 1990s all a pilot needed to exit our U.S. airspace and land on foreign soil were FAA documents for the plane and pilot, a birth certificate, and a photo ID such as a driver's license. Today, not so: the events of 9/11 and, more recently, COVID-19 have added a little complexity to flying from our nation to a foreign country.

For the purpose of discussing flying to a foreign country, my remarks will consist of only the three countries mentioned above, because those are the only foreign countries to which I have flown. Yes, small private aircraft can fly further and visit other foreign countries. Europe can be seen via eastern Canada, Greenland, Iceland, and Great Britain. Russia is a short hop west of Alaska. Africa is a quick flight south of Gibraltar. Dozens of tropical islands across the southern Caribbean Sea are only minutes away by island-hopping. Central and South America are reached without overwater flights.

But these flights may require extensive planning, special equipment, and considerable cash. Foreign trips north or south of us, or east of Florida, are readily accessible, not expensive, and planning the trips is not arduous. In fact, there are resources to make the planning and execution rather simple.

Another advantage of these three countries is the language. English is a common language in all three. The native language of Mexico is Spanish, but everywhere I have been, English was spoken. While eastern Canada speaks French, I never encountered problems speaking English. The Bahamian people speak English.

## What a Pilot Needs to Know

To avoid legal difficulties, a pilot and aircraft owner should understand that departing one country for another and exiting one country's airspace for another requires considerable knowledge about what each country requires.

Exiting the United States and entering a different country requires an understanding of the aircraft, pilot, and flight regulations of both countries. Additionally, pilot and passengers should know about customs regulations for entering or reentering both countries. For example, a U.S. FAA private pilot is authorized to fly a private plane in the three countries mentioned above. If the pilot is not instrument rated and current, then some restrictions may apply such as no VFR flights at night. Knowledge of the foreign country's flight rules is essential.

Rules and regulations often appear frivolous or contrary to common sense. Yet, as inane as some seem, we must obey them. Sometimes, what is or is not required regarding our plane in the United States may be exactly the opposite in another country. It is up to the pilot to understand these differences and to confirm that their aircraft comply with foreign requirements. Two common discrepancies are the size of our plane's N-numbers and having a radio station license for your plane.

FAA Advisory Circular No. 45-2E Identification and Regulation Marking describes what markings must be on U.S. registered aircraft. The plane's N-numbers must be 12 inches high, but there are exceptions. Unfortunately, some foreign countries may not allow smaller numbers, even if legal in the United States.

In the United States, the usage of aircraft radios is regulated by the Federal Communications Commission, not the FAA. When I first started owning airplanes the FCC required my plane to possess a federal radio station license, and I had to have a radiotelephone operator permit. In 1996 this requirement was altered. Today aircraft operating within the United States and using VHF two-way radios, radar, or emergency locator transmitters are not required to have an aircraft radio station license or a restricted radiotelephone operator permit.

But if the plane is operating internationally, both are required by the FCC (see FCC Form 605). The radio station license is for a plane and good for 10 years. The operator permit is good for life. Information on how to obtain both is available on the FCC website.

Another thought: Do you have a medical certificate, such as a third-class, or do you fly with BasicMed or your driver's license? Some countries require a regular medical exam certificate, so this is another aeronautical requirement to check out.

## Thirteen. Flying Outside of the United States

It is the responsibility of the pilot to be fully aware of what rules and regulations must be complied with upon entering the airspace of a foreign country. Fortunately, today a pilot has more foreign travel resources available than I ever did. The internet is your best friend and ally to learn what you need and where to get it.

Amazon and other internet booksellers carry guidebooks to flying a small private plane almost anywhere. YouTube has extensive videos on flying to our most popular foreign destinations. The Bahamian and Canadian governments promote private aircraft travel within their borders. Mexico not so much.

For adjacent foreign private airplane travel, AOPA is the first place to start your research. AOPA should have the latest information on where to go, how to get there, and how to remain safe and regulation compliant. Additionally, our U.S. State Department website provides current information on security and health issues in foreign countries.

Having flown my own plane into Mexico, Canada, and the Bahamas well over two dozen times, I do have experience with air travel in these three countries. My involvement in flying into and through Canada and the Bahamas was nothing short of great. Landing my planes in those countries and clearing their customs was much easier and more pleasant than returning to the United States.

My flying into Mexico was always a wonderful experience. Mexico was different as sometimes the air traffic controllers' English was so heavily accented that instructions were hard to understand. Also, it seemed like every aviation-related service, such as filing a flight plan, obtaining a weather briefing, etc., required a separate cash payment. Personally, I do not see flying into Mexico as that much fun as compared to Canada or the Bahamas. I have pilot friends who flew in and out of Mexico all the time prior to Covid-19, declaring it very safe. For almost four decades I have lived close to the Mexican border. Being this close to the country has convinced me that I would have a concern traveling around Mexico in my own plane. Although I have done it in the past, and nothing untoward happened, my safety was not an issue, and my experiences were pleasant and fun. But that was yesterday, and today is different. Several American businesses do promote private aircraft flying into Mexico as a safe endeavor, but the government of Mexico does not promote vacationing in their country by private air as Canada and the Bahamas do. One caution: all countries do require that various health rules be followed because of Covid-19, and these are subject to change.

To fly outside of the United States, pilots and private aircraft must comply with various regulations allowing legal travel out of the United States and into a foreign country. Here are some of those regulations.

## User Fee Decal

Private U.S. registered aircraft and vessels 30 feet and longer must pay a U.S. customs fee upon reentering the United States. This can be done two ways. Every time a plane reenters the United States it can pay the customs fee, or an annual fee can be paid to receive a decal stating that the customs fee has been paid for unlimited reentry into the United States. Customs and Border Protection prefers the annual decal as it reduces time spent going through customs. This decal may be purchased via the CBP.gov website or by mail.

## eAPIS

Electronic Advanced Passenger Information System is a web-based computer application for Customs and Border Protection to collect manifest passenger and crew information on all private aircraft travelers departing or entering the United States. The data must be entered at least 60 minutes before departure either in the United States or in a foreign country if flying back to the United States. This data can be entered days or weeks prior to departure. This way, if there is no computer with internet connection at your destination, you can enter your return manifest data at the same time you enter your departure information. The pilot entering the data must be enrolled in eAPIS. The purpose of this system is to allow customs to check all people in an airplane to verify that they are approved passengers for security reasons. More information on eAPIS can be found on the CBP.gov or AOPA websites.

## Passports

A passport is needed to enter a foreign country and to reenter the United States. Information is found on the U.S. State Department website. A passport is valid for 10 years (under age 16, five years). It typically takes two to three months to receive your passport, so it makes sense to apply several months before needing it.

## Aircraft Requirements

Flying internationally may require different documents be aboard than expected in the United States. In addition to what has been cited above, a pilot usually needs an airworthiness certificate, aircraft registration, insurance coverage approved by the country being entered, weight and balance information, operating limits, identification data plate, 12-inch numbers, transponder with Mode C, emergency locator transmitter (121.5 or 406 MHz), and appropriate aeronautical charts. If your aircraft is not a factory-produced civil aircraft (i.e., experimental or warbird), additional aircraft data may be required. Each country will have a list of aircraft requirements, and it is up to the pilot to know this. Also, some aircraft legal in the United States may not be legal in the foreign country, such as light sport aircraft or other smaller personal aircraft. Two items that can cause serious legal problems in private aircraft are weapons and drugs. Best advice: leave them home!

If flying to the Bahamas, a U.S. Coast Guard–approved life vest flotation device is required for every person in the plane. A life raft is not required but is recommended. Both can be leased from the departure FBO in Florida if it is set up to assist private flights to the Bahamas. Because my wife and I would fly to the Bahamas often, we purchased our own life vests. When their expiration dates arrived, we sent them back to the maker to be opened, inspected, recertified, and repacked.

If flying to or through Canada for hunting in either Canada or Alaska, permits must be obtained in Canada to transport the hunting weapons. Only nonrestricted hunting weapons are allowed—no handguns. Internet research will state which weapons are legal and how to obtain the permits. Canada is not a firearms-friendly country, so be careful to obey all their firearms laws.

One last remark: A pilot can fly VFR almost anywhere, and flying VFR is the best way to sightsee from the air. But being instrument rated and current is, in my mind, the safest way to travel. As I mentioned, some countries do not allow night VFR flights. Most often, especially in western Canada and Alaska, I would not fly IFR but would remain on the ground for a variety of reasons including that the mountains were too high, there was icing in the clouds, and there were few to no safe places to land if needed. Flight planning in those areas called for creating down days so that if you were grounded for a couple of days, the schedule could accommodate this without skipping planned events or trips. Having the instrument rating and knowing how to use it was the best safety insurance in all my foreign trips. It allowed me to fly safely, and since IFR flying in all three foreign countries was no different from in the United States, I knew what was expected of me in flight, regardless of any language barriers. Just another degree of safety.

## Entering Canada

Prior to arrival in Canada, the pilot must contact CANPASS (Canadian Passenger Accelerated Service System) to establish the landing and for clearing customs. In eastern Canada, I was met and checked by customs officials. In western Canada, after I landed, ground control would taxi me to a building, and I would park, enter the building, and make a call on a phone in the building (no person, just a phone). I would talk to a customs person somewhere, get a number, write it on a piece of paper to place on top of my glareshield. This number represented my permit to land in and fly around Canada. Western Canada had the easiest customs clearances I ever experienced.

Most trips into western Canada were to follow the ALCAN (Alaska–Canada) highway into Alaska. This highway was constructed by the U.S. Army Corps of Engineers in 1942 as a main overland supply route and to ground connect a series of World War II military airbases so U.S. combat aircraft could be flown to Alaska to give to Russia as part of our lend-lease program.

In the 1990s and into the first decade of the twenty-first century, these flights were still across the wilderness of western Canada and the Northwest Territories. The most spectacular scenic flying I have ever done was in small private planes along the ALCAN highway. Most airports were unchanged since World War II, and this trip of several days would be like returning to the 1940s. Anita and I never tired of our many trips up and down the ALCAN highway.

Instrument flying in western Canada could be primitive compared to my experiences in the United States or even eastern Canada. Some of the old World War II airports along the ALCAN highway had excellent, lengthy, paved runways with multiple instrument approaches, but no

**In the Mooney 231 (N231HB) flying over northwest Canada en route to Alaska.**

towers or even manned radios. Upon landing, you found that your plane held the only humans for miles around.

One instrument approach I made will never be forgotten. We had overnighted in Whitehorse, then departed in the morning eastbound for Watson Lake Airport, about 250 miles away, to refuel. The weather was mild IFR but warm. There was some moisture—rain clouds all the way—but no icing. The terrain was fairly flat all the way, mostly three thousand to four thousand feet high, with occasional peaks rising just above five thousand feet MSL. We cruised at 11 thousand feet MSL, the outside temperatures above freezing. Upon departure and all the way to Watson Lake we were under the control of Edmonton Center. The weather at Watson Lake reported ceilings of about two thousand feet above the runway with excellent visibility.

Around 50 to 60 miles west of Watson, Edmonton turned me loose. I was cleared for the Watson Lake ILS approach to runway 08. Watson Lake had no tower, but I was provided a remote ground frequency to close out my IFR flight plan. When Edmonton said goodbye, I radioed back that I did not know what to do. Edmonton said I was the only plane in the sky and to just follow the instrument procedures on the approach plate. I asked when I should begin my descent and was told whenever I wanted.

I was not sure what to do. For every instrument approach I ever made, I was talking to someone who guided my descent and headings. Edmonton said goodbye while I was almost 8,800 feet above the airport and almost 30 minutes away. So, what was I to do? I calculated that a descent of 400 feet per minute would allow me to intercept the glideslope far enough out to make a good landing. I began going down, maneuvered to intercept the localizer, and continued down until I found the glideslope. We broke out a few miles west of runway 08 and made an uneventful visual landing.

This was the first and only time I made a complete instrument approach and landing all on my own without talking to anyone. Anita and I both thought I did surprisingly well.

Most times I crossed western Canada I was going to Alaska, the most spectacular flying I have ever encountered. Flying a small plane across Alaska is unlike any other flying I have ever done. Above the most scenic land ever, mountains rising two to three miles above you, glancing across your wing, eyeball to eyeball with mountain goats just feet away grazing on mountain sides. Flying around Alaska is the goal of every pilot who desires flight experiences never found elsewhere.

Information on flying to Alaska and through Canada can be obtained from AOPA. The book *The Milepost*, created for people driving the ALCAN highway, is an excellent guide for pilots, providing considerable information on what lies beneath you while flying across Canada to Alaska. I do not

**Anita standing in front of the Tiger, N1196L, at Fort Yukon, Alaska; Dirt strip airport, north of the Arctic Circle.**

know of any current videos or books describing the flight to Canada in a small plane. All used books on this subject are 30 to 40 years old, or older.

## *Flying to the Bahamas*

The most amazing aspect of flying to the Bahamas is being over the water for an hour or more, flying a compass heading, not seeing anything but the bottom of the Caribbean Sea, and hoping and praying that you will sight your destination island before running out of gas. Well, it is not quite like that today. With computer screens and GPS navigation equipment, you can see where you are relative to your island destination.

Even though you cannot see that far ahead, your equipment clearly shows that you are on course and that you will reach your destination in 34 minutes. You no longer sit and pray; you have your trust in your equipment. You know that it will not fail you.

Whether you fly to a quiet island and land on a short strip along a beach or execute a precise landing at Nassau, you enter an exciting new land with different people to meet, different historical sites to see, exotic foods to taste, a different life to experience. Perhaps you'll even converse with a local and discover common ground.

One day Anita was visiting local antique shops, and I was just tagging along. At one that had a small book nook, she found a book, *The Island Airman and His Bahama Islands Home*, just published by legendary Bahamian professional pilot Paul C. Aranha. She bought the book for me. It was so fascinating that I stayed up all night reading it. The next day, shopping again, we returned to the shop, and I told the owner how much I enjoyed the book. He was a friend of Paul Aranha, so he called him and gave the phone to me. He invited my wife and me to spend Easter Sunday with him and his wife, Kim.

Consider six degrees of separation, the idea that any two people are six or fewer social connections away from each other. In his book, Paul describes his neighbors growing up in Nassau. One of Paul's neighbors was a young girl, Joy. In 2007 Joy was a principal in a Naperville, Illinois, school where my granddaughter was a student. In the early 1700s, Kim's relatives founded the town of New Milford, Connecticut, where my father was born and grew up and where I was born and lived for the first eight years of my life. Also, Paul and Kim's youngest son, Scott, was a student in a private school in a small town in Connecticut near where I grew up.

Flying into the Bahamas is different from flying into Canada. More paperwork, more formalities. The best way to start is with an FBO on the eastern coast of southern Florida, such as Fort Pierce, Palm Beach, or Fort Lauderdale. Select an FBO that has experience assisting pilots flying to the Bahamas. With their help, flotation devices can be leased, aeronautical charts purchased, and the Bahamian customs entry paperwork completed. Also, they will assist upon return and clearing U.S. customs. Make sure your destination airport in the Bahamas will have access to customs upon arrival.

The outer islands may not have customs on the island but may be able to arrange to have one available upon landing. If landing in Nassau, an FBO can assign an assistant who will walk you through customs efficiently and without hassle.

## *Final Comments on Flying Outside the United States*

I have not been a fan of flying commercially for a variety of reasons. Today successful airline travel requires certain degrees of sophistication and knowledge. My adult daughters do this with aplomb and self-assurance, qualities I lack. Probably because for years I departed according to my schedule, my times, my decision, with zero hassle.

I checked the weather, filed my flight plan, drove to my hangar, loaded my plane, moved the plane out of my hangar, obtained my clearance, and taxied for takeoff. I did not spend hours or days trying to locate the cheapest tickets. I did not have to wrestle with the proper combination of schedules to avoid lengthy wait times between flights or arriving at dawn to clear security.

I did not have to worry that somehow a forbidden container of something would end up in a carry-on piece of luggage. No wands announced to the world I have a prosthetic hip and leg made of titanium, and my shoes stayed on. And I never lost any baggage, ever!

Upon arrival in a foreign country in my private plane, I was always treated as a respected and welcomed guest. I was never hassled, never treated with scrutiny or suspicion. In my opinion, this is why visiting a foreign country in your plane is an experience always cherished and never forgotten.

## Fourteen

# Aging

## What Happens as We Age?

### Aging and Medical Science

In 1903, when the Wright brothers first flew, the life expectancy was 49 years for American males and 52 years for American females. In 2023, American males have gained almost 30 years to age 78, while women reach 82. Clearly in the 120 years we have had airplanes, our life expectancy has increased astronomically. Today the average age of pilots is 44 years, yet many pilots in their seventies and eighties are still active.

With this prevalence of longer lifespans comes both good news and unwelcome news. The good news is that medical science allows us to live longer. The bad news is that health issues that would have terminated our lives a century ago are now around to slow us down and restrict what we can do. An aging neighbor tells me, "Getting old is hell, but it is better than the alternative."

At the end of 2007 the FAA changed the mandatory retirement age of commercial airline pilots from 60 to 65. Due to pilot shortages, however, some consideration is being given to raising the age limit to 67. There is no mandatory upper age limit to ground private pilots. To continue to fly a plane, though, pilots must undergo and pass periodic medical exams and currency flying evaluations and satisfy insurance requirements.

This means that pilots must be physically fit to continue to fly, and as humans age this can become more difficult. What happens to our bodies as we get older?

### The Aging Process

The aging process can be viewed as affecting the physical, intellectual, psychological, and genetically influenced performance of our bodies. There is more to aging than hair graying or even disappearing. The functioning of the brain can diminish, and as our nervous system ages, transmitted impulses may be slower or injured where they fail to function properly. Our skin thins, muscles weaken, body mass decreases, and motion becomes more difficult. Internal organs lose efficiency, and some may fail as we get older. Our hearing, eyesight, and balance may also deteriorate.

As we grow older our bodies wear out. Our ability to function diminishes. Yes, there are 70-year-old folks who still compete in marathon races, and there are 20-year-olds so obese that they can hardly walk. The effects of aging are an individual process, and not all people experience it the same way. Also, prior injuries may increase the aging process dramatically, while genetics may stave off some aging consequences. Additionally medical advances may allow parts of us to function normally for years beyond the expected usage period. For example, genetics has kept my hair full and brown into my mid-eighties. Cataract surgery has allowed my eyesight to remain acute without glasses, but prior injuries have made walking very difficult.

But how does aging affect pilots?

## Physical

As we age, our strength weakens. Pushing a plane into the hangar becomes harder. Our flexibility decreases. I first became aware of this in my late sixties when turning my head around in the cockpit to look over my shoulders, trying to spot traffic. Joints stiffen due to past injuries or arthritis, and movements become painful. Reaction time decreases.

Sensory deficits increase. Vision and hearing require assistance such as glasses and hearing aids.

Older people probably most notice a lessening of endurance. Walking, standing, sitting, and working all tire us more quickly. We need more rest, and daytime naps may be required to allow us to function into the evening.

Injuries that occurred in our youth, healed properly and quickly, and caused no problems into our fifties or sixties will possibly become problematic in our seventies and eighties. In my younger days I broke numerous bones below my waist due to parachute landings, gunshot wounds, and motorcycle accidents. In my early eighties I began to experience difficulty standing, which grew into mobility and balance problems by my mid-eighties.

Unkind side effects from medications are another real concern. Medical science involves the creation of drugs that stave off encroaching diseases of aging. For the pilot some side effects could possibly interfere with safety in the cockpit creating confusion, drowsiness, dizziness, decision-making impairment, or increased urge to urinate. This usage of lifesaving medications with undesirable side effects is becoming an increasing problem with older pilots.

## Intellectual

Some elderly people experience some form of cognitive decline as they age. This can develop in a wide variety of ways. Most common is becoming forgetful. Memory loss, dementia, or Alzheimer's may begin slowly and progress so gradually that people may deny what is happening, because the onset is not immediately recognized by many until something bad happens like leaving a stove on, or forgetting to turn off a car parked in a garage, or becoming lost on familiar streets.

More common with declining intellectual functioning is the slowing of processing information and the inability to make decisions. Learning may become harder and slower. Distractions become tougher to avoid or ignore, and immediate decisions more difficult to process.

In the cockpit, under instrument conditions, decisions become harder to manage, resolutions more difficult to render, and confusion comes quicker and more often. These cognitive mishaps can lead to increased stress and fatal mistakes. Around busy airports cognitive decline can create real hazards when controllers expect pilots to respond immediately to hurried requests to make abrupt flight changes or switch runways when on final approach.

## Psychological

Psychological disabilities can affect any age. But age-related situations can increase psychological or emotional dysfunction. Losing a spouse, forced retirement, financial issues, declining performance, memory loss, declining health, or fearing not passing the FAA medical exam—all related to one's age—can lead to emotional stress. Excessive worrying, increased anxiety, inability to rest or relax, or issues the FAA has with your flying all contribute to psychological difficulties creating problems in the cockpit.

If a pilot is experiencing severe problems in their life and not handling them effectively, the emotional responses can interfere with the safe piloting of a plane. Often, as one gets older, psychological difficulties become harder to properly process or ignore, creating unhealthy stresses that negatively impact safe cockpit behaviors.

## Genetics

Here are three facts. There are more than six thousand known genetic disorders. As we age, we become more susceptible to chronic health disorders. Yet only 25 percent of our genetic makeup relates to our longevity (see "Is longevity determined by genetics?" in MedlinePlus, National Library of Medicine).

Therefore, as we grow older, we become more prone to having a genetic inheritance disorder such as heart disease, cancer, Alzheimer's, arthritis, diabetes, or obesity.

While genetics play a role in our expected longevity, there are so many other factors that interact that our family history of genetics does not accurately predict how long we may live. Medical science, injuries, and lifestyles may override our genetic makeup. For example, my wife's mother lived until she was 104 and her father died in his nineties. But my wife's life was cut short due to health issues unrelated to genetics; she died at 82.

## Lifestyle Behaviors

Which factors contribute to longevity are not disputed by science. Exactly how much these various longevity factors influence one's lifespan is still subject to discussion. What is agreed upon is that genetics, lifestyle, gender, and one's life environment are all important factors impacting how long one lives. There is no medical or scientific doubt that one's lifestyle can increase or decrease one's life.

A poor diet, no exercise, dependence on drugs or alcohol, smoking, and continuous life stresses all contribute to a shorter life. Eating healthy food, avoiding tobacco and drugs, limiting alcohol, vigorous exercising, and minimizing life stresses are behaviors that increase longevity.

Farmers, ranchers, and laborers get plenty of physical exercise. Writers, office workers, and pilots do not. We spend most of our working hours sitting down, hardly moving our legs or arms. Those of us with sedentary routines must exert extra effort to make time for the physical activity our jobs omit.

But it is clear that a healthy lifestyle begets a longer life, which translates into more hours in the left seat.

## What This Means for the Aging Aviator

Aging is a process that affects each person differently. But it is undeniable that as we age our physical abilities and performance decline. For some people this diminishing of abilities may begin in their forties or fifties. For others, their performance may not begin to decline until their late seventies or even their eighties.

Aging can be seen as having two functions: primary aging and secondary functioning. Primary aging is irreversible physiologic functioning free from disease or injury. It refers to the normal process of the body aging and diminished capacity to perform. Some debilitating effects of aging can be compensated for with glasses, hearing aids, walking canes, false teeth, and other health aids.

The secondary aging process relates to outside body influences such as lifestyle, genetic disposition, or external factors such as the Agent Orange that destroyed my heart. It still functions with medications but must be constantly monitored, and inside my chest is a pacemaker and defibrillator to correct the heartbeat when it goes awry.

Google "performance studies of older pilots," and you will find that chronological age is not a meaningful predictor of performance. Other factors should be considered. It is a fact that pilot performance does decrease with age, but that fact alone does not mean that older pilots are a safety hazard.

## Aging and Insurance

### Is Age Just a Number?

Is your age just a number with no relation to your physical or mental abilities? Not for general aviation insurance companies. Many pilots believe that being 65 or 80 or 85 does not automatically render one physically and intellectually diminished. But I believe that it is not the age by itself that renders insurance coverage difficult for older pilots to get but a variety of other factors in addition to age.

Insurance risks are based on broad factors of statistics, actuarial tables, scientific data, the probability of risk, the influence of competition, and the size of the insured pool. So, the age of a pilot has an assigned risk factor based on considerable data to determine risk covered and cost, and the willingness of the company to insure that risk. This section discusses the availability and cost of insurance for an airplane owned and flown by an older pilot.

Many older people do not view themselves based just on their age. I am one of those. While I am 86 years old, I do not perceive myself as that old. My cognitive abilities have not declined. The presence of diminished capacities and my continued strengths are not different than most aging Americans. What is different is at what age we begin to decline and what parts of our body are affected. While we all age differently, we all will age.

It is a fact that our mental and physical performance will diminish. That may happen to some in their sixties, while others may function perfectly into their eighties or nineties. Another fact of life is that 70 percent to 80 percent of aviation accidents are caused by people. It should not be a stretch to understand why, if humans cause most aircraft accidents and if aging results in declining capabilities, insurance companies are not keen to cover aging aviators. Especially those of us who fly without copilots, which is to say the GA pilots.

## The GA Insurance Industry

It is important to realize how the insurance industry operates. They expend considerable time and money analyzing what risks are involved and the statistical chance of an event or behavior occurring that will require them to pay out for a mishap. They must calculate the chance of something happening that will cost them money. The greater the risk involved and the higher the value of the plane, the higher the cost of being insured.

Insurance companies operate on the strategy of handling risk and the investment management of their income. Because they provide a service, their income is not subject to covering the cost of goods sold, just paying for operating expenses (agents, insurance experts, etc.) and any costs relative to an aircraft accident. So typically, the income is invested to earn interest until needed.

Consider that in the United States there are 286 million registered vehicles on our roads. That means a potential pool of 286 million vehicle insurance policies exists. Probably most of the money paid out by auto insurance companies is to repair vehicles. This also suggests that ample auto and truck parts must be available to fix the busted vehicles. With the millions of vehicle drivers and more than 20 thousand accidents every day, the auto insurance business is enormous.

With this amount of business, it becomes apparent that auto insurance is very competitive, resulting in lower insurance policy premiums. Also, with this amount of business, there is ample data to be examined to assess risk and payout costs more accurately.

The general aviation insurance industry, though, is a totally different animal. The pool of policyholders is considerably smaller because there are only about 205 thousand general aviation aircraft in the United States. While there are 1,500 insurance companies servicing automobiles, only 15 companies offer aircraft insurance. This means little competition, which results in fewer policy costs discounts.

Additionally, the state insurance regulators determine how insurance companies may operate within the state. Some insurance companies may find that the cost of compliance within a state, and the size of the potential pool of policyholders, is not worth the cost of doing business in the state. This drives the cost of aircraft insurance policies up while also making the policyholder eligibility requirements more stringent.

Let us examine the pool of older pilots to be insured. The general aviation pilot population is around 267 thousand men and women. Compare this to the 228 million licensed drivers in the United States. There are just under 47 thousand U.S. pilots between 70 and 79, with fewer than 11 thousand pilots aged 80 or older.

The bottom line is that the pool of older pilots is relatively small for insurance companies. Most older pilots own and operate single-engine aircraft, which account for 68 percent of all general aviation accidents. The federal or state government provides little oversight of general aviation or personal aircraft operations. And lastly, most aviation accidents are caused by the pilot. For pilots over 80, the risk is high and the pool of policyholders shallow.

## What Aviation Insurance Companies Need to Know

Insurance for aircraft includes coverage for the value of the plane itself, called hull coverage, coverage for any damage done to property, and personal injury. Policies have a variety of specific coverage such as other pilots, maximum coverage per seat, coverage in motion (taxiing), not in motion (parked or in hangar), in flight, and others. Another important aspect is the amount of the deductible. The greater the deductible, the cheaper the policy cost simply because the pilot is carrying more of the risk. Most of the policy cost goes to hull insurance, so some older pilots eliminate any hull coverage.

There are four primary factors for determining insurance premium costs for pilots. The aircraft being insured, the pilot owning and flying the plane, where the plane is located, and how the plane will be used. All become extremely essential for the aging aviator for obtaining aircraft insurance. Insurance providers will evaluate all aspects of the plane and pilot to determine the risk of each individual pilot. The higher the risk, the higher the premium cost, or the lower the chance of being insured.

## The Aircraft

The more complex your airplane, the harder it is to fly. The fewer of that model manufactured, the fewer spare parts around for repairs. The equipment in your instrument panel is also important because it aids in flying your plane. Both an autopilot with altitude hold and a GPS navigation system with a moving map reduce pilot workload. Even better is if it is IFR certified. Also, the number of seats factors into premium cost, because more seats mean more people in the plane. This increases injury costs in the event of an accident.

Insurance companies will see high performance, complex airplanes as requiring more focus, concentration, and skill to fly. And these are the human performance abilities that fade fastest. Some insurance companies will not insure pilots in their eighties unless they own and fly single-engine, four-seat, fixed-gear airplanes.

The airplane you own and its equipment compared with your experience and skills in the airplane help determine how risky you are as the pilot.

## The Pilot

Your entire life as a pilot is being evaluated. Your certificates and ratings attest to your skill level as a pilot. A private pilot certificate is acceptable, but the instrument rating is almost a given for older pilots. Why? Weather is responsible for many aircraft accidents, especially where poor visibility is involved. Competency in instrument flying can be crucial if encountering hazy weather conditions or very dark nights.

Currency is essential, so spend time with your favorite flight instructor. I would get an instrument proficiency check ride every six months, even if I were current through IFR flying. Every year I would also complete an FAA-sanctioned flight review (see FAA Advisory Circular 61.98D).

Several aircraft model organizations offer pilot proficiency safety programs, both classroom and flight training, with some lasting two to three days. The training is specific to your airplane. Attending a course such as this is viewed as a positive by insurance decision-makers.

The more sophisticated your training, the better. A couple hours a year with your favorite flight instructor is fine, but for older pilots, attendance at a factory type or an aircraft organization's extended annual training course is much better. Frequent simulator training is also greatly appreciated by aircraft insurance companies. Flying with your CFI a few hours a year is good, but spending the time and money to attend aircraft-specific safety classes, both classroom and in flight, shows how much you prioritize safety and assuring your skills as a safe pilot. You are a much better insurance risk.

Returning to flight training to obtain other certificates and ratings clearly indicates a propensity for becoming a better and safer pilot. Advanced specific training increases a pilot's skill set, resulting in both professional upgrades and enhancing one's performance. Both are appreciated by insurance companies.

How often you fly is also critical. Older pilots need to fly often. Less than 100 hours a year is not seen as sufficient. The more you fly, the longer you retain familiarity and proficiency with your plane. Today's glass panels can be so complex that without constant usage, instinctive responses get rusty. Fumbling to figure out how to program an approach can be costly, adding more anxiety to an already stressful situation. Your flying is best evenly spread throughout the year, not concentrated in late spring through early fall, with almost no flying in the winter months.

Another consideration is any FAA inquiries regarding incidents or other infractions. Any unfavorable actions by the FAA against you can be reason for insurers to refuse to insure you without obscene premiums or impractical obligations.

## Where Your Plane Is Located

Your home base becomes important and influences premium decisions. Parking your plane outside renders it susceptible to hailstone damage, high winds, or even theft. Being hangared eliminates this.

Your airport also may come into play. Being parked on a 2,500-foot dirt strip at eight thousand feet elevation increases the risk factor considerably, especially for a 2 p.m. departure in July or a night approach in January. The actual airport may also define risk. A well-maintained multi-runway airport offers more safety than a single, short runway in a poorly maintained airport. Does it have a tower, is it in the vicinity of a larger very busy airport, or is it home to corporate jets or hectic flight schools with aircraft coming and going 24 hours each day? Additionally, where the airport is also affects risk. Areas of our country with constant high winds, tornadoes, hurricanes, or long icy winters may make local flying more risky.

## What Flying You Do

This usually pertains to pleasure flights with less pressure versus business purposes. Business flying includes using your plane for traveling to business meetings or sales presentations or for visiting clients or customers—use that typically involves more pressure to make appointments and be on time—or commercial work such as flight instructing.

Also of interest is who flies with you. Most of my flights were just me and my wife. An owner-pilot mostly flying with a younger partner, likewise a pilot, could be seen as less risky than a pilot who always filled every seat with non-pilot friends who liked to take trips, or the business pilot who flies mostly solo, IFR at night returning home.

All these items apply to any pilot of any age. But, as we age, that by itself becomes a very discriminating factor in determining if we can still obtain aircraft insurance. While it is a fact that good, safe pilots in their mid-eighties find it very hard to remain insured, it can be done.

The cost of premiums will be higher, insurance coverage will be less than what you had years prior, and compromises must be made. But my pilot friends in their mid-eighties who still own planes they fly remain insured.

## Basic Aspects of Flying That Insurance Companies Pay Attention To

Aviation insurance companies prefer customers who are considered "seasoned pilots." These are pilots with experience, well-honed flying skills, considerable flight hours, and heavy involvement in aviation safety.

Pilots who belong to and are active in aviation organizations are preferred. If you hold a leadership position or teach safety seminars, this is better. Flying constantly year-round is desired. Currency training is a must—the more, especially related to your aircraft, the better.

The insurance companies look at numbers such as total flight hours, recent flight hours, years flying, training, pilot certificates, and ratings because the more you have, the better you look. If your flying record is clean, perfect. If not, beware. If over the past few years your annual hours have decreased, that can hurt you. Brokers indicate that those pilots changing insurance companies frequently to get lower premium costs or better deals may imperil their chances of renewal. Be careful about changing companies purely for cost reasons.

An active older pilot who has an impressive flight history, is instrument rated, belongs to and participates in aviation organizations, and still flies constantly will have a better chance of staying insured than the pilot whose annual hours are decreasing, is not actively involved in aviation organizations, and engages in no more training than the FAA-mandated biennial flight review, which is the minimum flight evaluation for a pilot.

## How to Continue to Be Insured in Your Eighties

First start your quest for insurance renewal early. Early means two to three months before your current policy expires. If issues such as your age arise, there should be time to resolve problems before your coverage terminates.

Second, work with your broker. An insurance broker represents you, the customer. The broker knows you, your background as a pilot, and your total involvement in aviation. The insurance agent represents the insurance company and prepares the insurance contract. The broker contacts insurance companies to locate the best coverage for you at the best price. The broker is the middleman between you and your insurance company.

When it comes to acquiring insurance for you and your plane, the broker becomes your best friend and confidant. Be honest with your broker. Neither you nor your broker wants a hidden issue to arise in the future and bite you. If your broker presents you with news that the insurance companies contacted are all saying no, don't blame the broker; they are just delivering the truth.

One friend, upon reaching 85, was notified that his insurance company would not renew the policy; he flew a complex, high-performance single. His broker then contacted other insurance companies. All said no. His broker, frustrated, explained to his client that he was not able to find insurance coverage for him.

Fortunately for my friend, he was deeply involved with general aviation, especially aviation safety, with 45 years as a pilot and no accidents or incidents. He began his own research regarding the aviation insurance industry. He watched an online video in which aviation insurance executives were describing how "good" their insurance companies were to "safe" pilots.

He identified one of the speakers, contacted her, and made his pitch. He explained his plight and how he was not a significant risk, despite his age. The insurance company and his broker worked out a policy that provided the coverage he wanted. He did not get hull coverage; he felt he could assume that risk himself. Other minor aspects were not covered, but he does have liability and medical coverage. He also agreed to take currency training and attend safety classes. But he was able to get insurance for another year.

Another company had also agreed to insure him provided that he met certain restrictive requirements, and the premium cost was appalling. One of the requirements was he could not fly and be covered without an experienced copilot. The cost to comply would be too high for him to afford and very impractical as often flights were only scheduled the day before.

This introduces the third requirement: compromise. As we age, we should change our flying habits to reduce stress and make our piloting requirements easier to manage. Some insurance companies will only offer insurance coverage if a pilot does this. One pilot, moving into his late eighties, owned and flew a high-performance complex single. His insurance company would not renew his policy. They did say that if he replaced his plane with a smaller, less powerful single-engine, fixed-gear plane, it would be covered. And that is what he did. He is not so happy flying lower and slower, but he can still fly and have his insurance protection.

Many older pilots will face this situation: pay exorbitant premiums, fly with a younger copilot, move to a less complex airplane, quit flying, or fly uninsured. Some will simply quit. Few will fly uninsured. Some who want to fly and be protected from potential financial disaster will downsize their aircraft. Those pilots who have excellent aviating pasts may be fortunate to be presented with options other than just abandoning flying.

## What Pilots over 80 Have Done to Remain Insured

Pilots in their sixties are not that concerned with aging and obtaining insurance. Those in their seventies are concerned about being able to acquire affordable coverage. Those in their eighties go from year to year and find the process of insuring their plane increasingly difficult and costly. Concessions are often required of the pilot.

I contacted several pilot friends in their mid-eighties to find out what they have done to remain insured. Their approaches to retaining their aircraft insurance are really nothing new. In fact, what they did is exactly what I did in my seventies to ensure that my coverage continued as I wanted and that the premium costs stayed affordable even after I suffered an accident that totaled my plane. When I expressed concern that being the pilot would be a black mark, especially for my insurance coverage, the NTSB investigator responded, "Anyone who reads this accident report will see that your training and flying skills did not total an airplane, instead you saved two lives."

Essentially what my friends did was to provide proof to the insurance companies that their entire flying careers have been devoted to sensible flying and promoting aviation safety.

These pilot friends are less of a risk than the average general aviation pilot because of their flight experience and their commitment to aviation safety.

They are experienced pilots with their total flight time exceeding six thousand hours, spread over more than 45 years of flying. Their certificates are either private or commercial, but all are instrument rated, flying high-performance, complex aircraft. This means that their level of training and experience is high.

The average age of their aircraft exceeds two decades, so the hull value of their aircraft is not that of a new one. Two factors become the exception between these pilots and most other general aviation pilots. These pilots are committed to aviation safety by either teaching safety courses and instructing or holding leadership positions in several state or national aviation and pilot organizations. Additionally, the training received every year is outstanding: online seminars, FAA WINGS seminars, teaching safety courses, airplane manufacturer organization owner training, and flight proficiency evaluations. These pilots are totally committed to aviation safety; they practice what they preach.

Another factor is that they fly only for personal reasons, using the BasicMed or a third-class medical. They fly year-round, averaging well over 100 hours a year to include IFR.

As one gets older, though, more can go wrong with your body without any signs or symptoms. Therefore, even the safest pilots enter a time in their lives when statistics rule against them, despite how good they are, mentally, physically, or aviation-wise. At that point in time, the risk becomes higher, and either insurance costs rise or coverage becomes impossible to acquire.

We are living longer. Defects that would kill us at age 60 a generation ago are now mitigated by medical science. Physical infirmities can be controlled today by medicines, operations, implants, or artificial components; thus, our lives can continue longer. In 1959 the FAA established age 60 as the upper limit for airline pilots. In 2007 the FAA increased the mandatory retirement age of airline pilots to 65. Moving into the mid–2020s, aviation advocates are suggesting the age be raised to 67. As we age, despite modern medicine, the risk of an undetected medical condition that incapacitates us rises to the point where an insurance company will not take on the risk.

At some point in our aviation lives, we must face the fact that the cost and/or risk of continued flying is too great and stop flying. Or consider other flight options. For that see Chapter 15.

## Medical Issues and Denial of Flying Privileges

### Medical Concerns

As pilots and aircraft owners age, most of us have no aviation fears greater than being told we will lose our insurance coverage or our medical. A professional pilot must fly under a Class II or I medical certificate (see Chapter 1 for a description of the various FAA medical exams pilots must pass). For the purposes of this section, I will be discussing the FAA medical requirements primarily as they pertain to pilots in their seventies and eighties or older, but the information should be of interest to pilots of all ages. After all, if we take care of ourselves and love flying, hopefully all will eventually become aging aviators.

I will focus on the nonprofessional pilot who is flying under a third-class medical certificate or BasicMed. But this section could also apply to older professional pilots such as a certified flight instructor with a Class II or I medical. Also, my focus will be on the older private pilot, flying a typical single-engine plane, not a recreational pilot or a sport pilot. The information regarding the FAA and medical requirements to fly are found in Code of Federal Regulations Title 14 Part 61, also known as FAR Part 61.

## The FAA Medical Exams Allow Us to Fly

To fly as a private pilot, one must possess a third-class medical certificate or qualify under the BasicMed program. Even so, to fly under Basic-Med, one must have had, in the past (after July 14, 2006), a third-class medical. For older pilots, some insurance companies may require a third-class medical certificate.

I did not become a pilot until I was 38. Being in the Army I was in excellent physical shape. I did not see a civilian FAA aviation medical examiner (AME) but instead was seen by my Army installation flight surgeon, an Army physician with special training in aviation medicine, who completed my FAA medical exams, being authorized by the FAA to do so.

As a younger pilot, I had no concerns about passing the FAA medical exams. At age 53 I was in a motorcycle accident that destroyed my left leg from above the knee to my pelvis. The initial operation tried to rebuild the femur and the hip but was not successful (the smashed bones died), so my leg became three inches shorter, and I could not walk unaided. For five months I was unable to fly. I had sold my plane a year before the accident and belonged to a local flying club.

On June 13, 1990, I received a check ride in a Cessna 172 by a CFI and was deemed okay to fly in spite of not being able to walk without crutches. Two months later, on three separate days, I spent 2.2 hours with a CFI obtaining refresher training, including 12 landings. Three weeks later, I spent one day and one night in the air for three hours becoming night current and passing an instrument check ride. I was back in the air again.

Now it was time for my 24-month third-class medical exam. While I could not walk, my eyes and ears were fine, the urinalysis passed, my heart was good, and in all areas I passed. But I still could not walk unaided. My left shoe had a three-inch lift, and I needed a cane to ambulate. I showed my logbook to my AME, who was also a pilot and aircraft owner. I had six entries signed by a CFI stating that I was competent for day and night flight and also instrument flying.

The AME studied my logbook, asked a few questions and said, "You have demonstrated to a flight instructor you are competent to fly a plane. You also qualify medically. The only problem is you need aids walking. But the FAA does not require you to walk to fly a plane." I received my third-class medical certificate.

Two years later, still walking with a cane, I had my medical renewed. One year later I had my left leg and hip completely rebuilt with the leg stretched again to regain the missing three inches. After a few weeks of rehab, I could once again walk unaided. Both feet touched the ground without any lifts. My next FAA medical was completed without question.

Bob exiting his Tiger, N1196L. After extensive surgery to replace his destroyed left hip and leg, he was able to fly again, but he walked with a cane (in his left hand).

## Disqualifying Medical Conditions

The FAA and its medical requirements, especially for the third-class or BasicMed, are not onerous if someone is in decent shape. If one has vision issues, glasses allow one to fly. Hearing problems? Hearing aids solve the problem. Medicine needed? The FAA has a list of prohibited meds in its *Guide for Aviation Medical Examiners*.

There are certain medical conditions that result in the denial of a medical certification, be it under a third-class certificate or BasicMed. Broadly speaking, they are cardiovascular conditions to include heart attacks (myocardial infarction), coronary heart disease, cardiac valve replacement, heart replacement, or having a cardiac pacemaker. In the United States heart disease is the leading cause of deaths.

Certain mental health conditions also prohibit pilots from flying. These include personality disorders, psychosis, bipolar disorder, and substance abuse or addiction. A Centers for Disease Control study (August 2020) found that over 40 percent of the U.S. population reported suffering from mental health or substance issues. Keep in mind this was during the Covid-19 pandemic. Most mental health issues are temporary and quickly resolved without disabling effects. Counseling and medication acceptable by the FAA can remedy more serious concerns. See Chapter 8.

I should point out that aviation, like every other career field and profession, faces the stigma regarding mental health issues, so pilots resist seeking support or professional help. Because of this, the aviation industry has a variety of means to address mental health issues.

Airlines such as American and Delta offer employees medical and mental health support programs. There are also peer pilot support groups. University flight training programs such as at the University of North Dakota and Embry-Riddle also offer mental health support for students by pilot peer counseling.

Some neurological conditions also disqualify pilots from flying. These include epilepsy, unknown consciousness disturbance, and unknown loss of control of nervous system functions. A major study released by *Lancet Neurology* showed that, in 2021, nearly one in three people suffered from some form of a neurological disorder. And there are more than 600 forms of neurological disorders.

Diabetes and insulin use may also be a disqualifier.

As has been pointed out in previous sections, the risk of having one of these medical conditions increases with age. While all are conditions terminating a pilot's authorization to fly, any denial of a medical certificate can be appealed. But here is where the slippery slope begins.

The appeal process must be done properly; it can involve lengthy medical procedures that are most likely expensive, and you can still lose. There are aviation medical clinics that specialize in preparing appeals and conducting the entire process. Most focus on restoring the medical certificates of professional pilots. These clinics can be located on the internet, and your AME may know one or an organization like the AOPA Pilot Protective Services may have information.

There are different ways to fly with disqualifying medical conditions. One is a waiver, and another is a SODA, or a Statement of Demonstrated Ability. A medical waiver is authorization from the FAA to exercise the privileges of a pilot despite a disqualifying medical condition.

A waiver or a special issuance is only a temporary approval to fly based on one's medical evaluation. A SODA is a permanent approval based on the condition being permanent such as loss of a limb or monocular vision, in which the pilot has shown they can safely pilot an aircraft despite the physical handicap.

Essentially, while the FAA is charged with ensuring to the public that aviators and flying are safe, it also is regulated to accept that there are health and medical exceptions. Therefore, regulatory procedures are in place to allow exceptions to the rule, if properly documented.

But, keep in mind, that an inactive or medically disqualified pilot can occupy a front seat in a friend's plane or that of a flight instructor, and physically manipulate the controls. However, time in the air for the former pilot cannot be logged.

## Your Health and Your AME

Many people have a primary care physician. Every pilot should have one. You do not want your AME to also be your primary doctor. Why? The AME is working for the FAA, not treating you as their patient. The job of the AME is to conduct a medical examination to determine your fitness to exercise the flying privileges you have earned. The AME has three options to pursue. The most likely outcome is to do the exam and issue your medical certificate to you.

The second option is a denial, which is rare. The AME may find a medical condition such that you are denied your airman's medical certificate. A denial may be appealed.

The third option is a deferral. This is a process in which the AME may have found a disqualifying condition that may be questionable. More information is needed, which may take time. The pilot may be able to fly until the current medical certificate expires; then the pilot becomes grounded until the matter is decided.

You never want to find that you have a disqualifying medical condition during your FAA medical examination. That is why you should have a different physician monitor your health, especially as you age. If any health issues arise, they can be addressed before your medical certificate expires. Having a denied medical causes a multitude of long-term problems if you want to continue flying. If you discover an FAA disqualifying medical condition while still possessing a valid medical certificate, other options are available.

For example, if you have a current medical certificate and have a heart attack, you are immediately grounded. So, you stop flying, but you have not been denied a medical certificate. Therefore, if you have a valid driver's license and your heart attack has been successfully treated, you should be able to fly under the FAA sport pilot rules (CFR Title 14 Part 61.23).

But herein lies the caveat. Regardless of what medical certificate a pilot possesses, or even being a pilot via a driver's license, the FAA mandates that any pilot must always self-assure that they are medically capable of flying and not violating any FAA regulation regarding one's health or medication ingested.

This means that any pilot, knowing they have or may have a disqualifying medical condition, should ground themselves until the condition is corrected. Even if you do not have a disqualifying condition but you know you are not safe in a plane in the sky, you are still required to ground yourself.

Some pilots do not do this. They hide medical conditions from their AME or refuse to accept that they are not safe. Their desire to continue flying outweighs their common sense. Medication that can make one sleepy or lose focus and concentration escapes their judgment. Fatigue and exhaustion are ignored, and high blood pressure is camouflaged with pills the pilot does not see as dangerous. All are conditions that require the pilot to remain on the ground, but the desire to fly overrides their wisdom. This condition can lead to accidents that could have been avoided if the pilot exercised acumen.

## Special Issuance

If you, as a pilot, are denied a medical certificate, or you develop a disqualifying medical condition, you can apply for a special issuance. It is essentially a "get-out-of-jail-free" card, allowing you to continue to fly, temporarily, despite a disqualifying medical condition.

The special issuance (SI) is a procedure that allows a pilot with a medical disqualification to pilot an aircraft. It can take time, it may require extensive medical testing, and it can be very expensive. To be successful it also requires the pilot and the assisting AME to fully understand the bureaucratic process of challenging the FAA. But this is a way the FAA agrees that some disqualifying medical issues have been contained where a pilot may not be a risk flying a plane.

At this point let me add my two cents. I have a Veterans Affairs disability rating of 220 percent due to Agent Orange and numerous combat injuries suffered in Vietnam. I have been on both sides of the appeal process. As a veteran I have appealed, more than once, to VA medical offices, and all appeals have been approved. As an Army medical clinician, I have served as part of an appeal board established to determine how disabled a soldier is.

In my experience with both military and federal government medical appeal issues, I believe that many boards are not looking for reasons to deny; instead, they look for solid, valid reasons to reverse a denial. Based on my knowledge, the key to receiving a SI depends on two factors. The first is whether there is ample medical documentation to show that your medical condition is at a point where you are not a medical risk as a pilot flying an aircraft. The second is how this documentation is presented. The FAA requires specific medical information to be presented in a specific manner.

Therefore, you need someone who represents you before the FAA to know, absolutely, what to do. Consider this fact: 90 percent of SI denials are based on insufficient medical information being presented to the FAA. Second and third re-appeal submissions tend to lose strength. Another FAA fact: of those appeals that provide all the proper medical documentation, almost 98 percent are approved. Make unequivocally certain that the first SI submission is complete, accurate, and complies with everything the FAA has requested.

Often disqualifying medical conditions slowly creep up on pilots as we age. In my acquaintance with older pilots, the two aging maladies most often encountered are cardio-related deficiencies such as hypertension (high blood pressure) and memory deficits including forgetfulness, difficulty concentrating, or loss of focus. But occasionally something can happen to someone suddenly. Small, innocuous instances that we ignore as unimportant, such as a slight cough or shortness of breath while sleeping, can be noted by significant others or our primary health care provider, who insist that they be examined more closely. Suddenly, even if we believe we are healthy and okay, we find we are at death's door and, unless some form of medical intervention takes place immediately, we will die.

This is exactly what happened to me.

## My Disqualifying Medical Condition

There are those who, like me, lose their freedom to fly suddenly. In my case, it was my heart. Two combat tours in Vietnam exposed me to Agent Orange, which has a propensity to damage soft tissue in the body in a variety of nasty ways. I was diagnosed at age 78 with ischemic heart disease, requiring immediate replacement of my aortic heart valve. The federal aviation regulations prohibit a pilot with a replaced heart valve from flying. If the pilot desires, after several months pass, they can undergo extensive (usually expensive and not covered by medical insurance) cardiac evaluations and, if passed, request a special issuance FAA medical certificate (FAR Part 67.104). When six months had passed, medical specialists who had experience helping pilots obtain their SI to fly again suggested that I apply for an SI.

One day in May 2015, a couple of weeks after my 78th birthday, I walked into my AME's office, filled out the requisite FAA forms for my third-class medical and waited to see the doctor. My name was called, and a technician performed some simple tests such as vision, hearing, and urinalysis. I don't wear glasses but have hearing aids. All tests were normal. Then the AME entered the office. We shook hands and engaged in "how have you been" banter for a couple of minutes (we were both pilots and pistol shooters), and then the exam began. He asked questions; he poked and prodded and listened to heart and lungs. He checked my file for previous visits and asked more questions. Consulting his list of what parts of me had to be evaluated, he concluded the examination and told me I had successfully completed my FAA medical and would receive my third-class medical certificate for another 24 months. Saying our goodbyes, I left, went to the front desk, signed more papers, handed over a check, and walked out with my medical certificate.

Normally I would undergo my personal annual physical exam before my FAA medical. This year, due to scheduling problems, it was not done until late June. My wife would sometimes attend my annual physical because often spouses note little things that can lead to serious things that the other spouse either forgets or ignores. During the question-and-answer period my wife mentioned my recent isolated but pesky coughing that bothered her. My health care provider noted that and ordered a chest X-ray.

The results of my physical were all normal, except the chest X-ray revealed an enlarged heart. A consultation with a cardiologist was scheduled. More appointments, more tests, and the realization that the heart was not functioning properly. A heart catheterization was conducted. This procedure inserts a catheter into the heart via arteries to help assess the condition of the heart.

My final diagnosis was that the aortic valve was not functioning properly, causing ischemic heart disease, or inadequate flow of blood due to blockage.

Normally this blockage would be due to plaque buildup in the blood vessels, not uncommon for elderly folks, but this was not the cause for me. It was my aortic valve that was damaged. The cardiologist noted, quite emphatically, that unless I had my aortic valve replaced immediately, the reduced blood flow could cause the heart muscles to die, leading to a fatal myocardial infarction (heart attack). He predicted that I would die in a few short weeks if the damage was not corrected. Understanding, we quickly arranged a visit to the Texas Heart Institute in Houston, Texas, some 800 miles away. The Texas Heart Institute at Baylor Saint Luke's Medical center is on the cutting edge of cardiovascular surgery and care. It was founded in 1962 by world-renowned heart surgeon Dr. Denton Cooley.

In Houston, more tests confirmed the original diagnosis. Unfortunately, the heart surgeon in Houston said, "You are too old for the procedure."

I replied, "So what am I to do? Go home and die?"

The surgeon thought and responded, "We can run more tests, and if all are okay to operate, we will."

I spent the next two days and nights being poked, prodded, pricked, and finally pronounced fit to receive a new, artificial aortic valve, scheduled for the morning of July 14, 2015.

The operation involved open-heart surgery where my heart was stopped for 20 minutes during the 2½-hour procedure. My heart now had a Trifecta tissue heart valve, serial number 15213625. Thirty days later, after a few weeks of intense rehab, I returned home.

Being an aviation journalist and familiar with the federal aviation regulations, I was aware that my heart valve replacement disqualified me from flying my plane, a Cessna 182, solo as PIC (pilot-in-command). FAR Part 67.311(d) requires the pilot holding a third-class medical certificate to have no history of cardiac valve replacement. And FAR Part 67.313 indicates that if I have a valve replacement, it renders me unable to safely perform my airman's duties as a pilot. Now what?

There are specific instructions to allow a pilot with a heart valve replacement to apply for a special issuance. First the pilot must wait for six months to pass before applying. The FAA will specify what testing must be completed to demonstrate the pilot can medically qualify to FAA standards with a new heart valve. The caveat here is the assumption that no new event has occurred.

I contacted the AOPA medical experts. I talked to pilot friends who had experienced cardiac problems and had received their SI and were back flying. I contacted a medical facility that specialized in guiding pilots through the SI process. We spent some time discussing the process, what I had to do, and their prediction that I could receive an SI. I was close to my 79th birthday and feeling fine. Several post-surgery examinations confirmed that the surgery had gone well. I was medically in great shape and no adverse side effects were noted.

While in Houston after the surgery, irregular heartbeats of atrial fibrillation (A-fib) were noted. A-fib is a condition where the electrical activity controlling the beating of the heart becomes erratic. Untreated it can increase the risk of dizziness, stroke, or a heart attack, causing death.

I underwent another nonsurgical procedure to correct the A-fib, and it appeared to work. But several months after returning home, irregular heartbeats were again perceived during cardiac exams. So, more medicine was prescribed. The A-fib had returned.

I discussed my latest problems with pilot friends who had also suffered cardiac issues and with aviation medical experts. Most agreed that the FAA would probably not authorize a special issuance due to (1) the heart valve replacement, (2) the A-fib, and (3) my age, regardless of how good the test results were. I now had three choices.

I could opt to apply for a SI, I could do nothing and not fly, or I could become a sport pilot and fly using my driver's license since I was never denied a medical certificate. I decided to do number three.

I did my research on light sport aircraft and located one for sale within the state. I flew in it and made an offer, which was accepted. It would be several weeks before the plane could be delivered.

Two weeks later, I woke up with my left leg paralyzed. I could not walk. A neurosurgeon diagnosed the cause as spinal stenosis, so back surgery was scheduled. In the meantime, I called the LSA owner, explained my situation, and stated that I couldn't buy his plane. He understood and even said he had another buyer who wanted the plane. The back surgery was successful, and I could walk again.

I considered my next move as a pilot. Ten weeks shy of my 80th birthday, I sold my 182. Between my open-heart surgery and the sale of my plane, seven months later, I added another 8.7 hours to my plane. During that time, I successfully completed an FAA flight review and an instrument flight proficiency check ride, although, due to my medical condition, the flight time could not be logged. Flight-wise I was a competent pilot; physically and legally I was a medically unqualified pilot. Such is life.

For 40 years I had occupied the left seat, mostly in one of my own planes. Ninety-eight percent of my flying had been cross-country flights, mostly with my wife in the right seat. Because of the weight limits of a light sport aircraft, any cross-country flights would have been limited to one-day trips as no luggage could be carried. I had a friend who had a cardiac-related medical issue, which was resolved, who owned an LSA. He would fly it cross-country, and his wife would drive to their destination to join him there. I did not see this as a viable compromise for my wife and me as we enjoyed traveling together in our plane or in our car.

Planes had been the way for my wife and I to travel together for business, fun, visiting friends and relatives, and new adventures. I could no longer do that. I realized that and accepted that that part of life was forever closed to us. Accepting that did not mean aviation was out of my life, though. I still write about it and share what I learned from 40 years in the sky with both seasoned pilots and students just beginning their lives in the air.

## Aging and Flying

As we grow older, our bodies tend to perform less than they used to. Being fit is a prerequisite for flying. Getting old diminishes that. At some point in life, we must admit that we are no longer young, no longer able to do what we once used to. At some point we must recognize that we are no longer physically capable of safely performing the duties required for flying an aircraft.

Certainly, we have options for flying, even with disqualifying medical conditions. But we must decide if the trouble and expense is worth it. Some may be allowed by the FAA to return to flying and be safe and competent pilots. Some may fail and never return to piloting again. Others, like me, may have that privilege abruptly snatched away and never sit in the left seat again alone in the sky.

Yes, I miss the opportunity to load up my plane and travel hundreds or thousands of miles away to enjoy new adventures or rekindle old ones. But I do not mourn. I enjoyed 40 years in the sky, over seven thousand hours in the left seat, owning and flying nine airplanes. Today, no longer a pilot, I am still a part of general aviation—an endeavor I love—as a writer.

## Fifteen

# Remaining a Safe and Proficient Pilot

### *What Does Research Say About the Performance of Older Pilots?*

I would guess the reluctance of insurance companies to insure pilots and their airplanes in their eighties is about age. Many pilots see age as a number rather than an absolute sign of unacceptable risk. Why? Ample research over the years reveals two facts: as pilots age, their performance does decline, but experience and currency may override or compensate for diminishing physical and cognitive performance in pilots. I am not going to cite the endless research studies that tend to show that older pilots who are experienced and continue to fly consistently are safe. I suggest you go to an internet search engine and type "performance of older pilots." This will bring locate numerous research reports and journal articles describing projects examining the performance abilities of older aviators.

Basically, these reports and articles document the declining cognitive performance of older pilots in the cockpit or in simulator settings. Yet these studies have found, time after time, that the ability to safely fly a plane remains. It seems that aviation-related skills gained over time and used frequently are retained in a process called crystallized intelligence, the preservation of task-specific knowledge.

Here is my explanation of how this works. It is the brain and memory of the pilot understanding what is happening based on extensive experience doing the same thing. Once I was on an IFR flight in my Cessna 182 into a small tower-controlled international airport in Mexico. While international airports must speak English, sometimes the controllers have difficulty with the language.

Approaching the airport, I received the landing information in English. But the approach controller setting me up for an ILS approach was not truly fluent in English. For example, he pronounced the word "roger" as "row-year." But, based on my stored knowledge accumulated over the years—my crystallized intelligence—I knew how to make the ILS approach, so I was able to anticipate his commands. Despite my failing to understand half his words, my experience in making the ILS landing allowed me to respond appropriately. I simply did what I had done hundreds of times previously, and all worked out fine.

Studies reveal that older, experienced pilots can perform safely, that age by itself is not a predictor of unsafe piloting abilities. Studies of age related to aircraft accidents show that accidents decrease as pilots age and gain experience. Then, as pilots begin to get older, accidents do increase. Does this suggest that older pilots are more at risk? It depends.

Most aircraft accidents are caused by human error. Older pilots with less experience and less flight currency are more prone to make mistakes as they get older. So, in these cases, yes, age is related to unsafe aviation practices. But experience and consistent recent flying can reduce pilot mistakes.

Bottom line: as pilots age, our performance skills do decrease. But our experience (and continued flight performance) can counter some deficiencies. Any specific age of an individual pilot is not an absolute indication of their failure to fly a plane. Age, by itself, is not an accurate means to judge how a pilot can perform. Here is what pilots can do to remain safe and proficient.

## As We Age, Stress Increases

Flying can be stressful. Often my wife and I would sit in our plane, parked on the ramp, waiting for clearer weather to depart. While departure would be legal, the ceilings and visibility would be so low that meteorological conditions would preclude a landing after departure if a problem occurred. So, we would wait. If we had planned a long, cross-country flight, our schedule would be compromised, requiring unwanted changes. This could become stressful. My wife and I accepted the weather. Nothing we could do about it, so why fret? It was better to remain safe than to be sorry. Stress reduced!

As we age, our endurance diminishes, and we tire more easily. Our reflexes relax, and our responses slow. Our focus and awareness fade. In short, our ability to sustain long flights, conduct night landings, or sustain challenging instrument flying lessens. Flying should be fun. As a pilot in my forties and fifties, long hours on extensive cross-country flights were easy—demanding, yes, but not dangerous or too difficult. But when we get older, our bodies can no longer sustain these long trips.

Stress is an unpleasant reaction when we are forced into doing things we don't want to or things we don't believe we can do successfully. Missing an appointment due to unexpected traffic makes us anxious. But facing unwanted weather delays with a definite time we must be home can create stress resulting in fatigue, headaches, or even sickness. As we age, the chance for this happening only increases unless we change our flying behavior.

As we add years to our life, we see changes in our endurance, strength, and flexibility, all of which are needed to fly a plane. Internally we encounter changes in our heart, lungs, and bladder, and the likelihood rises that we'll become afflicted by vision or hearing issues, cancer, heart conditions, dementia, arthritis, strokes, sleep disorders, and other aging-related afflictions.

If we are honest with ourselves, we should be able to note that our reaction times are slower, it can be harder to focus, our cockpit performance decreases, simple chores become difficult to accomplish, we are easily fatigued, and our plane wanders off course or altitude. Another aspect of aging is medications needed to function normally. There are several FARs that specifically refer to flying being prohibited if taking medications (see FARs 61.23, 61.53, or 91.17). Also, as we age, our bodies and minds are less able to withstand life's stresses, which we face every day.

So how can we recognize how aging may adversely impact what we do in the cockpit?

Do you forget checklist items? Is it harder to move your plane into or out of its hangar or to get in and out of a plane? Do you now have poor preflight, start-up, taxiing, or engine run-up procedures? Do you have problems concentrating on takeoff, climb, cruise, descent, or landing? Do you forget to retract flaps or gear? Do you encounter difficulties understanding or have a delayed response to ground, tower, approach, departure, or center instructions? Do you become frustrated or uneasy in high-intensity environments? Are controllers pointing out too many close calls? Are flight reviews or instrument proficiency check rides stressful to you? Do you have difficulty making "good" instrument approaches and landings?

There are two options for making flying less stressful as we grow older. One is to change how we fly, and the other is to change what we fly, that is to downsize our aircraft.

## *The Airplane*

Aviation is full of compromises. We want to buy a plane. Most of us must compromise between what we can afford and what we want. Perhaps it is a choice between departing today in harsh weather or waiting until tomorrow for clear skies. For others in their eighties it is to continue flying in a less complex plane or stay with your complex aircraft but fly uninsured.

Some pilots downsize because they are forced to remain insured. Others, like me, downsize to a less complex aircraft to make flying easier and less stressful.

In my late sixties I had a Mooney 231. It was fast but not easy to get in and out of with legs that have been busted up way too often. I wanted as much speed as possible with a plane that was roomier inside and much easier to enter and exit. My wife also encountered some difficulty climbing up over the wing and then twisting her body to lower herself into the seat. Exiting just reversed the taxing process. The 231 gave way to a retractable Cessna 182. Another problem arose. Full fuel tanks weighed almost 600 pounds, all over my head. The track at the bottom of the hangar doors had a lip, high enough so I could not push a full fuel plane into the hangar. A gasoline tug solved that problem.

For those who fly retractables, an old saw goes, "there are those who have and those who will," meaning that, if you fly a retractable-gear plane, sooner or later you will have a gear up landing. By my mid-seventies, I wanted less complexity, so bought a fixed-gear 182.

A single-engine, fixed-gear, two- to four-seat aircraft with a motor under 200 horsepower is viewed by insurance companies as safer than a high-performance, complex plane. There are two gains by downsizing airplanes. First is the workload in flying a less complex machine decreases considerably as well as maintenance costs. Second, insurance coverage becomes more available, and at a lower cost. Less workload flying results in less stress, yielding safer flights.

## The Pilot

Flying is an endeavor requiring that several intellectual, psychological, and physical tasks be accomplished individually and in tandem. Strength is required to remove a plane from its hangar, and the bigger the plane, the greater the strength needed. Mentally pilots must absorb, analyze, quantify, and act upon considerable information, often simultaneously. Pilots must deal with the stresses of harsh weather, aircraft malfunctions, time schedules, passenger issues, and personal difficulties. Any of these issues may create psychological concerns that interfere with safe flying.

Sadly, as we age, our strength, abilities, and skills tend to diminish. For some people this lessening may be slow over time while with others it is insidious and rapid, interfering with safe flying. Wise pilots recognize and accept these changes as we age. Others will ignore signs of fading capabilities and continue to fly regardless of the dangers involved.

As we discover that it takes more energy or agility or mental acuity to accomplish aviating responsibilities that were readily achieved 20 to 30 years ago, we become frustrated, worried, and stressed. All reasons for failure in the left seat.

Yesterday you could curl 35 pounds effortlessly, whip through a crossword puzzle in minutes, answer the phone, take notes, and use your computer, all at the same time. In the past, in severe IFR weather you could easily on final acknowledge a request to abort your present approach and switch to a different instrument approach to land. Your acute mental process accepted and understood immediately what had to be done and how to do it. Missed approach procedures were applied, radio frequencies changed, approach plates switched, and GPS reconfigured quickly and without undue concern.

Today, though, it's hard to curl 10 pounds, crossword puzzles require additional time to think about correct responses, and multitasking is impossible. Today you must take time to focus on what is required to achieve, and, if rushed, you become incredibly stressed. Confrontations arise when you have too many things to complete at the same time. In the cockpit, this is a recipe for disaster.

As we age and our abilities begin to fade, we need to recognize that this is causing more stress on flights so we should do things differently or with less challenges to reduce stress. And doing this is not that demanding if you desire to continue flying safely.

An uncomplicated way to reduce stress when flying is to alter flight plans. Into my sixties I could fly my 231 straight from my home in New Mexico to my parents' home in Connecticut, over two thousand miles in one day. Depending on the winds and refueling stops, this was a 12-to-15-hour trip.

As I grew older, I eliminated night flying, then cut back each day's flying to two easy legs, terminating no later than midafternoon. I did less "hard" IFR flying, willingly waiting for better weather. I would spend time flying locally, practicing the usage of all my instruments for instrument flights. Even if I only had one long cross-country in a month, I was still remarkably familiar with all the gadgets in my plane.

Since most of my flying was cross-country, I now began to plan my trips for the easiest flight, not the quickest. Instead of seeking the cheapest gas en route, which usually meant smaller uncontrolled airports, I preferred larger airports with control towers to assist me in landing, but not busy airports like Memphis or Phoenix-Mesa Gateway or airports with busy flight schools. Additionally, I would select airports with an ILS approach to make it easier to set up the best flight path for landing and then let the autopilot lock on and fly to touchdown. Now I would go around mountains rather than over or through them.

Some people thrive on sticky notes. These are notes to remind me of phone calls to make, bills needing to be paid, appointments not to be missed, even grocery lists.

The cockpit is just as important. Checklists specific to your airplane become your convenient sticky notes for the left seat. Some pilots use what is in their pilot operating handbook, others make their own; I preferred the plastic-covered checklists made by CheckMate. It lay readily accessible in the console between the front seats. While I believe my brain is good, I know I can't remember everything, so a checklist ensures that what I do in the plane is correct. Where is your checklist?

One of the best ways to stay proficient with your plane is to fly often. Practice in airports with towers, responding to the directions of controllers. Use your checklists all the time; do not depend on old habits or memory. Practice IFR flying and approaches and use all the navigation and communication equipment in your plane often. Fly with a CFI or friend to practice emergency procedures and IFR flying.

Everything I mention would go a long way to reduce or eliminate stressful flights. Another suggestion: AARP provides a defensive driving course called Smart Driver, also available online, which is not a skill-driving session but an in-class tutorial to make one a smarter driver. It exposes older drivers to threats and dangers, often never realized. Taking this course makes people very much aware of how aging negates what we may once have been able to do. I found that taking this class also made me a better pilot, mostly by increasing my awareness of functioning in the cockpit.

## The Flight

Why one flies has a lot to do with cutting back. For me, the plane was primarily for cross-country trips. In my forties to my sixties when most of my flights were business-related, my flight planning goal for most trips was to arrive at my destination as quickly as possible. Speed was of the essence, so that meant long legs, infrequent stops, IFR weather, and flying into the night. I was younger, stronger, and physically fit. And my aircraft were designed for fast flight, covering ground quickly.

Moving into my sixties I found that trivial things would cause more concern than they had a decade earlier. Anxiety could arise when flight planning long trips that would last after dark, or require hours in IFR weather, or require departures before the sun rose.

Cross-country flights would now be planned to avoid potentially stressful flights. Shorter legs, more frequent stops, and no night flying, although I would remain current by practicing at night at home. Flying through clouds, or light rain occasionally, was okay. But challenging IFR weather would be avoided. The goal was to make our cross-country trips easier, smoother, less of a challenge, where speed in getting there was no longer the goal. Often summer trips terminated in the early afternoon and we spent time relaxing in hotel swimming pools rather than slugging through heavy rains or dodging thunderstorms.

Avoiding stress is easy to do. Never go below one-third of a tank of fuel. Follow weather patterns a few days before a trip to understand what the weather is doing. Avoid very high-intensity airports and avoid very small rural airports with cheap fuel but without maintenance facilities necessary to repair a flat tire or replace a battery.

Consider carrying sectional and terminal charts as backup to your iPad. Most pilots have never experienced trouble with their electronic flight bag (EFB). Many carry backup electronic equipment as well as spare batteries/charging devices to supplement their iPads so paper charts become obsolete or redundant.

This is a personal decision. Equipment can fail, so having other options may be important to you. Practice with your EFB equipment before a trip to be very familiar with it. Before a trip check on FBOs, hotels, ground transportation, etc., to ensure that what may be needed is available.

In the air and on the ground, avoid situations that can become stressful. Do not be rushed, remain relaxed. All of the above can make flying easier and safer as you age. It is a matter of recognizing that in our sixties or seventies, we do not function as we did 20 to 40 years before. Be aware of how we perform now and do things to be safer and less stressful.

## *Being Safe and Proficient*

Older pilots and their passengers can remain safe and proficient by slowing down. Fly less complex aircraft, plan shorter trips, avoid flying in bad weather, trade a fast cross-country trip for a leisurely planned sojourn. Be prepared for weather delays and avoid stress-producing trips. Retain the joy of flying but in a more relaxed manner. Understand how aging has affected you, understand your limitations, and proceed accordingly. Make each trip enjoyable and relaxed, not a challenge.

This section presented several suggestions on what elderly people can do to reduce the negative effects of aging. It begs the question: if aging reduces the qualities pilots need to fly safely, are there things a pilot can do to remain a safe and proficient pilot while growing older? The answer is yes, and the next section will tell you how.

## *Ways to Mitigate Aging as a Pilot*

### Pilots and Aging

As we age the ability of our body to perform declines. Strength, mobility, flexibility lessen or become restricted. Not everyone ages at the same rate or even loses the same attributes or abilities. But eventually the aging process does affect everyone. Some may discern it in their fifties, while others don't notice getting older until they are in their seventies. We can't reverse the aging process, but there are many ways to slow it down, allowing us to fly safely longer.

Flying a plane requires two separate behaviors and skills. First are the skills needed to fly the plane. Second are the skills necessary to operate within the flying environment. Aging mostly affects the second set of skills. Why? Here are the needed skills: cognitive acuity; central processing speed; memory; physiologic and perceptive motor skills such as vision, hearing, and eye-hand coordination; and attention such as focus and concentration.

Aging may be offset by the individual pilot. The pilot's lifestyle, behaviors, physical condition, expertise, current experience, and attitude all relate to the ability to mitigate some of the reduced performance due to aging.

People can develop skills and behaviors over time to compensate for diminished capacity. These successful behaviors can become automatic and intuitive. This concept has a lot to do with the domain in which the person is performing in. In the pilot's case it is the cockpit. For example, a 30-year-old basketball player on a basketball court may encounter few problems outplaying a 60-year-old opponent because the demands of the domain (the basketball court) are physical, while the demands in the cockpit domain are mostly intellectual.

Piloting a plane can be complex and demanding. The aviator's performance depends on cognitive, psychomotor, and perceptual skills but also knowledge and judgment relative to the flight and the ability to perform in varying flight conditions.

Age by itself may not be a factor related to decision-making. But experience and ability to respond to stress is. Judgment and decision-making come from experience and the outcomes.

Consider that when U.S. Airways Captain Chesley Sullenberger III ran into a flock of geese after takeoff, the plane lost power in both engines. Decision time: find a place to land or attempt to return to LaGuardia.

Realizing he was too low to safely return to any airport, Sullenberger decided to put the plane down in the river, landing safely in the Hudson. He claimed that his success was due to his 42 years of experience, education, and training. He was 57 years old.

Good judgment comes from experience and outcomes. Positive outcomes are the result of a pilot's confidence in themselves. Generally, the older the pilot, the more experience. Younger pilots may lack flying hours. In aviation it is said, "Younger pilots use their youth and superior reflexes to get out of bad situations that older pilots avoid because of their superior experience."

## How to Slow the Aging Process

To be able to legally fly, a pilot must be current, having a flight review and having logged required flying time along with meeting physical or medical standards, that is, be in decent shape. What shape are you in? Statistically, you probably could use some help. Why?

Unfortunately, 42.4 percent of adults in America are obese. This could lead to heart disease, type 2 diabetes, stroke, or some forms of cancer, all of which could result in a medical disqualification to pilot a plane. Only 25 percent of American adults meet the Centers for Disease Control and Prevention (CDC) physical activity exercise guidelines, which recommend getting at least 150 minutes of moderate exercise each week.

The most prominent means of slowing aging is making lifestyle changes. This refers to increasing some daily activities while reducing others. Here is my list of lifestyle activities that medical science has determined have an impact on aging (see "The new truth about aging," *AARP Bulletin* 63, no. 5, June 2022).

To be honest, slowing the aging process must begin with truthful appraisal of yourself and a frank assessment of what you must do and what you must avoid. Thirty years of bad habits and unhealthy behaviors cannot be changed overnight. But starting at 50 or 60 may be better than not starting at all. Especially if you want to continue to fly.

## Lifestyle Activities Related to Slowing the Aging Process

| | |
|---|---|
| Exercise | Sleep |
| Nutrition | Reducing stress |

| | |
|---|---|
| Happiness | Health supplements |
| Socializing | Increase intellectual |
| Positive mindset | activities |

## Exercise

CDC recommends that each adult do 150 minutes of moderate cardio activity, such as brisk walking, a week and participate in muscle strengthening activity twice a week. The American College of Sports Medicine and the American Heart Association both recommend the following exercise regime.

Aerobics: 30 minutes a day, five times a week of moderate intensity aerobic (cardio) exercises each week.

Resistance: weightlifting or use of resistance bands to increase muscle strength at least twice a week.

Flexibility: stretching/twisting exercises for 10 minutes twice a week such as yoga, Pilates, or standing and sitting stretching.

Balance: exercises that maintain or improve balance such as standing on one leg and raising the other, heel-to-toe walking, rising and sitting without using hands, walking while raising the knees.

Of course, running, basketball, tennis, and other athletic activities do just as well. The point is that our sedentary lifestyles seldom involve vigorous behaviors; therefore, we must specifically include in our daily routine robust workouts to remain healthy.

## Nutrition

After my open-heart surgery, one of my nurses was educating me on proper eating habits and nutrition. Her recommendations were: if it comes in a package or can, don't consume it. If it grows on a tree or comes from the ground, eat it. While her advice is very rigid, her point is that fresh fruits and vegetables comprise a good diet.

I will not attempt to issue instructions on what to eat, but I will offer this. A person's body weight is controlled by calorie intake. If calories ingested exceed calories expended, we gain weight. If we consume fewer calories than we burn up, we lose weight. As we age, our level of activities naturally decreases. This suggests that if we don't want to gain weight, we either have to decrease what we eat or increase our level of activities or exercising.

Bottom line: eat healthy; eat in moderation; eat earlier in the day, not in the evening; and limit foods that are heavy in fats, sugar, and salt.

## Sleep

A pair of Brazilian professors conducted a 2019 study of pilot performance and sleep deprivation on a sample of Brazilian airline pilots ("Aspects of work and sleep associated with work ability in regular aviation pilots," *Revista de Saude Publica* 53, 2019).

What they found is that pilot performance flying airliners decreased with less sleep. Less sleep could be attributed to stress in and out of the cockpit. During this study, the researchers also found that those pilots who exercised less than 2.5 hours each week suffered most from lack of sleep. Those pilots who exercised over 2.5 hours per week reported less fatigue and better sleep, resulting in better pilot performance.

Is fatigue also a problem with general aviation pilots? According to the FAA, 70 to 80 percent of GA accidents are caused by pilots. Between 15 to 20 percent of fatal general aviation accidents are caused by fatigue. Most general aviation aircraft are flown by a single pilot, so there is no copilot to assume flying chores if the pilot succumbs to fatigue or stress. So, yes, fatigue is a hazard for general aviation.

Another aspect of fatigue may be distraction. Distraction is a loss of focus; the mind drifts away from what it should be attending to. Fatigue increases the probability of becoming distracted. Obviously one way to avoid being distracted is to be rested. Another way is to maintain a sterile cockpit, prohibiting nonessential activities during critical phases of flight. Use checklists; have a plan and follow it.

Older people do not require more sleep than younger adults. Sleep requirements vary by each individual but not by age. But because we are not as strong in our sixties and beyond as we were in our twenties and thirties, we may find it difficult to function with less rest. As we age, adequate sleep is important for peak performance.

## Reducing Stress

The need to be in top physical and mental condition and the stress of military pilots results in their reaching their peak performance in aeronautical abilities and skills in their early forties. Airline pilots fare better (less stressful than military) because they reach peak performance in their mid-fifties. General aviation pilots, those of us who fly smaller aircraft for our own use, have no defined peak age because there is no organization monitoring how we perform as pilots, although there are FAA physical exam requirements and periodic check rides.

Stress is a physical and emotional response to situations or conditions to which we do not react favorably. It happens when the person is challenged to respond but either does not have the ability or believes they cannot respond properly to the demands or pressures placed upon them. It can be a feeling of failure, anxiety, or physical reactions such as vomiting, crying, screaming, becoming paralyzed, or panicking.

The simple answer to avoid stress is to avoid situations leading to stress. For many that is almost impossible to do. If you are a first responder, a combat infantryman, a physician, or a farmer or rancher, your life is filled with stress, requiring decisions for situations totally out of your control. You must react to situations or demands placed upon you, not of your choosing.

My response has been that if something happens to me that I have no control over, I do not worry about it. I will do my best recognizing this and will accept the results regardless of how that impacts me. In many cases this means that you have confidence in your response. You lose your engine. That is stressful, right? You can mitigate the stress by focusing on landing the plane as safely as possible, or you can give in to the stress and crash.

Avoid placing yourself in stressful situations. Don't spend more money than you earn. Constantly train for emergencies in your plane so that if one arises, you know how to respond. Learn how to foresee possible stresses in your life and prepare yourself to deal with them. It boils down to three situations: avoid stressful situations or prepare yourself to deal with the situation or panic.

Flying while severely stressed is dangerous. Pilots can lose focus and concentration and become forgetful. Attention can sway from flying the plane to the stress itself, leading to unsafe conditions. There are some organizations that offer stress management training to pilots and student pilots to alleviate anxiety and enable them to better handle stressful situations.

Thorough flight planning can spot potential stressors, and constant emergency flight training prepares one for the worst. Recognizing harsh weather appearing during a planned trip and staying home avoids stress. There is an old saying among pilots: "It is better to be on the ground wishing you were in the sky than being in the sky wishing you were on the ground."

## Happiness, Socializing, Positive Mindset

Happiness usually is a part of how you respond to people and how they treat you. Happiness is how content you are with your life. Interacting with people positively is very important to one's mental health. Bitter people have few friends and are usually unhappy. Friendly people are sought out by others. Humans are social beings; we grow up in families and develop friendships in school and work. We seek out others with similar passions in life and create our own families. Successful people are typically happy.

As we age, though, life changes. We retire, we downsize. We may become empty nesters. Our parents die, our friends die, we may lose spouses. But death is what everyone is born for. For some it comes too early. For others, it arrives after a long and productive life. Life will move on, with or without us.

Two male friends and I, all in our eighties, lost our wives within a few months of each other. We miss our spouses very much. I will have a thought while writing and turn to tell my wife something only to realize that she is no longer by my side. I miss that. But the three of us recognize that becoming depressed, avoiding others, and becoming reclusive is not in our best interests. We must stay active, embrace other endeavors (two of us are writers and the other runs a workshop), and socialize daily, which we do.

A healthy lifestyle, socializing with others, staying active, and having a positive frame of mind all add to one's longevity. As we age, death of close others becomes more constant. A gap in our lives becomes real and hurts. One must accept this loss but focus on a different future rather than dwelling on what has vanished.

## Healthy Supplements

I am not a physician, so I cannot prescribe what supplemental vitamins one should ingest. For many people additional vitamins and minerals are not needed. But as we age our diet may change or the body's ability to absorb nutrients may alter, requiring additions to what we consume in our food. Or we may have health issues requiring specific amounts of vitamins or minerals not sufficiently provided in our diets. This question should be discussed with your physician and any recommendations then followed as prescribed. Ads in the back of our magazines may appear enticing, but professional advice may prove more effective.

## Increase Intellectual Activities

Our brains have been servicing us for many decades. As some get older, they may find it difficult to remember or hard to process daily problems. And as we age, others may note that these brain functions are declining even if we don't see it ourselves.

First may be memory and our forgetting things such as where we put a pen or a book or someone's name or where they live. Confusion may arise trying to figure how long to heat a cup of water for coffee. Or problems arise completing a newspaper crossword puzzle.

There are intellectual activities that can help the brain function over time. These include engaging the mind in meaningful activities requiring thinking, memory, and problem solving. If the mind is required to function, like your muscles, it may retain its ability to perform.

Something as simple as interacting with new people or visiting friends requires the brain to work. Asking questions, remembering responses, and providing answers necessitates brain function, stimulating performance. Learning new skills, doing puzzles, having conversations, reading, visiting new places, and playing board or card games all involve memory activities.

As a nonfiction writer I begin my books with outlines and use research such as the internet, books, magazines, documents, and records to expand the outline into chapter summaries. While writing the chapters I constantly must instill credibility by more research. I read one or two novels a week plus daily newspapers. I am an officer in two very active organizations and teach writing and business seminars. Additionally, I write articles on different subjects for magazines. In short, I keep my brain active and working very hard for me.

## Other Options to Keep Flying

### When Is It Time to Quit Flying?

It is a fact of life. Eventually every pilot quits flying. Some do it voluntarily while others are forced to abandon the cockpit. But before that time comes, consider some options that may be available to continue flying.

Some of my pilot friends quit because flying became too expensive. Military pilot friends provided numerous reasons why they quit. One said that flying general aviation aircraft just could not compare to his jet fighter, so when he retired, he stopped flying. Another Army friend quit upon retiring, saying that flying was too dangerous and he no longer had to fly. He had two combat tours in Vietnam as a helicopter pilot. Another friend, who retired as a colonel fighter pilot at 48, declared that he was too old to continue flying.

Most pilots I know who quit voluntarily report that the stress of obtaining weather, flying IFR or in congested areas, maintaining proficiency, staying current, worrying about insurance coverage, and remaining technically competent became more of a chore than the fun it used to be.

If a pilot lives for extensive cross-country trips, enjoys the challenges of hard IFR flights, and relishes the cockpit of their super-fast, retractable-gear pride and joy, lesser flying options may hold no appeal.

But for those pilots who find peace and comfort lazily boring holes in clear blue skies, there are options. These options may come with a price or compromise. Assume the pilot in question is at least a private pilot and flies with a third-class medical certificate or BasicMed. Further assume that the pilot has a valid state driver's license and is in danger of not qualifying to pass their next FAA medical exam. If the pilot has never been denied a medical certificate, there are ways to continue to fly.

The type of flying most likely will not replicate what the pilot is used to, but the passion for flight can continue. I had an acquaintance who was in at least his mid-eighties. He was short, skinny, frail, and weak. He loved aviation. Long, long ago, he was an Air Force fighter pilot. He owned a hangar that housed a small, high-wing light sport aircraft. Once he invited me to enjoy a short flight with him.

I met him at his hangar. Inside, everything was immaculate, everything perfect. Everything had its place, and all was properly located where it belonged. Removing the chocks, he maneuvered a tug before the front wheel, hooked his tug to his plane and slowly crept the plane out of the hangar onto the apron connected to the taxiway. This was no easy chore for the feeble man, but he managed it, not without difficulty.

Demonstrating the preflight to me, he appeared less delicate and more in charge. He opened the right door, explaining what I should do, then advised me on buckling up. Closing his hangar door, he slipped into the left seat, strapped himself in, and handed me a headset. Placing his own on, he began moving his hand and fingers around the instrument panel, touching switches, pulling or pushing knobs. The engine started. With the radio on, he explained what he would be doing. First, he listened to ATIS and then adjusted more knobs to set the altimeter and compass.

Speaking on the radio, he announced his movement to the active runway, held short to complete his run-up. More radio talk, and then, swinging onto the runway, pushing throttle forward, we began to roll down the runway, perfectly aligned with the white center line.

Throughout the time since he started the engine, his feet and hands moved comfortably around, head constantly swiveling from panel to wind screen, left and right. All motions were sharp, coordinated, and crisp. Into the air we went, then joining a left-hand pattern around the active runway. Two things were immediately apparent. My pilot was the consummate professional. His control of the aircraft and his radio procedures were perfect. Maybe on the ground he appeared as a frail old man, but in his plane he had total control over everything. Also noted was how cramped I was in his LSA. The cockpit was so small and tight that I could hardly move. Accustomed to the room in my 182, I felt so restricted I was very uncomfortable. I knew then that I could never feel relaxed flying this LSA.

## Fifteen. Remaining a Safe and Proficient Pilot

Thirty minutes later we landed, and he taxied to his hangar. Struggling with his tug, I helped him place his plane in his hangar. Thanking him for the experience, I wondered at his transformation from an older, fragile man into his former fighter pilot self. For him the LSA was perfect to allow him to be in total control of a plane once again. But just flying around the pea patch was not my cup of tea. My plane was my ticket to travel, to explore, to enjoy new adventures, and to share my flying passion with my wife. Alas, an LSA could never allow this to happen.

But for some older pilots, there may be alternatives to continue to fly that could be appealing.

### Flying Alternatives

There are alternatives to flying with a third-class medical in a typical single-engine, four-seat airplane. While you can still prowl around the sky without an FAA medical or BasicMed, there are compromises. There are limits to the weight of aircraft, which severely reduces the aircraft carrying capacity. There are also limits on the type of flying one can do, impacting IFR or night flying, as well as altitude and airspace restrictions.

Assuming the pilot considering alternate options to flying is at least a private pilot, the additional training will primarily involve learning how to safely fly the alternative aircraft. Keep in mind that exercising flight privileges depends on being medically qualified by FAA standards, even if flying via your state driver's license (see FAR 61.23, "Medical certificates: Requirement and duration"). If your medical certificate has been denied, revoked, or suspended, you may not be allowed to seek an alternative means of flying.

Alternate aircraft include ultralights; light sport aircraft; some smaller, older, U.S.-manufactured general aviation planes; gyroplanes; gliders; and balloons.

### Ultralights

To me an ultralight (FAR Part 103) is a hang glider with a passenger pod and small engine suspended from the bottom of its wings. In fact, some say that ultralights came about because hang glider users wanted powered flight back in the 1970s and '80s. An ultralight is probably the smallest powered flight vehicle available.

An ultralight is not required to be registered as an aircraft with the FAA. Legally it requires no certification or training to fly one, but training is strongly recommended. And there are limitations: one has to weigh under 254 pounds, carry no more than five gallons of fuel, and fly under 64 miles per hour. Also, it must be flown solo; there is only a single seat. It is a

**Bob, ready to take a flight in a tandem ultralight in Alaska.**

day-only, VFR-only vehicle and restricted to unpopulated areas and uncontrolled airspace. An ultralight is very affordable and an easy way for a private pilot to continue to spend time in the air. Because of its slow landing speed and short stopping distance it doesn't require much space to land.

Ultralight pilots describe flying in one as going back to the days of World War I planes with open cockpits. Others describe them as motorcycles in the sky. While they are designed and controlled by regulations for recreational or sport flying, they are used for more than that. Many pilots use them for trips but only in daylight and clear weather. Some see their ultralights as the perfect camping companion, sleeping under the wing in the wilderness.

I have flown in a two-seat ultralight trainer, although it had two seats and was registered as a light sport aircraft. It was different, as I was hanging in the air only by metal tubing, a seat, and straps. My regular plane was like a high-speed automobile in the sky. For me, an ultralight was not practical. But for aficionados of true flight, nothing beats flying an ultralight.

Ultralights come in several forms. There is the typical ultralight: wings, a tail, a structure to sit in, and an engine. Other forms include a powered parachute; an amphibian; or a trike, which is a powered hang glider in which the pilot uses their weight/strength to manipulate the shape of the wing to maneuver the aircraft.

## Light Sport Aircraft

The FAA, in FAR Part 1.1 ("General definitions"), describes a light sport aircraft (LSA) as an aircraft, not a helicopter or powered-lift, that must meet a long list of specifications. This list includes a takeoff maximum weight of 1,320 pounds for land or 1,430 for water operations, no more than two seats, and a maximum speed of 120 knots. These aircraft can be flown with a sport pilot certificate (no FAA medical). Currently there are more than 200 makes and models of LSAs available in the United States.

There are limitations for both the sport pilot certificate and the LSA. These include for the pilot: no night flying, VFR only, and airspace and altitude restrictions. For the plane there are speed and weight restrictions. Essentially, flying is restricted to nice days, and long trips for two adults are not practical. After all, the FAA still sees the average U.S. male weighing 175 pounds while they actually weigh almost 200 pounds. Putting two normal guys in the seats can easily overload the plane.

Newly made LSAs come with the latest in glass cockpits and fly as smoothly as any of the larger aircraft we are used to. And they are expensive. For a single pilot who enjoys low and slow in clear weather, an LSA can allow traveling in style. With a private pilot certificate, an instrument rating, and a suitably equipped LSA, the pilot restrictions would no longer apply, so night and IFR flight could be accomplished.

Certain U.S.-manufactured aircraft, mostly from the 1940s and '50s, such as some models of Aeronca, Ercoupe, Interstate, Luscombe, Piper, Porterfield, and Taylorcraft, also qualify under FAA regulations as LSAs.

Essentially, a new LSA looks like and flies like a plane we have flown in for much of our lives. It just flies lower, slower, and only in daytime and nice weather. It can be flown without an FAA medical, but one must possess a valid state driver's license.

## Gyroplane

Gyroplanes are described in FAR Part 1.1 as rotorcraft (i.e., helicopters) with unpowered rotor blades. I describe it as looking like a helicopter but flying like a plane. It needs a short strip to take off (maybe 300 to 500 feet) and less to land (100 feet). The gyroplane uses its engine and a propeller for thrust and the unpowered rotor (as air passes under it) for lift. Sort of unconventional to say the least. The FAA considers a gyroplane a rotorcraft that depends on its rotors' lift for support during flight. Other names are gyrocopter and autogyro.

A gyroplane may be flown with a sport pilot certificate and under light sport aircraft rules, if the aircraft meets LSA requirements. Originally gyroplanes were sold only as kits, so they came under experimental aircraft regulations. The gyroplane is in the FAA category as a rotorcraft and gyroplane class.

Gyroplane flying can be expensive. Some are available as U.S.-produced,

FAA-certified gyroplanes, but most for sale are experimental aircraft. One can purchase a new kit and, maybe in 300 hours, build a minimal gyroplane. Usually the aircraft kit is sold without an engine, which is purchased separately. Used ones—again, mostly experimental—are available. A person with a fixed-wing sport or private pilot certificate can obtain the gyroplane training in around 30 hours and receive a gyroplane endorsement. As a sport pilot, one can fly without an FAA medical.

## Gliders

Gliders (sailplanes) are fixed-wing aircraft without engines, although some do have small motors. Gliders use the dynamics of the air to maintain lift. Some gliders use small engines to take off, but most are towed by another plane and, when airborne, detach themselves from the lift plane. Some gliders may use a cable attached to a winch on a truck to pull the plane to create lift. Gliding is also called soaring.

Gliders are constructed for maximum aerodynamic efficiency out of very light materials. Other forms of gliders are hang gliders, rigid frames covered with fabric and launched by the pilot's legs, running. Another is a paraglider, in which the pilot sits in a harness seat under a fabric wing (just like a parachute) and departs by running (or being pulled by a vehicle or even a small boat). For our purposes I will discuss only the fixed-wing glider.

In the United States, gliders are considered light sport aircraft and therefore can be flown using a sport pilot certificate. A pilot must hold at least a recreational pilot certificate, never have had a medical certificate denied (or revoked or suspended), not have any disqualifying medical conditions, and obtain the glider flying instructions.

To add a glider rating to a powered aircraft pilot certificate, one needs glider training, 40 hours of pilot-in-command time in an airplane, three hours of glider flight time, 10 glider solo flights, and to pass the FAA glider flight exam with an examiner; no written exam is required. A medical is not required. Glider students may begin training at age 14 and fly solo but must be 16 to be certified.

Because soaring requires rising air for lift and air currents for lateral travel, glider training and lift aircraft are not located at most airports. One should seek out glider training and soaring centers on the internet. The organization Soaring Society of America (www.ssa.org) is an excellent place to start learning about glider training.

## Hot-Air Balloons

Hot-air balloons are the oldest form of aviation, being over 200 years old. In concept they are rather simple, consisting of three main components. The uniqueness of balloons is that they depend on heated air inside the balloon for rise and descent. Lateral movement is dependent on wind currents. Experienced pilots use their wisdom and the vertical movement of the balloon to locate favorable winds for distance travel.

The balloon consists of a large, fabric (usually nylon) covered, inverted teardrop envelope to hold hot air. Attached to the balloon by metal cables is a basket or gondola to carry passengers. The basket is comprised of a steel frame, covered by wicker. The air is heated by bottled liquid propane-fueled burners. The heated air, being less dense than the ambient air, fills the envelope, which then rises.

Hot-air balloons come in two types. The Montgolfier is a pure hot-air vehicle invented by two brothers in the late 1700s. The second type is a hybrid that has a compartment holding helium or hydrogen to assist in lift. The hybrid is usually used in competition where distance is the goal. Having lift assistance saves on propane.

Hot-air ballooning is for competition and recreation only, as a slow and lazy way to enjoy a sightseeing trip across the countryside. Since balloons are dependent on winds aloft for their course of travel, one does not know exactly where they will end up. Therefore, a ground crew has to follow the balloon and arrive at the landing site to pick up the passengers and recover the balloon.

As with the glider, a private pilot who is professionally trained and has never had a third-class medical denied, revoked, or suspended can pilot a hot-air balloon using a sport pilot certificate and a valid state driver's license (no FAA medical). As with any FAA pilot certificate, the pilot must be free of any disqualifying or incapacitating medical condition.

## *Additional Comments*

All of the aerial vehicles described above require specific training and maintenance. Most airports probably do not provide all that is needed to be trained and have the properly qualified service facilities available. Being trained in and owning an LSA means that repair personnel must be available where you are based or nearby.

I strongly recommend that a pilot wanting to pursue an alternate form of flying take the time to research the topic. Begin with the internet to become familiar with the form of flying. Understand all the FAA rules and regulations pertaining to the certificate you will need for the flying you want to pursue. Ensure that you understand and can comply with the medical requirements necessitated by the FARs.

Contact other pilots currently flying what you are considering and see whether they can provide a demonstration ride. Contact CFIs or flight schools that provide the training you need.

Consider the costs and, to be safe, estimate the maximum training time needed, not only the minimum.

Lastly, contact local, regional, and national flight organizations devoted to the sport flying you are interested in. You can locate these organizations on the internet and at the end of this book. Excellent information can also be obtained from manufacturers and sales vendors for the aerial vehicle you are interested in.

Above all, do your research. Understand what you want to do and make sure you can legally fly the alternate aircraft. Understand the maintenance requirements and know where that maintenance can be done. Having a close-by CFI can keep you safe. The FAA reports that problems arise because a pilot misinterpreted the FARs regarding what a sport pilot can do or what constitutes an LSA. Do not be one of these. Know as much as possible before committing. But one of these alternatives to what you are accustomed to may allow you to continue to fly safely.

# Epilogue

## My Aviation Life After Open-Heart Surgery

### What I Miss and Do Not Miss About Flying

At age 38, I learned to fly. My job required travel, and pilot friends suggested that I learn to fly since often it was quicker and easier than relying on airlines. I did, occupying the left seat for 40 years and over seven thousand hours. During that time, I owned nine planes, flew in 49 states (I missed Hawaii), visited three foreign countries, and flew as far south as Mexico and the Caribbean and north of the Arctic Circle. Due to adventures as a soldier (combat wound and injuries), my flying days terminated.

Asked if I miss flying, the simple answer is no, but the reality is much more complex. I miss certain aspects of flying, yes, but others not so much.

Because I am still involved in aviation, I am around pilots and their aircraft. And this reminds me of what I miss and what I do not. Part of understanding my thinking is to realize that my life has, if anything, never been consistent. In fact, the only constant in my life has been my wife, Anita. We were together as a team for 64 years, married for 62.

As I enter my ninth decade on this planet, I have changed careers many times, never looking back, never harboring any regrets, and always focusing on the present and the future.

So, when I decided that not flying was best for me, it was not with regrets. I had a flying career few others have achieved. Being able to fly your own plane, anywhere, whenever you wanted was great, and that is a main reason why I loved to fly. There are some aspects of flying that will not be missed. Most of my flying involved long, cross-country flights, many of these in IFR weather.

Probably atop the not-missed list is the anxiety of flying in very bad weather. As an experienced IFR pilot, I had the best equipment possible for instrument flight. Yet, launching into rain or dark clouds or knowing that an instrument approach into an unknown airport awaited me at the end of the day required me to be at my best for prolonged periods of time. While I had confidence in my ability to handle intense weather situations, the element of "what if" was always there. Anyone who has flown in "hard" IFR conditions knows what I am referring to.

Being on a long, cross-country trip and arriving at the airport in harsh weather or loading the plane in rain or fog so thick that the FBO, 30 feet away, is a blur makes one have second thoughts about flying. Often takeoff would be delayed until the weather improved (my rule was: never depart from an airport in which the weather would not allow landing).

With all the IFR flying I have done, this aspect of flying occurred often, and I do not miss it at all. But what I miss the most is what flying was all about.

Despite what I said about IFR weather, being instrument rated did allow completion of trips impossible for VFR-only pilots. Living in San Antonio, Texas, sometimes low layers of clouds would cover the city, requiring an IFR clearance to depart. Typically, within 40 or so miles, the cloud deck (usually only a couple of thousand feet thick) would dissipate. After having a few flights canceled due to this weather, I started my IFR training. Receiving this rating allowed me to complete my flights. I could now fly anywhere in the world my plane could go.

My plane was my magic flying carpet. It allowed my wife and me to experience our country, as no other form of transportation could. Once we were in San Francisco, attending a conference. The conference wrapped up on a Friday, but I wasn't due back at work until Monday. In the local paper was an ad promoting Frank Sinatra Saturday evening at Caesars Palace in Las Vegas. I booked a room at Caesars as well as tickets to Sinatra's show. We flew to Vegas on Friday, attended the concert, and were home on Sunday. Using my plane made this a simple arrangement.

Another time we were heading home to New Mexico from the east somewhere. Our line of flight, in perfect VFR summer weather, had us crossing the Mississippi River around western Kentucky. We were flying our new American General Tiger, which had a sliding canopy. We discussed the idea of sliding the canopy back, dropping down to 500 feet AGL and following the river to Baton Rouge (the 500-foot floor was to remain above any power lines, etc., which seemed to cross the river often). We enjoyed an aerial trip down the river seeing sights few people could ever see. Only a GA aircraft would allow this.

I could relate more than a thousand flights where my aerial magic carpet allowed us to enjoy trips only possible in a small plane. The only advantage to larger and faster planes is that they arrive quicker, but they do so at a cost of missing the beauty and grandeur of seeing our country from above but up close.

This is what I miss most, being able to start in the morning and, by afternoon, be almost a thousand miles away (which covers about half the United States from our home). This is why I learned to fly and what I miss most. The ability to get far away, quickly, easily, and without the stress and hassle of the airlines or two days driving.

# List of Aviation Organizations

More information about each organization may be found by conducting an internet search. I believe all have websites, but some websites may not be active. This list is not a final authority on all the aviation organizations or associations available to pilots, but what I have found from a variety of sources. Because many organizations depend heavily on volunteers, some of these listed may no longer be viable. This list was compiled in 2023. A Google search by the reader may discover an aviation organization other than those listed here. Some of these organizations have foundations or scholarship funds to support aviation education and training. Some known aviation organizations are not on this list simply because they are a subpart of an organization already on this list.

Air Care Alliance (has a list of volunteer pilot organizations that transport people, pets, supplies, disaster relief materials, etc.)
Air Line Pilots Association, International
Air Transport Association
Aircraft Owners and Pilots Association
American Aviation Historical Society
American Helicopter Society International
American Institute of Aeronautics and Astronautics
Antique Airplane Association
Association for Unmanned Vehicle Systems International
Black Pilots of America
Civil Air Patrol
Commemorative Air Force
Experimental Aircraft Association
Helicopter Association International
International Air Transport Association
International Miniature Aerobatic Club
International Society of Women Airline Pilots

## List of Aviation Organizations

LeRoy W. Homer Jr. Foundation
National Aeronautic Association
National Air Transportation Association
National Association of Flight Instructors
National Business Aviation Association
National Center of Excellence for Aviation Operators
National Congress on Aviation and Space Education
National Intercollegiate Flying Association
NGPA (world's largest organization of LGBTQ pilots)
New Mexico Pilots Association
Ninety-Nines
Old Bold Pilots Association
Organization of Black Aerospace Professionals
Quiet Birdmen
Recreational Aviation Foundation
Seaplane Pilots Association
Sisters of the Skies
University Aviation Association
U.S. Army Black Aviation Association
U.S. Pilots Association
U.S. Powered Paragliding Association
U.S. Ultralight Association
Whirly-Girls
Women in Aviation International

# Index

accidents *see* FAA/NTSB investigations, accidents; off-airport landings
advanced aviation training devices (AATD) *see* flight simulators
*Aeronautical Information Manual* (AIM) 7, 14, 131, 134, 143
aging pilot: flying tips 219, 220–223; insurance 197–204, 219; medical concerns 205–214; process 193–197, 205, 214, 216–220, 223–224; slowing the process 224–229; time to quit 205, 214, 229
Air Defense Identification Zone (ADIZ) 14–15, 131–135, 143
Aircraft Owners and Pilots Association (AOPA) 40–*42*, 45, 56, 59, 80, 86, 100, 106, 111–112, 114, 117, 185–186, 189, 208, 213
airline transport pilot (ATP) *see* certificate, commercial pilot
airplane: annual inspection 54, 63, 67–68, 105, 107; engine rebuild 52, 65–66, 68–69; maintenance 54–55, 57, 62–63, 65–68, 93, 107, 110, 219, 222, 236; modifications 63, 65–66, 70–71
airports 6, 13–17, 20, 55, 64–65, 169, 170, 191, 195, 201, 216, 220–222
airspace 6, 14–16, 23, 67, 82, 159, 183–185, 231, 232, 23
American General Tiger (1992/N1196L) 31, 54, 63, 81–*82*, *83*–84, 117, *190*, *207*, 238
Association of Aviation Psychologists *121*–122
associations *see* organizations and associations
aviation industry 5–6, 17–18, 113, 119
aviation medical examiner (AME) 125, 206, 208–211
aviation publications 113–115; *see also* magazines, general aviation

Bahamas, flying in the 81, 88, 185, 187, 190–191
balloons, hot-air *see* hot-air balloons
basic aviation training devices (BATD) *see* flight simulators
*Basic Survival Skills for Aviation* 171
buying an airplane: basic considerations 51–53; cost considerations 52–56, 59; financing 54, 59; pre-buy inspection 48, 58–60, 75, 79, 90; searching for 55–57; steps 53–60

Canada, flying in 49, 72, 88, 147–148, 169–170, 183, 185, 187–*188*, 189–*190*, 191
certificate: commercial pilot 9, 28–29, 31, 33 (*see also* commercial aviation pilot; flight training, civilian); private pilot 8–9, 10, 27, 31, 233, 234 (*see also* flight training, civilian); recreational pilot 20, 205, 232–234; sport pilot 8, 149, 205, 232–234
Certified Flight Instructor (CFI) 6, 9, 13, 20–23, 27, 28, 33–35, 57, 78, 92, 146–148, 158, 161, 200, 205–206, 221, 236
Certified Flight Instructor Instruments (CFII) 29–31, 75, 90, 154, 158
Cessna 172 (1965/N8233U) 29, *47*, 48–50, 62, *72*–*73*, 74, 96, 147, 153, 171–*172*
Cessna 182 (1971/N9277G) 62, 64, 90–91, 213
Cessna 182 (1979/N96551) 62, 64, 74–*75*, 216
Cessna 182 RG (1981/N4696T) 56, 62, 64, *87*–*88*, 89, 135–137, 219
Cessna Pilots Association (CPA) 88, 91
Civil Air Patrol (CAP) 94–95, *96*–*97*, 98–100, 144, 165
*Code of Federal Regulations* (CFR) 139; CFR Title 14 6–7, 112, 152, 205, 209; CFR Title 49 126, 138
cognitive decline *see* aging pilot, process

243

# Index

Commemorative Air Force (CAF) 177–179, 182
commercial aviation pilot 3, 5, 9, 12, 17, 20–21, 124, 149, 193, 226; *see also* certificate, commercial pilot
crash landings *see* off-airport landings

emergency landings 143, 161–162; *see also* off-airport landings; surviving a nontraditional/emergency landing
emergency locator transmitter (ELT) 67, 131, 164, 166
endorsements *see* ratings/endorsements and certifications
engine failure 160–161; *see also* emergency landings
examination, physical *see* medical exams and certificates
Experimental Aircraft Association (EAA) 40, 114

FAA (Federal Aviation Administration) Advisory Circulars and publications 13, 57, 59, 66, 101, 112, 141, 184, 200
FAA aviation safety inspector (maintenance) 48, 67, 68
FAA flight examiner 8, 9, 28–30, 234
FAA investigations, incident 3, 7, 126, 127, 131–135, 137–138, 140–144
FAA investigator 129–130, 138–140
FAA/NTSB investigations, accidents 3, 56, 126, *127*–129, *130*–131, 135–138, 141–144, 161
FAR (*Federal Aviation Regulations*) 6–7, 94, 126, 131–132, 134–135, 138, 141–143, 235–236; *see also* individual FAR Parts (i.e. *FAR Part xxx*)
*FAR Part 1* 232–233
*FAR Part 42* 74
*FAR Part 43* 66–67, 69
*FAR Part 61* 8–9, 20, 23, 25, 33, 101, 151, 205, 218, 231
*FAR Part 67* 211, 213
*FAR Part 71* 14–15
*FAR Part 91* 13, 110, 134–135, 141, 147, 152, 168, 170, 218
*FAR Part 99* 135
*FAR Part 103* 231
*FAR Part 107* 8
*FAR Part 141* 20–21, 25–26, 33
firearms 169–170, 187
flight simulators 24–*25*, 26–27, 34, 150, 154–155, 158, 200, 216
flight training device (FTD) *see* flight simulators
flight training: civilian 6, 8–9, 19–28 (*see also* certificate, private pilot; certificate, commercial pilot; Part 141 pilot school); military 19–20
flying alternatives 231–234
flying as a business expense *see* ownership, as business expense
flying, physical examinations *see* medical exams and certificates
flying with family 34–35, *36–37*, 38, *172*, *190*

general aviation (GA) 3, 5–18, 40–46, 122, 198–199
General Aviation Manufacturers Association 62
*General Aviation News* (GAN) 44, 100, 104, 108, 114, 117, 177
gliders 231, 234; training 150–151, 161, 234
Green Sheet *see General Aviation News*
ground school 6, 8–9, 22, 24, 154
Grumman Tiger (1979/N4515U) 31, *79–80*, 81
gyroplane 233–234

hang gliders *see* ultralights
health: mental 119, 121, 123–125, 195, 207–208, 227; physical 118, 165, 193–194, 216–217, 223–229
hot-air balloons 234

incidents *see* FAA investigations, incident
instrument flight proficiency check ride 92, 140, 149, 154, 158, 200, 206, 214, 218
IFR (instrument flight rules): equipment 29, 49–50, 56–57, 63, 67, 70, 75, 79–80, 85–86, 88–89, 158, 199, 237; flying 13, 18, 29–30, 32–33, 53, 55, 67, 74, 76, 79–82, 86, 89, 90, 98, 105, 128, 132, 134, 139, 157–159, 167, 187, 189, 200–201, 204, 206, 216–217, 220–222, 229, 231, 233, 237–238; publications 92, 94–95, 101, 112 (*see also* ownership, IRS and taxes)
instrument rating/endorsement 9, 10, 28–31, 32–33, 49, 184, 187, 200, 202, 204, 233, 238
insurance *see* ownership, insurance

leasing an airplane *see* ownership, leasing vs.
legal services, AOPA 45–46, 60, 106, 133–135, 140, 142–144
license *see* certificate, commercial pilot; certificate, private pilot
light sport aircraft (LSA) 5, 10, 20, 55, 187, 213–214, 230–236

magazines, general aviation: *Midwest Flyer* 114–115; *Plane and Pilot* 100, 114; *Private Pilot* 80, 100; *see also* General Aviation News
medical exams and certificates 8–9, 43, 124–125, 149, 184, 193, 195, 204–209, 210–211, 213, 226, 231, 233–235
Mexico, flying in 148, 183, 185, 216
Mooney Aircraft Pilots Association (MAPA) 84–85, 154
Mooney 201 (1979/N4538H) **84**–85, ***127***, **128**–***130***, 131
Mooney 231 (1979/N231HB) 70, 85–**86**, **87**–88, 153, ***188***, 219
Mooney 231 (1982/N1159G) 70, 74–75, **76**–77, 84, 87–89, 153, 158

National Transportation Safety Board (NTSB) 12, 122, 126–127, 129–131, 137–139, 141–142, 151, 157, 161, 204
New Mexico Pilots Association (NMPA) 45, 114, 148
nontraditional landings *see* off-airport landings

occurrence *see* FAA investigations, incident
off-airport landings 2, 85, ***127***–131, 135–137, 144, 156–161, 164; *see also* emergency landings; surviving a nontraditional/emergency landing
older pilots *see* aging pilot
organizations and associations 2, 21, 39–46, 51, 55, 58, 63, 94, 111, 114, 117, 152, 154, 200, 202, 204, 208, 227, 229, 236, 241–242; *see also* individual associations and organizations (e.g. Aircraft Owners and Pilots Association; United States Pilots Association)
ownership: as business expense 93, 94, 95, 100–105, 107–112; costs and expenses 43, 51–53, 61–66, 71, 167, 198–199, 201, 219; insurance 17, 28, 32, 53–54, 57, 63–65, 88, 90, 93, 105–107, 110, 124, 146, 155, 186–187, 197–204, 206, 219; IRS and federal taxes 10, 63, 92–95, 100–104, 107–111; leasing vs. 71, 93; record keeping 66–67, 93–95, 107–109, 112; state taxes and laws 48, 54, 58, 63. 110; ways to cover costs 95–107

paragliders *see* gliders
Part 141 pilot school 20–22, 29–31, 33
paying for certificates and advanced training 21, 33, 44
personal locator beacon (PLB) 164–166
personal stories 2–3, 21–24, 28–31, 33, 34–38, 44–45, 47–51, 56, 61–62, 63, 71–91, 92, 93, 95–100, 100–101, 102–104, 106, 116–117, 127–137, 142–144, 152, 171–172, 174–***180***, 181, 185, 187–192, 206, 211–215, 216–217, 220–221, 230–231, 237–238
physical examination *see* medical exams and certificates
Piper J3 Cub *1*
publications, aviation *see* aviation publications
purchasing *see* buying an airplane

radio station license 184
ratings/endorsements 8–10, 26, 28–29, 31–33, 57, 147, 148–151, 181, 234
Recreational Aviation Foundation (RAF) 148
renting an airplane *see* ownership, leasing vs.

safety 14–15, 34–35, 63, 66, 69, 105, 185, 187, 194, 197, 201–202, 226, 229; education 15, 34, 40–41, 45, 122, 146, 150, 154, 200, 202, 204
sailplanes *see* gliders
seaplane or floatplane rating/endorsement 148–149
search and rescue (SAR) 95, 97–99, 101, 164, 165–166, 178
Soaring Society of America 150, 234
special issuance (SI) 91, 208, 210–211, 213
state driver's license 8, 9, 183–184, 209, 213, 230–231, 233, 235
Statement of Demonstrated Ability (SODA) 208
Sullenberger, Captain Chesley, III 223–224
survival training *see* surviving a nontraditional/emergency landing
surviving a nontraditional/emergency landing 162–***172***, 173

Temporary Flight Restrictions (TFRs) 14–15
training, proficiency 26, 28, 146–155, 158, 160, 171, 200, 202, 204; *see also* ratings/endorsements; certificate, commercial pilot; certificate, private pilot

ultralights 5, 10, 20, 231–***232***
United States Pilots Association (USPA) ***44***, ***45***
University Aviation Association (UAA) 21
unscheduled landings *see* off-airport landings

very high frequency omnidirectional range (VOR)  13, 49
visual flight rules (VFR) flying  13, 27, 29–30, 49, 53, 55, 99, 105, 128, 132, 134–135, 139, 153, 159, 167, 171, 184, 187, 232–233, 238

warbirds, World War II  104, 117, 174–*178*, 179–*180*, 181–182, 187

www.ingramcontent.com/pod-product-compliance
Lightning Source LLC
Chambersburg PA
CBHW032036300426
44117CB00009B/1085